Parthia:
The Forgotten Ancient "Superpower" And Its Role In Biblical History

By

Steven M. Collins

Dedication

This book is dedicated to the Glory of the Creator God and the Restoration of His Truth and Knowledge.

The Parthians

"Acts 2:9-11: 'Parthians, and Medes, and Elamites...we do hear them speak in our tongues.' To their cities the exiles of Israel were carried. (2 Kings xvii. 6) The Parthi — Parthians — meaning exiles, were unknown in history till the 6th century, B.C. In 140 B.C. their vast empire reached from the Indus to the Euphrates, and from the Euphrates to the Caucasus. Bishop Laurence, who wrote in 1838, said the Parthians were in the northern districts of the Caspian and Euxine, and likely to be one of the tribes carried away by Shalmaneser, who never returned." —*Bible Notes, J. Bell, 1907, p.402*

About The Cover

Our cover depicts a map of the very powerful empire of Parthia and a striking example of its forgotten technology. Parthia was one of the largest and most powerful empires of the ancient world, but it is almost never discussed in history texts. It was contemporary with the Roman Empire at its height, and Roman writers acknowledged Parthia as an ancient "superpower" rival of Rome. The object superimposed on the map was an ancient electric battery! Scientific and academic articles have been written about Parthia's electric batteries, but this evidence of Parthia's advanced technology has also been excluded from mainstream history texts. This book will detail for you the fascinating history of this "forgotten" empire and its notable achievements. You will also learn why modern history texts scarcely mention the history of Parthia!

Parthia:
The Forgotten Ancient "Superpower" And Its Role In Biblical History

Book Three of the Series:
"The Lost Tribes Of Israel"

By
Steven M. Collins

Published by:
Bible Blessings
www.bibleblessings.net
Box 1778
Royal Oak, MI 48068-1778
USA

Parthia: The Forgotten Ancient "Superpower" And Its Role In Biblical History

Written by Steven M. Collins

Editor-In-Chief, Pastor Jory Steven Brooks

U.S. Library of Congress Control Number 2002116972
I.S.B.N. 0-9725849-2-7
This book includes material published previously under
Library of Congress Copyright Number TX-4-266-787

Website: www.israelite.info

First Edition

COPYRIGHT NOTICE:

COVER ARTWORK:

The Parthian battery was painted for us by Ruth Amelia Lincoln, an accomplished artist who has many beautiful paintings to her credit. The back cover map was designed by Wayne Laurence, Historic Research Group, 66 Boundary Road, Whangarei 0101 New Zealand.

ORDERING INFORMATION:

For information on ordering copies of this book, other volumes in this series, and other books published by *Bible Blessings Book and Tract Ministries,* see our website or the order notice at the back of this book.

About The Author

Steven Collins' first book was *The "Lost" Ten Tribes of Israel...Found!* During its second printing, that book attracted sufficient attention that its subject matter was substantially expanded into this four-book series tracing the history and modern locations of the biblical Israelites.

Mr. Collins is a former *National Merit Scholar,* and a graduate of the *University of Minnesota* with a B.S. in Public and Personnel Management.

While employed in the office of the Mayor of St. Paul Minnesota (1973-1974), Mr. Collins researched the fields of air transportation and radiation safety as well as applicable government regulations while drafting the nation's first airport ordinance (at *Minneapolis-St Paul International airport*) monitoring the air transportation of radioactive materials. This ordinance was examined by CBS Television on a national telecast entitled *"Magazine"* in 1974.

The author was employed by the *Minneapolis-St. Paul Metropolitan Airports Commission* in a number of capacities from 1974 to 1983, the most recent position being that of Personnel Manager. In addition to personnel management duties, the author performed many research and writing projects, and also prepared formal exhibits for air route hearings of the former *Civil Aeronautics Board* (CAB). These projects involved research and analysis of a wide variety of economic, demographic and air transportation data, and in an International Route Case, the author also served as an oral witness as part of the CAB proceedings.

After a career-ending injury, the author directed his research skills to a comparison of secular historical records with the historical accounts of the Bible. This led to the publication of his first book, *The "Lost" Ten Tribes of Israel...Found!* The author is a former Board Member of the *Association for Christian Development* (ACD), based in the Seattle area, and a member of the *National Epigraphic Society.* However, this book represents the analysis and judgments of the author, and does not claim to represent the views of any organization.

Steven Collins is also the founder and president of *The Evangelistic Two-House Information Center* (ETHIC), an organization formed to develop and present new research concerning the nation of Israel in history and prophecy. ETHIC is a non-sectarian effort to combine the knowledge and research of Christian, Messianic Hebrew, and Jewish scholars in this field, and is open to all who are interested in this topic regardless of background. A large amount of research, publications, and other information is now available. For more information, please visit ETHIC's web site: **www.israelite.info**

PARTHIAN JUGS AND JARS.

Acknowledgements

This series of books on the history of the Israelite tribes is the result of years of research, writing and ongoing review. The process of writing four books involves considerable effort and time, but it has been a "labor of love" for me. During this time, I have been aided by the assistance and encouragement of others, to whom gratitude must be expressed.

I would first like to recognize the profound pioneering work of the late Dr. Barry Fell, Harvard University Professor Emeritus who was the Founder and President of the National Epigraphic Society. Dr. Fell deciphered many ancient inscriptions which confirmed that several Old World civilizations were present in the ancient Americas. The books and writings of Dr. Fell and other contributors to the publications of The Epigraphic Society have been most helpful in providing source material for historical facts and observations cited in this book. Indeed, it was the striking information in Dr. Fell's books, *America B.C.* and *Saga America* which inspired my own writing efforts. Whenever I personally contacted Dr. Fell to seek his assistance in directing me to past publications of the National Epigraphic Society dealing with specific research topics, he was always most helpful and cordial. He was that rarest of individuals: a person who possessed great talent while displaying personal humility.

I am also indebted to the late Dr. Charles V. Dorothy (a graduate of Claremont Graduate School, Claremont, CA, and formerly the Director of Biblical Research for the Association for Christian Development, Auburn, WA), for checking many of my transliterations from ancient languages into English. Dr. Dorothy studied Hebrew, Greek, Aramaic, Syriac, Akkadian and Ugaritic at the Fuller Theological Seminary in Pasadena, CA., and was an Assistant Professor of Biblical Studies at Faith Lutheran Seminary in Tacoma, Washington before his untimely demise. Like Dr. Barry Fell, Dr. Charles Dorothy combined scholarly and academic ability with personal humility. I have been privileged to know two such individuals.

There are a number of individuals whose assistance and support has made this current series of books on Israelite history a reality. I want to thank Pastor Herb Teitgen for performing the data conversions necessary to upgrade my data disks to a "modern" software format suitable for publication. I am one of those people who is most comfortable writing at a keyboard with word processing software that is now archaic. While doing so enables me to write more effectively, the downside is that no modern computer or publisher can utilize my old software's data. Herb was able to perform the data upgrades accurately and effectively.

Special credit must be given to Pastor Jory Steven Brooks, Editor-In-Chief, for his able assistance in providing additional research, source documentation, and illustrations. This series of books has greatly benefited from the inclusion of material from his own research at various libraries and historic sites. He has also assisted in editing my books, and in preparing them in desktop publishing software for publication. His support in the preparation of these books has been crucial to the success of this effort.

Finally, I also wish to thank the many people who have contributed in various ways to the inspiration for, and writing of, these books. Their collective contributions have provided valuable assistance and encouragement to me during my writing efforts.

Steven M. Collins

ISRAEL'S CONNECTION TO PARTHIA

Reproduced below is a portion of a map appearing in the frontis of the book, "The Bible Handbook" by Dr. Joseph Angus, published by The Religious Tract Society, London, England, in 1864. In the center of the map below is the legend: "PARTHIA (Jews numerous)." The close Hebrew connection to Parthia is the subject of this book.

Illustrations

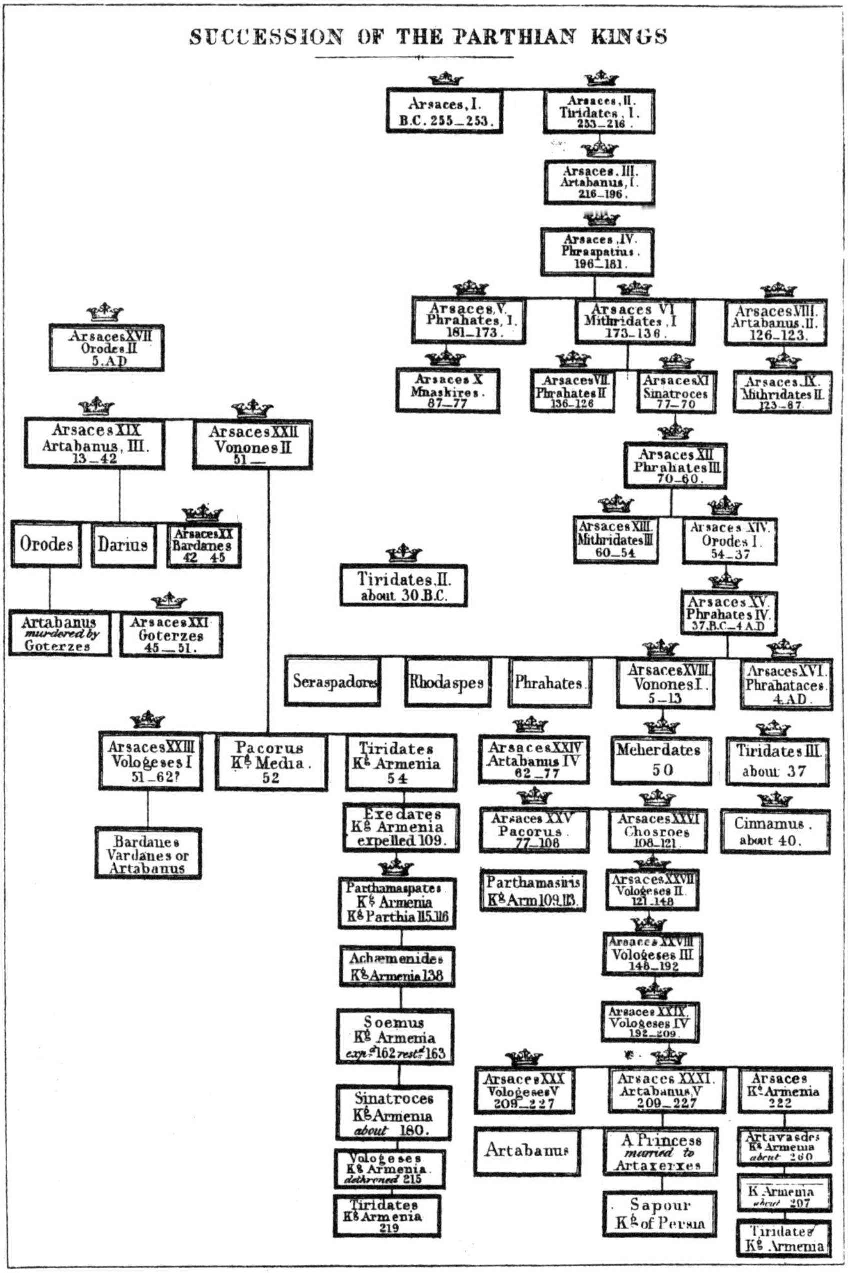

See the Chronological Table of the Reigns of the Parthian kings on page 232

Table of Contents

Chapter 3: The "Untold Story" of Jesus Christ's Life

Introduction

This third book in the series on Israelite history continues the narrative about the "forgotten" ten tribes of Israel. As the readers of the first two books know, the tribes of Israel were never truly "lost," and God continued to confer upon them the special blessings of the Abrahamic Covenant. God pledged to make Abraham's descendants extremely numerous and powerful. God further pledged to give them material wealth and geopolitical advantages. We have seen that God gave the best promises to Abraham's "birthright" descendants, found among the ten tribes of Israel.

In Hosea 1:6-10, God promised that the populations of the ten tribes of Israel would be multiplied beyond calculation **after** they were expelled from the Promised Land. Given God's immutable promise that the ten tribes would become a vast multitude on the earth, how could they ever be "lost?" How do you hide a vast multitude?

The first two books revealed that the ten tribes of Israel were never "lost" at all. Greek, Roman and Jewish historical sources wrote much about them, and it is not difficult to identify them among the ancient nations. Efforts to locate them have failed because of a hopelessly "minimalist" approach: Looking for isolated little bands of people with vestigial Hebraic customs. When one looks for the ten tribes of Israel utilizing the "maximalist" approach required by biblical accounts and prophecies, the tribes of Israel are easily found!

The tribes of Israel dominated the Phoenician Empire. After their diverse migrations from Palestine, they built new empires in Carthage and Scythia. European and British Celts also descended from the colonies and refugees of the Phoenician empire. Given the extraordinary blessings of the Abrahamic Covenant which they inherited, the tribes of Israel must be found among the great nations and powers of the earth in every historical period.

In this book, we will examine the fascinating, but widely-suppressed, history of the Parthian Empire. Parthia ruled one of the largest and most powerful empires that existed in ancient times, becoming an ancient "superpower" that often dominated its great rival, the Roman Empire, when they met in warfare. You didn't think Rome had "great rivals" which often defeated it in major wars? Your history courses have utterly failed you! Rome's own writers and historians wrote extensively about the Parthian Empire and its many victories over the Roman Empire. Given the fact that Rome's own writers acknowledged the major historical role of Parthia, it is most curious that modern history texts routinely ignore and obscure the history of this great Asian empire.

This book will document that the Parthian Empire was formed and governed by Israelites who had been relocated into Asia. It also offers extensive evidence concerning Parthia's Israelite/Semitic origins. Parthia's kings were from the same Judaic dynasty as Israel's King David, and the city where the first Parthian King was crowned was named after Isaac, the son of Abraham. It is Parthia's glaringly-obvious Israelite origins which likely has caused it to be censored out of today's "politically-correct" educational system. Modern academia, in which evolutionary dogmas are so pervasive, recoils from historical truths that confirm the Bible and offer evidence that a Creator God is actively overseeing the progression of world events. This book will restore the Parthian Empire to its rightful place in world history.

We will also see evidence that Parthia was an Empire governed by the same feudal system which resurfaced in Europe many centuries later. Indeed, Parthia pioneered some of the institutions of modern elective government, choosing its emperors via a bicameral vote, extending "home rule" to many cities and respecting the rights of minority groups and religions.

We will also resume our discussion of the Scythians, the Asian "Sacae" who had a large empire of their own. The eastern Scythians eventually migrated into the Parthian Empire and their history became inseparably linked to that of Parthia. The Western Scythians stayed in the Black Sea region, but they were increasingly known in historical accounts by their Roman name (the Goths) instead of their Greek name (the Sacae). As late as the first century A.D., the Apostle Paul, who lived in a Hellenist society, still referred to them as the "Scythians" in Colossians 3:11.

This book will also present striking new information and insights about Jesus Christ's life, which cannot be fully appreciated apart from the larger context of Parthian-Roman politics. For example, the famous "visit of the Magi" to the young Jesus Christ takes on dramatically greater meaning when it is realized the Magi were a delegation of Parthia's powerful nobility who selected Parthian Emperors and searched for male relatives of Parthia's kings. A plausible account of the whereabouts and activities of Jesus Christ during the Bible's eighteen-year gap in his life is offered in this book, based on information from both secular and biblical accounts.

After centuries of power and wealth, Parthia repeated the cycle of previous Israelite Empires: It decayed internally and the divine blessings of the Abrahamic covenant were withdrawn. When the Parthian Empire fell, it's collapse was sudden and spectacular. Paradoxically, just before Parthia fell it defeated the Roman Empire in a titanic struggle which was one of the largest battles in ancient history. This great war is rarely mentioned in history texts, but this book will reveal its details and significance.

Continuing a theme from the first two books, this book will include evidence that the sailing routes to the New World were still known to Old World civilizations in the early centuries of the modern era. The reader should be prepared for some surprising facts about world history which will make the past "come alive" as never before.

Parthian helmet
from, George Rawlinson, "Parthia" page 398
(compare to the Israelite hat shown on page 57)

Chapter 1
PARTHIA:
An Israelite Empire Rises In Asia

Many readers may ask the question: "Who or what was Parthia?" It is a testimony to the woeful lack of historical knowledge in the modern world that this question could even be asked. Parthia was a vast ancient empire, which ruled in Asia at the same time that the Roman Empire ruled over the Mediterranean region. Although Rome launched many wars of imperial aggression against Parthia, none succeeded in their aims of subjugating the Parthians. Conversely, Parthia administered many crushing defeats to Roman armies as these two ancient "superpowers" opposed each other for centuries. In spite of the fact that much is known about Parthia's history, it is almost totally ignored in history texts. How accurate a picture of ancient history would we have if textbooks dwelt extensively on Parthia's empire and neglected to mention Rome? It would yield a very distorted view of ancient history. Yet we now have an equally distorted view of world history as a result of Parthia's omission from texts on ancient history.

The famous nineteenth century historian, George Rawlinson, wrote two books extensively documenting the history of the Parthian Empire. They were entitled *Parthia* and *The Sixth Great Oriental Monarchy*. The Greco-Roman classical writers recorded a voluminous amount of information about Parthia, and Rawlinson wrote about the "defective" view of history, which resulted from ignoring Parthia's major role in world history. He introduces *The Sixth Great Oriental Monarchy* with these words:

> "...**the picture of the world during the Roman period... put before students in 'Histories of Rome,' was defective, not to say false, in its omission to recognize the real position of Parthia**...as a counterpoise to the power of Rome...**a rival state dividing with Rome the attention of mankind and the sovereignty of the known earth**. Writers of Roman history have been too much in the habit of representing [Rome] as...a Universal Monarchy, a Power unchecked... having no other limits than those of the civilized world...the truth seems to be that...from the first to the last...there was always in the world a Second Power, civilized or semi-civilized, which in a true sense balanced Rome, acted as a counterpoise and a check...**This power for nearly three centuries (B.C. 64 — A.D. 225) was Parthia**."[1] *(Emphasis added)*

The fact that Rome had equal rivals in the ancient world will surprise many readers. This chapter, and the following chapter, will attempt to restore a balanced perspective on ancient history by a thorough discussion of the origins and history of Parthia.

The abysmal lack of information on Parthia results from the fact that history has been taught almost exclusively from an ethnocentric, Greco-Roman perspective. The preoccupation with Greco-Roman history has led to major misunderstandings about the realities of the ancient world. In the previous books of this series on Israelite history, we learned that widespread ignorance about Phoenician and Carthaginian history has led to modern man's unawareness of the role of North America in ancient history. This was due to the fact that the Phoenician and Carthaginian fleets controlled Gibraltar and, for almost a millennium, denied the Greco-Romans any maritime access to lands beyond the Mediterranean Sea. As a result, Greece and Rome were far less advanced than the Phoenicians and Carthaginians in nautical skills and in understanding world geography. Also, we learned in the previous book that the Scythians (the Sacae) were a civilized people, and that their power was so great that they devastated the Assyrian Empire and twice defeated the Persian Empire. Yet you read almost nothing about them in history texts either.

We shall now learn that modern man's neglect of Parthian history has led to more gross misunderstandings about the ancient world. These misunderstandings affect us today. The reader will see in the fourth book of this series how our misunderstandings about ancient history distort our perceptions of what is really happening in today's world events.

The Hebrew-Israelite Origins of Parthia

Who were the Parthians? There is no record of their presence in Asia at all until the Persians refer to them in the sixth century B.C., and "there is no mention of them in the Old Testament, or in the Assyrian inscriptions, or in the Zendavesta."[2] The Persians called them the "Parthva," and named them as a subject people involved in a revolt in 521 B.C.[3] Herodotus mentions the Parthians as being one of the subject nations in the Medo-Persian army which attacked Greece under Xerxes, the Persian King.[4] Herodotus also mentions that the Parthians were subjects of King Darius, and that they lived in an adjoining province to some of the Sacae.[5]

Those who have read the previous book in this series know that the "Sacae" were Scythians named after "Isaac," the Israelite patriarch. The Parthian homeland was located southeast of the Caspian Sea.

The Parthians are clearly identified by historians as having a common origin with the Scythians. Rawlinson states, "there was a strong conviction on the part of those who came in contact with the Parthians, that they were Scyths,"[6] and adds "that the Scythic character of the Parthians is asserted in the strongest terms by the ancient writers."[7] Rawlinson cites the classical historians Strabo, Justin and Arrian in stating:

> "The manners of the Parthians had, they tell us, much that was Scythic in them. Their language was half-Scythic, half-Median. They armed themselves in the Scythic fashion. They were...Scyths in descent, in habits, in character."[8]

The Scythian origin of the Parthians is further confirmed by the fact that many times in their history, the Parthians sought the aid of the Scythians in various wars. Ousted Parthian kings sometimes sought asylum in Scythia. This recurrent Parthian reliance on the Sacae tribes of Scythia in times of trouble confirms that the Parthians and Scythians were natural allies.

There is a record from Diodorus, a Greek historian of the first century B.C., that the Parthians had:

> **"passed from the dominion of the Assyrians to that of the Medes...to a similar position under the Persians."**[9] *(Emphasis added)*

Rawlinson also notes concerning the Parthians:

> "...it was believed that **their name meant 'exiles.'** Hence it was necessary to suppose that they had migrated into their country from some portion of Scythia."[10] *(Emphasis added)*

The previous book documented that the Assyrians exiled two waves of Israelite captives into Asia, and that some of them were located in the cities of the Medes. After the fall of Assyria's empire, it is logical that some Asian Israelites would come under the dominion of the Medes and Persians. The above evidence that Parthia's language was "half Median" indicates that the Parthians had lived in very close proximity to the Medes for a considerable length of time. Some of Israel's exiles were placed in "the cities of the Medes" (II Kings 17:6), confirming that many Israelites would have lived among the Medes and become familiar with the Medes' language.

The last chapter of the previous book provided abundant evidence that the Sacae Scythians were relocated members of the ten tribes of Israel. Since ancient historians affirm the Parthians were kinsmen of the Sacae Scythians, and since there is no record of any Parthians being in Asia until **after** the Israelites were placed there, it is evident that the Parthians were also part of the ten tribes of Israel. The fact that ancient writers regarded them as a nation of "exiles" supports this identification. The ten tribes of Israel in their Asian locations were, indeed, there as "exiles" from Palestine.

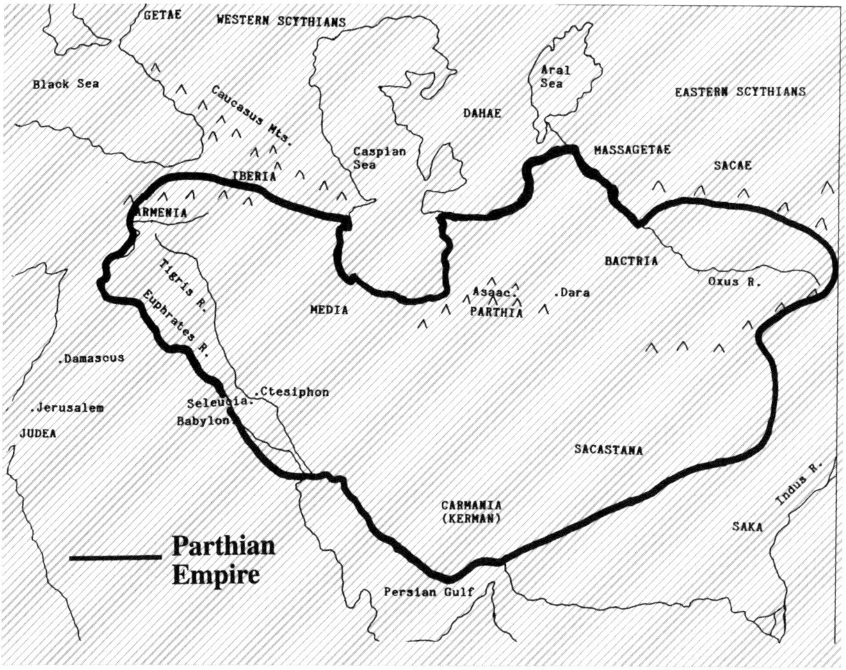

Rawlinson cites an account of the ancient historian, Diodorus, that the Parthians "revolted from the Medes and placed themselves under Scythian protection."[11] This confirms that from the time of their first efforts to gain independence, the Parthians looked to the Scythians as their natural protectors and liberators.

The *Encyclopedia Britannica* records that:

> "The alphabets in use in Persia, at least **from the time of the Arsacid dynasty onwards, are based upon the Aramaic**...The earliest records of Aramaic go back to about 800 B.C. and were found...in northern Syria... **Other developments of Aramaic are modern square Hebrew**..."[12] *(Emphasis added)*

The "Arsacid dynasty" refers to the Parthian kings. That the Parthians utilized an Aramaic alphabet — a Semitic alphabet related to Hebrew — confirms that the Parthians originated in the region of Syria and Palestine where the Aramaic language developed. Their use of a Semitic alphabet clearly indicates that the Parthians had a Semitic racial and linguistic origin! Also, since ancient historians strongly maintain that the Parthians were a Scythian people, the Semitic nature of Parthia's language reinforces the Semitic origin of the Scythians. That the Parthian language was related to the Hebrew language strongly indicates that the Parthians were the descendants of the ten tribes of Israel, who had been relocated into Media and other Asian regions.

What little is preserved of the Parthian language confirms a Semitic origin for the Parthians. **Rawlinson states the Parthian word for "city" was "karta"** or "kerta."[13] In the previous book, the Semitic-Israelite origin of Carthage was discussed, and it was noted that the original Semitic name of Carthage was "Kirjath Hadeschath." **The Semitic name of Carthage is also rendered as "Kart** Hadasht," meaning "new city."[14] The Semitic origin of Carthage is well known, and both the Carthaginians and Parthians used the word "kart" for "city," indicating that they both shared a common Semitic origin. That common origin was in the old Kingdom of Israel, called "Phoenicia" by the Greeks.

In the next chapter, we shall examine the role of the Parthian "Magi," an influential portion of Parthia's ruling classes. An early Carthaginian ruler was named "Mago,"[15] again indicating a common linguistic heritage with the Parthians.

A modern website on Parthia notes the following about the Parthian language:

> "The Parthians used the Aramaic alphabet for writing...Another example is the Aramaic title MLKYN MLK (=King of Kings)...They also used the word BRY (=My Son in Aramaic)..."[16]

The Parthian Aramaic word for king ("MLK") is also the Hebrew word for king, and it appears over 2,500 times in the Bible.[17] The word "BRY" is an obvious cognate word to the Hebrew word "BR" or "BAR," which also is translated "son" in the Bible.[18] The "Aramaic-Parthian" (or "Semitic-Parthian") linguistic link could just as easily be called a "Hebrew-Parthian" link, but establishment sources are not likely to acknowledge that connection. Doing so would lead to the inescapable racial-ethnic link between the Parthians and the tribes of Israel who had been transplanted into Asia.

A prominent family of Parthians was called the "Suren" family,[19] and one of their hereditary rights was to crown Parthian kings.[20] The word "Suren" (it also appears as "surena" or "surenas") is a Hebrew composite word. The Hebrew word "**sur**" includes the meaning "reign" or "make princes."[21] The Hebrew word "**en**" (rendered "ayin") means "eye," sight" or "presence."[22] **The Parthian name "sur-en" is Hebrew for a person whose "presence makes princes" or "reign in his (eye) sight**." The Parthian Suren did exactly what the Hebrew words signify, showing the parallels between the Hebrew and the Parthian language were no coincidence.

Would the strong linguistic relationship between Hebrew and Parthian exist if the Parthians had a Mongoloid origin from the interior of Asia? Obviously the answer is "no," However, linguistic links to the Hebrew language, as found among the Parthians, are exactly what we should find among the descendants of the ten tribes of Israel who were displaced to Asia. Later, we shall also see that many of the personal and place names of the Parthians were not merely Semitic, but specifically Israelite in nature.

After Persia's Empire fell, Parthia was ruled by the Greeks under Alexander the Great. When Alexander's kingdom was divided after his early death, Parthia was placed in the Seleucid Greek Empire. There was an apparent fulfillment of an obscure biblical prophecy about the house of Israel, the ten tribes, at the time that Alexander the Great destroyed the Persian Empire. In Ezekiel 4:3-5, an unusual prophecy is found in which God instructs Ezekiel to do the following:

> "**This shall be a sign to the house of Israel**. Lie...upon thy left side, and lay the iniquity of the house of Israel upon it: according to the number of the days that shalt lie upon it thou shalt bear their iniquity. **For I have laid upon thee the years of their iniquity, according to the number of the days, three hundred and ninety days**: so shalt thou bear the iniquity of **the house of Israel**." *(KJV)*

For centuries, the Parthians had been captives of the Assyrians, Medes and Persians. The Israelite kingdom ended when Samaria fell in 721 B.C. The kingdom of Israel was the "house of Israel" (the northern ten tribes), so if a 390 year punishment began at the fall of

ARISTOTLE TEACHING ALEXANDER

Under Aristotle, the greatest of Greek thinkers and teachers, Alexander learned to know and love all that was best in Greek art and science

Samaria, a singular event should occur in the year 331 B.C. (721 B.C. - 390 years = 331 B.C.). In that year, one of history's major turning points occurred, and it released the Israelites from their centuries of captivity. It was also predicted in Biblical prophecy. Daniel 8:5-22 prophesied that a great Grecian king would destroy the Medo-Persian empire, and that four kingdoms would replace his empire. Alexander the Great fulfilled this prophecy.

In 331 B.C., Alexander the Great's outnumbered army routed the Persian army of Darius III at the battle of Gaugamela, also known as the battle of Arbela. After that battle, the Persian Empire disintegrated, releasing its grip on many captive nations. The battle of Gaugamela ended the captivity of the Israelites to the Medo-Persian Empire, exactly 390 years after the fall of Samaria. Technically, the Parthians were still within Alexander the Great's Macedonian Empire. However, Alexander's Macedonians conquered the Persian Empire with a small army, leaving few troops to garrison or control conquered nations. Also, Alexander was seen as a liberator by many of the nations freed from Persian rule.

In the Munich Glyptothek

ALEXANDER AT TWENTY

He was possessed of high physical courage, impulsive energy, and a lofty intellect

After conquering Persia, Alexander adopted Asian customs and actively recruited soldiers into his army from the Asian nations that had been under the Persian yoke. The March, 2000 issue of *National Geographic* magazine includes an article on Alexander's conquest of the Persian Empire and the battle of Gaugamela. That article points out that by 327 B.C., Alexander's army of 75,000 men included 60,000 Asiatic recruits and only 15,000 Macedonians![23] A Persian army which had unsuccessfully invaded the Scythians in the 6th century B.C. numbered 700,000 men, so Alexander's army was puny in size compared to the gigantic armies of the Persians. The small size of Alexander's army and the fact that it came to be composed mostly of Asians confirms that many nations ruled by Persia as captives were happy to serve as Alexander's allies. This testifies that the Asian nations, including the Israelites, who had been freed by Alexander from Persian rule, enjoyed considerable local independence as long as they acknowledged Alexander's supremacy.

Alexander died a few years later, and four kingdoms replaced his empire, each headed by one of Alexander's generals. This fulfilled the Daniel 8:22 prophecy that four weaker kingdoms would supplant Alexander's empire. The Parthians were within the territory of the Seleucid Greek Empire, and they revolted after being vassals of the Seleucid king for a few decades.

> ***"Yet the number of the children of Israel shall be as the sand of the sea, which cannot be measured nor numbered; and it shall come to pass, that in the place where it was said unto them, Ye are not my people, there it shall be said unto them, Ye are the sons of the living God."***
>
> **-Hosea 1:10**

In 256 B.C. (some sources put the date at 250 B.C.), Parthia and Bactria revolted against Seleucid Greek rule, and declared their independence. There are conflicting details about this Parthian uprising, but there appears to be a consensus that the revolts and independence of Parthia and Bactria were intertwined.[24] Some historians record that Arsaces, the first king of the Parthians, was a Bactrian, but most accounts agree that he was the chieftain of a Scythian tribe who slew the Greek satrap and liberated his Parthian kinsmen.[25] The name of Arsaces, the first Parthian king and founder of Parthia's dynasty, included the name of the Israelite patriarch, Isaac ("Ar-**sac**-es").

The Tribe of Ephraim Leads Parthia

In Hosea 1:6-10, God promised that He would make the Israelites too numerous to count **after** He expelled them from Palestine. The Jewish historian, Josephus, confirmed that the population of the ten tribes was exceedingly numerous by the 1st century A.D. With the Israelites' population increasing explosively, they came to be known by their clan names as well as their tribal names. Portions of the Bible record genealogies of ancient families and the tribes of Israel. Some call these sections the "begats," and they are often regarded as the most boring parts of the Bible. However, for historical research, these sections can be invaluable! These genealogies preserved the names of the individual clans (subtribes) of the tribes of Israel, and some of these names can be located in geographic and proper names in the post-exilic period.

For example, Numbers 26:35-36 records that three clans of the Israelite tribe of Ephraim were named the **Bachrites**, the **Eranites**, and the **Tahanites**. The Seleucid province of **Bactria**, which revolted along with Parthia, bore the name of one of the clans of Ephraim in a Hellenized form. An Israelite origin for Bactria is supported by an account from Richard Frye's book, *The Heritage of Persia*, which states that the Bactrian language "...was related to Saka, or at least underwent strong influences from Saka tongues."[26] The Persian word "Saka" referred to the Sacae Scythians. The record that the Bactrians welcomed a Scythian ruler who freed them from a Greek satrap, and the fact that the Bactrians shared a linguistic heritage with the Parthians argues that the Bactrians were also Sacae (or Saka) who had descended from the ten tribes of Israel.

Henry Rawlinson, in his book *Bactria*, states: "there seems to be very little doubt that the population of Bactria was largely Scythian"...[and cites Justin, a classical author, who wrote] "The Bactrian Empire was founded by the Scythians."[27]

Numbers 26:36 also notes that another clan of the tribe of Ephraim descended from **Eran** and was known as the "**Eranites**." A group of people known as the **Eranians** was present in the region of ancient Persia and Parthia.[28] Assyria had transplanted the defenders of Samaria (an Ephraimite city) into "the cities of the Medes." Therefore, we should expect to see Ephraimite names in the Medo-Persian region. The "**Eran**ians" manifested the **exact Hebrew name** of one of the clans of Ephraim in the area of Medo-Persia. This name has survived into modern times as the English name for modern Persia is **Iran**. The terms "Iran" and "Eran" are interchangeable. The *Encyclopaedia Britannica*, in its Index section, simply states "Eran: see Iran."[29] The capital of Iran, Teh**eran**, also preserves the name of this Ephraimite clan. This book does not assert or imply that modern Iranians are Israelites as it is clear from history that modern Iranians are principally Medo-Persian in racial origins. However, the name "Iran" is derived from the name of a clan of Ephraim, who were placed in Medo-Persian territory by the Assyrians and lived there for many centuries.

Most historical accounts assume that the name "Eran" originated from the term "Aryan." However, historical accounts generally have not considered an Israelite alternative for the origin of the Eranians. Indeed, historical accounts seem unwilling to even look for the large masses of Israelites who were relocated into Asia. The case for an Israelite origin for the Eranians is very strong. Not only are the Eranians found in Medo-Persia, the correct geographical location where Israelite tribes and clans were placed, but there were many other ancient names in that region with an Israelite origin!

There is evidence of considerable Semitic influence in ancient Persia. In commenting on the ancient Pehlevi (or Pahlavi) language of Parthia, Zenaide Ragozin states:

> **"Pehlevi...does not seem to be Persian at all, but rather Semitic. That is, an enormous proportion of the words — nouns, pronouns, verbs, adverbs, prepositions, conjunctions — are Semitic**, while the grammar and construction...**are Eranian**..."[30] *(Emphasis added)*

The obvious reason why Pehlevi, the Parthian language, had such strong Semitic content is that the Assyrians forcibly resettled a large portion of the ten tribes of Israel (a Semitic nation) in Medo-Persian areas. Additionally, large numbers of Jews were settled in Mesopotamia by the Assyrians and Babylonians. The descendants of those captive Israelites later became part of the Persian Empire. Indeed, many Jews — Daniel, Esther, Mordechai, Nehemiah and Ezra — had very high governmental positions in the Persian Empire. Since both the Jews and the more-numerous Israelites were Semites, they influenced the language of Persia in a Semitic direction. Later, when the Parthians, descendants of the ten tribes of Israel, ruled Persia for centuries, their Semitic language was the dominant language in Persia. The *Encyclopaedia Britannica* notes the Semitic nature of the Parthian Pahlavi language:

> "**The name [Pahlavi or Pehlevi], which means Parthian**, can be traced back for many centuries...The great peculiarity of the language is that though it is Iranian, **it is full of Semitic (Aramaic) words**..."[31] *(Emphasis added)*

It is not at all "peculiar" that Pahlavi, the language of the Parthians, had strong Semitic content. The reason is that the Parthians were Semites, descended from the tribes of Israel. Even the name of the Parthian language, "Pah-**lavi**" or "Peh-**levi**," contains the name of **Levi,** one of the tribes of Israel! The fact that the Eranian language had strong Semitic content confirms the Eranians were Semites, not Aryans.

In some historical accounts, the **Dahanites**, another Scythian clan, had a role in the founding of Parthia. They are likely the **Tahanites**, a third clan of the Ephraimites mentioned in Numbers 26:35. If the Dahanites were the Tahanites of Ephraim ("d" and "t" are linguistically similar consonants), it would mean that Parthia's independence began as a result of three clans of the tribe of Ephraim acting in concert. **The Bactrians, Eranians and Dahanites were most likely the Ephraimite clans of the Bachrites, the Eranites, and the Tahanites**. If the Hebrew connection was limited to a single name, it could be considered a coincidence, but these multiple connections add further weight to the conclusion that these names had Israelite origin. In addition, the subsequent stability of Parthia indicates that its component clans were closely related and had much in common. This stability is understandable if the above clans were all part of the tribe of Ephraim.

Since Ephraimite names clearly predominate in Parthia's origin, and since the Massagetae were one of the foremost tribes of their Scythian kinsmen, it indicates that Ephraim and Manasseh (the leading tribes of the old kingdom of Israel, and the inheritors of the "birthright" promise of Genesis 48 that included national greatness) were the dominant tribes of the Parthians and Scythians, respectively. No wonder that history records a close alliance existed between the Scythians and the Parthians. Ephraim and Manasseh were "brother" tribes who had descended from Joseph, the "favorite son" of Jacob, whose name was changed to Israel.

It also indicates how exceedingly numerous the Israelites had become in their new Asian homelands that large regions of Asia came to be known by Israelite tribal and clan names! God had abundantly kept His promise in Hosea 1:10 to multiply the numbers of the ten tribes of Israel after they were exiled from Palestine!

The Parthians and Scythians were obviously the people written about by Josephus as the very numerous descendants of the ten tribes of Israel. Josephus penned these words about the status of the ten tribes of Israel in the first century A.D.:

> "...**the ten tribes are beyond Euphrates** till now, and are **an immense multitude**, and not to be estimated by numbers."[52] *(Emphasis added)*

The evidence affirms this statement of Josephus. At the very time that Josephus wrote those words, **the Euphrates River was the recognized border between the Roman and Parthian Empires**. For Josephus to write (from his perspective within the Roman Empire) that the ten tribes were "beyond the Euphrates River" was another way of saying the ten tribes were "in Parthia," even as many Americans would recognize the phrase "beyond the Rio Grande" to be a euphemism meaning "in Mexico."

Josephus, Jewish historian

Many past efforts to locate the post-exilic, ten tribes of Israel have failed because of their "minimalist" expectations about locating tiny bands of Israelites scattered in obscure places. **Based both on Biblical prophecy and Josephus' secular account that the ten tribes of Israel had a huge Asian population by the first century A.D., the ten tribes must be found among the biggest nations in Asia during the millennium after the fall of Samaria and during the lifetime of Josephus**. That is exactly where the ten tribes of Israel can be found. We have already seen that the Sacae Scythians, one of the largest masses of people in Asia, were Israelites. We will now examine additional evidence that the numerous and powerful Parthians were also Israelites.

"The sceptre shall not depart from Judah, nor a lawgiver from between his feet, until Shiloh come; and unto him shall the gathering of the people be."
-Genesis 49:10

King David's Descendants Rule Parthia and Scythia

God foretold that the tribe of Judah would produce kings and rulers — **the "sceptre" promise of Genesis 49:10** — and King David was promised that his **descendants would always rule over the house of Israel.** *(Jeremiah 33:17)* Jeremiah's prophecy was made after the relocation of the house of Israel, the northern ten tribes, into Asia. Because Jeremiah's prophecy was made at a time when the ten tribes were living in Asia, we should expect to find descendants of King David ruling over the ten tribes of Israel in Asia.

Throughout the Parthian-Scythian sphere of influence, kings are found with names based on the word **"Phares,"** a marker of David's royal bloodline. **Matthew 1:3-6** confirms King David was a descendant of a Jewish patriarch named Pharez (Phares). A Parthian-Saka king who ruled in the area of West India was named **Gondophares**,[32] and several kings ruling over the Scythian kingdom of **Iberia** in the Caucasus Mountain region were named **Pharasmanes**.[33]

The second book in this series noted that the term "Iberia" is derived from the root word, "Eber," the father of the Hebrews. Strabo records that the Asian Iberians were the **kinsmen** of the Scythians,[34] whose Israelite origin has already been demonstrated. The above examples show that David's descendants of the House of **Phares** were ruling over widely separated nations of the ten tribes of Israel in both the Caucasus Mountains and the region of modern India. Also, many

Parthian emperors had names indicating that they were also members of the Davidic line of Judah. Some of their names include the key consonants of **PH-R-S** in the Hellenized forms of their Parthian names. Parthian kings with the names **Phr**aate**s**, **Phr**aorte**s**, and **Phr**aatace**s** include the consonants of the root-word "PH-R-S." God remembered His promise to David by guiding world events to ensure that David's descendants ruled over many Israelite nations — Parthia, Saka-Scythian and Iberian — in Asia.

How did David's descendants, from the defunct kingdom of Judah come to rule over the descendants of the ten tribes in Asia? God can easily intervene in world affairs to keep His promises, and the Bible indicates how it happened. In II Kings 24:8-15, we read that one of the last kings of Judah, Jehoiachin, and his wives were carried captive to Babylon by Nebuchadnezzar. Was this the end of him? Hardly! II Kings 25:27-30 shows that after 37 years of captivity, a later king of Babylon:

> "...did lift up the head of Jehoiachin king of Judah out of prison; and he spake kindly to him, **and set his throne above the thrones of the kings that were with him in Babylon**..." *(KJV)*

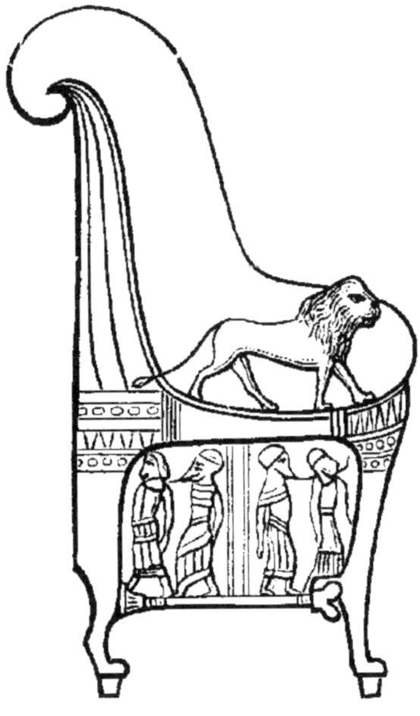

A ROYAL THRONE.

The king of Babylon ruled the Babylonian Empire, but he was served by many subordinate rulers who were vassal kings over assigned areas. That a Babylonian king gave Jehoiachin a **throne** indicates that Jehoiachin was made a vassal king over part of the Babylonian Empire. Indeed, the account states that he was set "above" the other vassal kings, meaning this royal descendant of King David was given a prominent rulership position in the Babylonian Empire! Since there were many descendants of the ten tribes of Israel who were subjects of the

Babylonian Empire—which inherited them when it conquered Assyria — it is likely that Jehoiachin was made a ruler over Israelites within Babylon's Empire. Since Jehoiachin was descended from both King David and the patriarch "Phares," his sons perpetuated a dynasty that ruled over portions of the ten tribes first as vassal kings, and then later, as kings of independent nations and empires. I Chronicles 3:16-24 records that the royal house of David did not die out after the fall of Jerusalem. Indeed, these verses record that Jehoiachin fathered many sons and grandsons, all of whom carried on the royal line of King David in Asia.

David's House had no shortage of royal princes to rule over the descendants of the ten tribes. Since the Babylonian king made Jehoiachin a favored vassal king, he likely set some of Jehoiachin's sons in positions of power as well. Perhaps the Babylonians felt that the captive nations of the Assyrians, whom they inherited as subjects, would exhibit less rebelliousness if they were given their own hereditary rulers as vassal kings. A search would have found Jehoiachin, an hereditary Israelite ruler from the tribe of Judah, alive in a prison. Thirty-seven years in prison would have made Jehoiachin very grateful when he was not only released from prison but also installed as a favored vassal king in the Babylonian Empire! His descendants were vassal kings to the Babylonians, then the Medo-Persians, and finally became independent kings over the Parthian Empire.

However, Jehoiachin's sons were not the only source of Davidic rulers over the ten tribes of Israel. The kings of Iberia — often named Pharasmanes — in the Caucasus region near the Black Sea were not captives of Assyria or Babylon. How did David's descendants come to rule in that region? One historical account states that the descendants of the ten tribes who escaped Assyrian captivity by migrating northward into the Caucasus were led by a "chief or **prince** whom they appointed."[35] This group of Israelites fled Palestine before the fall of Samaria, abandoning the last king of Israel to his fate. This indicates that they made a clean break with whatever dynasty was ruling Israel in its final days, and that a new hereditary "prince" was made the ruler over the escaping Israelites. At the time they fled to the Caucasus

Royal Line of King David

Israel/Judah:	Judah	⇨	Phares	⇨	David
Iberia/Scythia:	King Pharesmenes				
Parthian/Saka: (India)	King Gondophares				
Parthia/Sacae:	Kings Phraates, Phraortes, Phraataces				
Christ's Linage:	Phares	⇨	David	⇨	Jesus Christ

region, there was only one other Israelite dynasty from which a "prince" could have come. That dynasty was the bloodline of King David, whose descendants were still ruling over the kingdom of Judah.

The fact that Iberia's rulers included the name of "Phares" argues that this migrating body of Israel's ten tribes picked a "prince" of David's royal line as their new leader. They migrated in 724-721 B.C., and by 653 B.C. a leader of a Scythian-Cimmerian-Median alliance against Assyria was led by a person named "Phraortes."[36] The name "**Phr**aorte**s**" includes the root word **PH-R-S**, indicating a link to David's royal line of Phares. The name of Phraortes is similar to the names of later Parthian kings ("**Phr**aate**s**" or "**Phr**aatace**s**.)" This indicates that Phraortes was a Scythian bearing a "Parthian" royal name even though "Parthia" would not become independent for another 400 years! It is apparent that Davidic rulers of the line of Phares were ruling over Scythians about a century **before** Jehoiachin was made a vassal king of the Babylonians circa 555 B.C. The above evidence confirms that after Judah fell, there was **never** a time when David did not have descendants ruling over some portion of the ten tribes of Israel. This also confirms that God guided the destinies of the ten tribes of Israel even after they left Palestine.

Arsaces, the first king of Parthia, is credited with having a Scythian origin when he liberated the Parthians from the Seleucid Greeks. His descendants ruled Parthia for the entirety of its existence (almost five centuries). Since Ar**sac**es and his dynasty (the Ar**sac**ids) bore the name of **Isaac**, and since some of the Arsacid rulers included the root word of Phares (**PH-R-S**) in their names, it is evident that Arsaces was a descendant of King David.

While David's descendants were ruling several Israelite nations and empires in Asia, the reader should not assume that their reigns were always enlightened ones. David was given the blessing that his seed would perpetually have rulers over the ten tribes of Israel; however, David's descendants were also under a curse. When David committed adultery with Bathsheba and afterwards arranged the death of her husband, Uriah (both acts were tremendous abuses of power), Nathan the prophet was sent by God to deliver a curse upon David. In II Samuel 12:10, Nathan gave to David God's decree that:

> "the **sword** shall never depart **from thine house**." *(KJV)*

The "sword" symbolizes that death by violence and murder would be commonplace among David's descendants. This curse began in David's own lifetime as Amnon, David's eldest son, was killed by Absalom, David's favorite son. Absalom was then killed during a rebellion against David, and another of David's sons (Adonijah) was killed by King Solomon (David's son via Bathsheba). This curse was also evident in the ruling house of Parthia. As we shall see in the next chapter, many of Parthia's kings killed their royal relatives in order to eliminate potential rivals to the throne. Yet, no matter how many murders the Arsacids perpetrated among themselves, the Parthians always insisted that their rulers had to be blood members of the Arsacid family. Parthia is an unusual case among the empires of the ancient world. While most empires had many different dynasties, Parthia's empire lasted almost five centuries and had only one dynasty. The ancient kingdom of Judah also had only one dynasty during its four centuries of independent existence. The dynasties of Judah and Parthia were both descended from King David. God's unconditional promise to the House of David was the reason for the unbroken dynasties in Judah and Parthia. *(II Samuel 7:8-16, Jeremiah 33:17)*

Parthia's "Israelite" Cities

One prominent Parthian city was named **Asaak**,[37] where Arsaces was crowned king. The name, **Asaak**, clearly represents the name "Isaac." The name of Isaac had been attached to the "Sacae" Scythians long before Parthia ever became independent. Strabo records that Alexander the Great noted a region named **Asaacanus**, which was traversed in Alexander's expedition to India.[38] The presence of the name of Isaac in both Parthian and Scythian contexts confirms the many secular accounts that they were related kinsmen.

As further evidence of the Israelite origins of the Parthians, some Parthian cities were given Israelite names. An early capital of the Parthians was named **Dara**,[39] which is the **exact** name of one of the patriarchs of the tribe of Judah. *(I Chronicles 2:3-6)*

The Parthian province of Media Atropatene was located south-west of the Caspian Sea. The famous historian, George Rawlinson, records that (in Parthian times) "Its chief city was **Gaza**."[40] This city was apparently named after the Canaanite-Philistine city of Gaza, which is mentioned often in the Bible. This further indicates that the inhabitants of Atropatene had come from Palestine. II Kings 17:6 records that the Assyrians had placed Israelite captives in the "cities of the Medes," so it is not surprising that we later find a city of the Medes bearing the name of a city of old Palestine.

In the Parthian province of Hyrcania (located southeast of the Caspian Sea), we find that two of its chief cites were named "**Samariane**" and "**Carta**."[41] These names are clear evidence of the presence of Israelites from the former ten-tribed kingdom of Israel. Israel's capital city was named **Samaria**, and II Kings 17:6-7 records that its inhabitants, after a three-year siege, were transplanted by the Assyrians into Asia after the city fell. Centuries later, we find a Parthian city, Samariane, bearing the name of the capital city of the former kingdom of Israel! Only displaced Israelites would name a city after the capital of the kingdom of Israel. The city named "**Carta**" bears the same Semitic root word that was present in the name "**Carth**age." The words "Carta" or "Kart" are derived from the Hebrew word "Kirjath" (for "town" or "city"), as was documented previously.

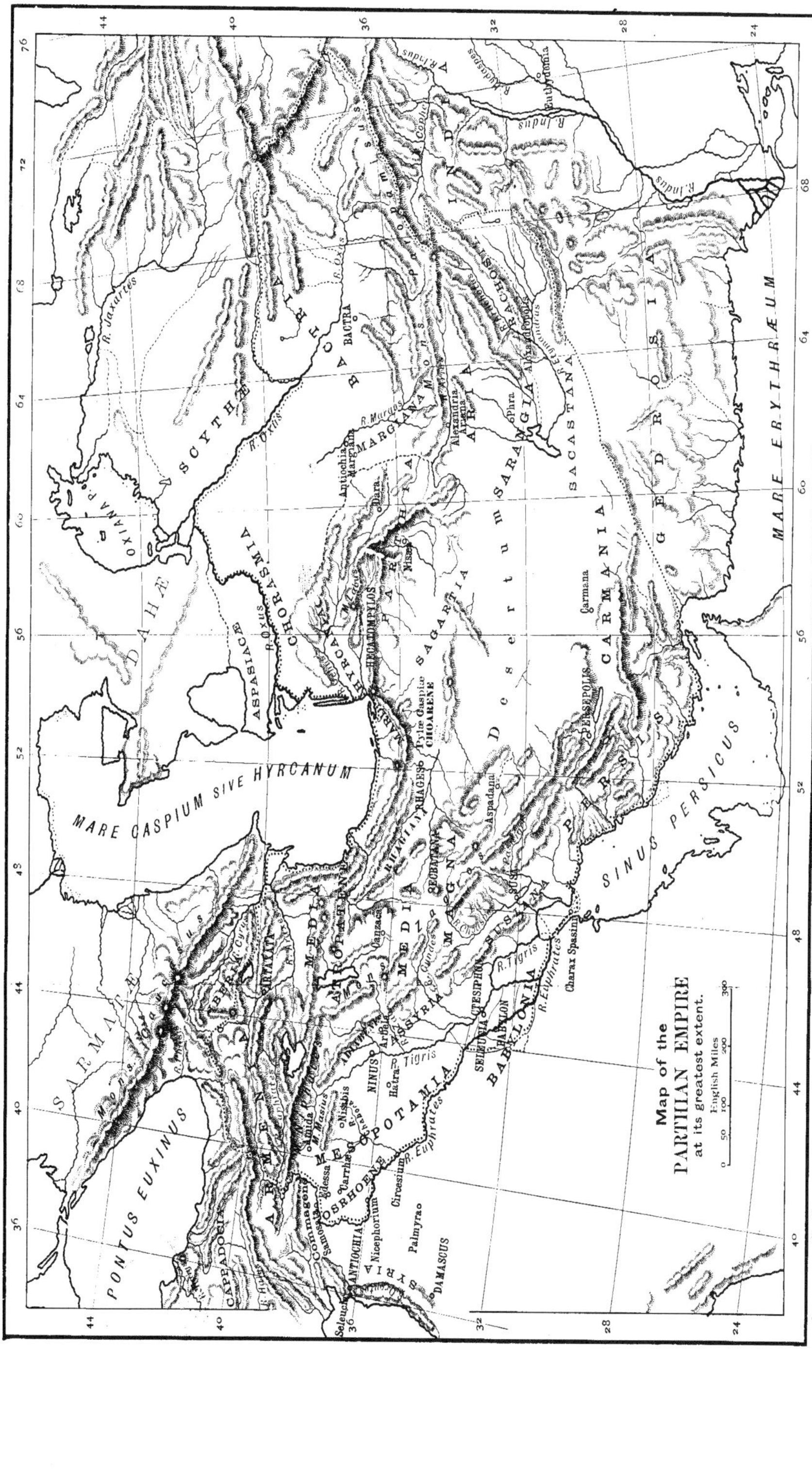

LONDON: T. FISHER UNWIN, PATERNOSTER SQUARE, E.C.

There is even more evidence to support the Israelite origins of the Parthians. Initial Parthian coins were inscribed in Greek, but later Parthian coins bear Semitic inscriptions.[42] The Parthian coins clearly depict their kings as having Caucasian features; supporting a Semitic racial origin for the Parthian nation.[43] Whether we look at their language, history, names or faces, all hard evidence indicates a Semitic origin for the Parthians, debunking baseless speculation that the Parthians were a Mongoloid (Oriental) race from the interior of Asia.

It is a myth that the ten tribes of Israel became "lost" after they relocated to Asia. Matthew 10:6 states that Jesus Christ told His twelve apostles to go to "the lost sheep of the *House of Israel.*" Biblical references to the *House of Israel* identify the ten tribes of Israel, not the Jews, who were called the *House of Judah*. **Since Jesus Christ commissioned His apostles to go to the descendants of the ten tribes of Israel, it is clear that Jesus knew that the Israelites could be found in specific homelands during His lifetime**. The apostles expressed no surprise at this commission as not one of them said: "No one knows where the ten tribes are!" or "They were all 'lost' long ago!" We have

SAMARIA.

earlier seen the evidence that Josephus, who like the apostles, lived in the first century A.D., also did not regard the ten tribes of Israel as "lost." Indeed, he knew so much about their whereabouts and condition that he identified one of their physical borders and adds that their population had become very numerous by his lifetime.

While the previous book in this series documented that some Israelites settled in Europe, the British Isles, North Africa and even North America, the most numerous concentration of Israelites was in the vast Asian territories of the Parthians and Scythians. Because neither Josephus nor Jesus Christ considered the ten tribes to be "lost" in the 1st century A.D., and they referred to them as living in known geographical locations, it is apparent that the Asian locations of the ten tribes of Israel were widely known among educated Jews in the first century AD.

It is significant that the Apostle Peter wrote the book of I Peter from the city of Babylon. Babylon was a prominent city in the Parthian Empire during the Apostolic era of the early Christian church. I Peter 5:13 indicates Peter had heeded Jesus Christ's instructions to go to the ten tribes of Israel, as Peter declares that he wrote his epistle from a major city within the Parthian Empire. Historical accounts also assert that the Apostle Thomas traveled within Parthia. The early church historian, Eusebius, identified Thomas as an apostle sent to the Parthians, and Andrew as an apostle sent to Scythia.[44] There are historical records which link the Apostle Thomas to the Parthian-Saka king, Gondophares (mentioned earlier), who reigned in ancient India.[45] Jesus Christ had commanded the apostles to "go to" the dispersed members of the ten tribes of Israel, as their first priority, before evangelizing the whole world. Why then would Peter, Thomas and Andrew go to Parthia and Scythia unless their people were Israelites?

It is also noteworthy that there were Parthian believers in the God of Israel who made pilgrimages to Jerusalem for the annual Holy Days of God. Acts 2:1-10 states that Parthians were present at the Pentecost Day when the Holy Spirit was poured out to the Apostles. The Medes, Elamites and "dwellers in Mesopotamia" mentioned in Acts 2:9 had also all come to Jerusalem from regions within Parthia's Empire. Since part of the ten tribes had settled in Media *(II Kings 17:6)*, it is likely that many "Medes" who made the pilgrimage to Jerusalem were Israelites from the ten tribes. Some of these pilgrims were Jews living in Parthia, but many were not Jews. Verse 10 indicates that these pilgrims were "Jews and proselytes (non-Jews)." Since Israelites from the ten tribes were non-Jewish, the term "proselytes" could apply to them as well as to gentiles.

It is also noteworthy that the Apostle Peter, while delivering his Pentecost message to both Jews and the devout pilgrims who had come to Jerusalem from Parthian regions, addressed them both as "men *of Judea* (Acts 2:14) and "men *of Israel*" (*Acts* 2:22). Peter's choice of words, easily overlooked by modern readers of the Bible, indicates that he knew he was addressing a crowd which included both Jews and non-Jewish descendants of the ten tribes of Israel.

Parthia: The "Covenant" Kingdom

One more "smoking gun" piece of evidence concerning the Israelite nature of the Parthian Empire needs to be presented. This piece of evidence concerns the name "Parthia" itself. In the previous books in this series, it was documented that the Hebrew word for "covenant," (B-R-T or B-R-TH) was commonly used wherever the empire of Israel was dominant. This Hebrew word formed the basis for regions colonized by Israel ("Britain" and "Brittany") or for migrating groups of Israelites ("Brythonic Celts"). It was noted that the Phoenician-Israelite city of Carthage placed the Hebrew word "B-R-T" on its coins.

In the ancient world, the letters "B" and "P" were interchange-able; both are phonetically similar "labial" consonants. In his book, *Phoenician Origin of Britons, Scots and Anglo-Saxons*, L.A. Waddell points out that the "Phoenicians" interchanged the B's and P's in various forms of the word B-R-T. He lists many ancient forms in which the root word B-R-T was expressed. Words such as "Barat," "Prat," and "Britannia" are just a few samples of words based on the Hebrew word for "covenant."[46] Waddell notes the Phoenicians interchanged the B's and P's in the Mediterranean world, and adds that the Phoenicians of Cilicia called the city of Tarsus "Parthenia."[47] Notice the similarity between the Phoenician "Parthenia" and the later Asian empire, "Parthia."

ISRAELITES

THE "COVENANT" PEOPLE

The Bible records that the tribes of Israel, under Moses, made a "covenant" with God. The Israelites retained the unique awareness that they were the "covenant" people as an enduring part of their culture. The Hebrew word for "covenant" ("B-R-TH") was placed on people, places and Phoenician/Carthaginian coins. The presence of the Hebrew word for "covenant" on ancient peoples or places is a strong identifier for locating where the ten tribes of Israel migrated after leaving Palestine. Listed below are important examples.

HEBREW WORD FOR "COVENANT"

Without Vowels:	**B-R-T, B-R-TH**
With Vowels:	**BERITH, BARAT, BRYTH, BRIT, B'RITH, etc.**

TRIBAL AND PLACE NAMES ASSOCIATED WITH MIGRATING ISRAELITES:

BRITON, BRETON, BRITTANY, BRYTHONIC CELTS, etc.

Place Name		Greek Name
BRITANNIC ISLANDS	=	PRETANIC ISLANDS
BRITHIA or B'RITHIA	=	PARTHIA

The *Encyclopedia Britannica* confirmed that the Greeks interchanged P's and B's, recording that the Greeks referred to the Britannic Isles (the British Isles) as the "Pretani" or Pretanic Islands.[48] Aylett Sammes, a 17th century British historian, also noted that "B's" and "P's" were "easily convertible" in ancient contexts.[49]

Since it is documented that the Greeks interchanged P's and B's, their accounts of Parthia" could just as easily have been written as "Barthia," or "Brithia." In these forms the Hebrew word for covenant ("B-R-T" or "B-R-TH") is clearly evident. **Representing the "B" as a "P" (as was done in the ancient world), the consonants of "Berith," the Hebrew word for "covenant," become P-R-TH, the exact consonants of the word "Parthia!"** The identity of the Parthians is no longer a mystery. They were the "covenant" people of the ten tribes of Israel, and their very name declared to the world that they were the "covenant" people.

L.A. Waddell, the author of the book cited above, understood that words formed from the consonants B-R-T identified the Phoenicians, but he never grasped that the Phoenicians were the Israelites or that the B-R-T words designated the "covenant" people. Since his book contains Aryan racial themes, Waddell never saw this self-evident fact. He also did not realize that the terms "Jewish" and "Israelite" were not synonymous. In the appendix in his book, Waddell includes the following notation in an historical chart:

FRIEZE IN THE PALACE-TEMPLE OF HATRA.

"Israelites carried into captivity by Nebuchadnezzar, 587 [B.C.]."[50]

As the reader now knows, the Israelites of the ten tribes had left Palestine by 721 B.C., and were well established in the Black Sea region and the Russian steppes by 587 B.C. The "Israelites" were long absent from Palestine by 587 B.C. Waddell should have said the "Jews [were] carried into captivity" because it was Judah that was carried captive by Nebuchadnezzar in 587 B.C.

A modern epigrapher, Dr. Barry Fell, has also noted the interchangeability of the P's and B's in the ancient world. He gives the name "P-Celts" to a group of Celts who used "P" and "B" interchangeably. These "P" Celts were the "Brythonic" Celts, and they gave birth to the Breton, Welsh and Cornish languages as well as the ancient "Gaulish languages of central and eastern Europe."[51]

Some ancient cultures interchanged the letters "P" and "B" (both are labial consonants with similar sounds). The Brythonic Celts, who settled in ancient Britain, were known as P-Celts because of this trait. The ancient Greeks also manifested this trait, using the term "Pretanic Islands" for "Britanic Islands." Since the term Parthia has also come to us from early Greek writers, substituting a "B" for the initial "P" of this word results in BARTHIA or PARTHIA, a clear proclamation by the Parthians that they were descended from the "covenant" people of the Ten Tribes of Israel. The Brythonic Celts were Israelites who, retaining the name of the "covenant" people, migrated westward toward the British Isles and Europe. The Israelites who migrated northward and eastward

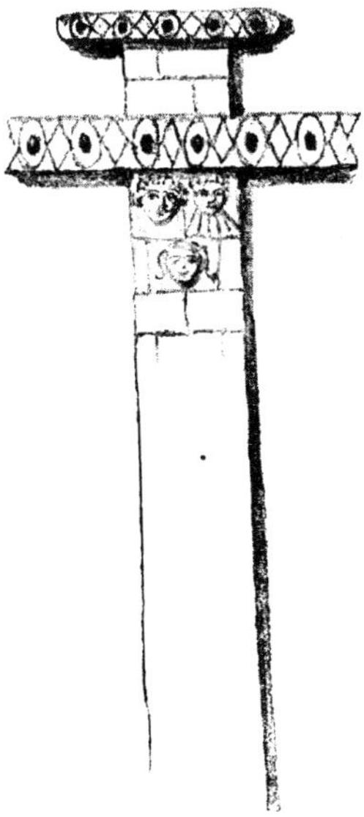

PILASTER AT HATRA, WITH CORNICE AND CAPITAL.

into Asia became the Iberians, the Sacae Scythians and the Parthians. Therefore, we can see that the interchangeability of "P's" and "B's" accompanied the Israelites migrating both eastward and westward from ancient Palestine.

In conclusion, let us briefly review the overwhelming evidence that the Parthians were Israelites of the ten tribes of Israel who had migrated to Asia. The Parthians were never recorded as being in Asia until **after** the ten tribes of Israel relocated to Asia. The Bible records that these tribes were placed in the "cities of the Medes," and Parthia's homeland adjoined the territory of the Medes. History records the Parthians were first under the dominion of the Assyrians, and that was also the fate of those Israelites taken captive by the Assyrians. We can easily see the names of the clans of Ephraim in the Parthian homelands, and history is clear that the Parthians were the kinsmen of the Scythian Sacae, who were shown to be Israelites in the previous book.

The Parthian cities of Asaak, Dara, Gaza and Samariane all bore Hebrew names. Many groups from the Parthian Empire were among the worshippers of the God of Israel who were in Jerusalem for a Holy Day of God, the first Christian Pentecost. The Parthians had many Hebrew-Semitic words in their language, and later placed Semitic inscriptions on their coins. The Parthian Ar**sac**id dynasty included the name of "Isaac" and many individual kings had names that included the term "Phares," fulfilling God's promise to David that his descendants would perpetually serve as rulers over the ten tribes of Israel. The very name "Parthia" preserves the Hebrew word "B-R-TH" (with the "B" shown as a "P"), proclaiming that they were "the covenant people." The facts are clear. The Parthian Empire was an empire of Israelites who, having thrown off the dominion of their captors, were now ruling over their previous masters.

If the history of the Parthian Empire was discussed in much depth in history texts, its Israelite origins would become obvious. Perhaps that is the reason why their history has been mostly deleted from history texts taught to the modern world. The secular modern world has a strong anti-biblical bias, and it does not want to find the "lost"

ROCK SCULPTURE OF GOTARZES AT BEHISTUN.

ten tribes because doing so would powerfully validate the Bible. Therefore, the true history of the mighty Phoenician, Carthaginian, Scythian and Parthian Empires have been mostly censored out of the historical record. **Is it only a "coincidence" that the major world empires dropped from modern history texts are all Israelite empires?** Instead of teaching the facts about the major Israelite empires, history texts now include the fiction that Greece and Rome were the only world empires and the only truly "civilized" people in the ancient world. As the famous British historian, George Rawlinson, noted in a quote at the beginning of this chapter, such a viewpoint is both "false" and "defective."

While Rome dominated the Mediterranean region and much of Europe, the Parthian Empire dominated Asian territory between the Euphrates and Indus Rivers and between the Persian Gulf to the Russian steppes inhabited by the Scythian tribes. The Parthian Empire stretched approximately 1900 miles from east to west and 1000 miles from north to south.[53]

Parthia and Rome interacted as "equals," yet few in the modern world have ever heard of Parthia's great empire! To demonstrate how dramatically the history of the Parthian Empire has been deleted from the modern world's awareness, go to any encyclopedia you can find and look up "Rome" and "Parthia." Count the pages devoted to each empire and you will see how little modern readers are allowed to learn about the history of Parthia. This de-emphasis of Parthia's real role in history as a superpower rival to Rome is especially hard to justify when the classical Roman writers themselves wrote an immense amount of material about the power and scope of the Parthian Empire.

Rome and Parthia had major wars, summit conferences and even a period of detente. Any detailed and honest comparison of the Roman and Parthian empires will cause the reader to reconsider the question of which of these empires was "barbarian" and which one merits the term "civilized."

The rarely revealed, but true story of this ancient, Israelite Empire of Parthia will now be revealed in the following chapter.

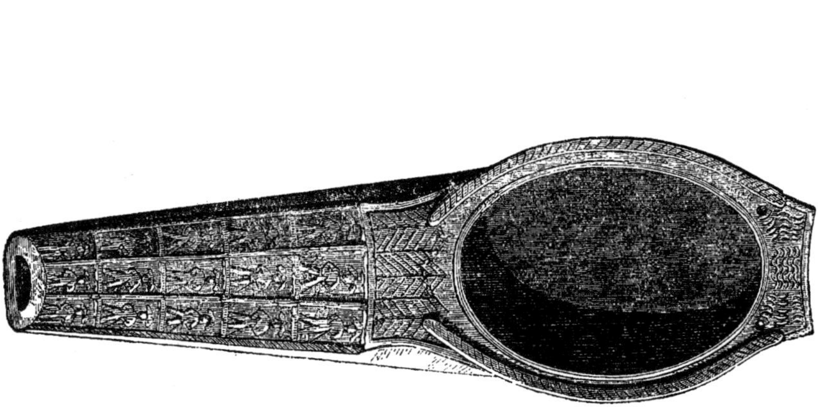

ENDNOTES: CHAPTER ONE

1.Rawlinson, The Sixth Great Oriental Monarchy, Preface, pp. v - vi

2.Rawlinson, Parthia, p. 27

3.Rawlinson, The Sixth Great Oriental Monarchy, p. 15

4.Herodotus, The History, 7. 66

5.Ibid., 3. 93

6.Rawlinson, The Sixth Great Oriental Monarchy, p. 19

7.Ibid, p. 20

8.Ibid, p. 19

9.Ibid, p. 26

10.Ibid, p. 19

11.Ibid, see footnote 1, p. 15

12.Encyclopaedia Britannica, Vol. 1, Heading entitled "Alphabet," pp. 683-684

13.Rawlinson, The Sixth Great Oriental Monarchy, p. 23

14.Charles-Picard, Daily Life in Carthage, p. 27

15.Church, Carthage, p. 13

16.Hopkins, Edward C.D., Attested Names of Parthian Rulers, website: www.parthia.com, see links: "Art and Culture" and "Language"

17.Young's Analytical Concordance to the Bible, see word "king," pp. 565-572, and "Index-Lexicon to the Old Testament," see word "melek," p. 25

18.Ibid, see word "son, subheadings 3 and 4," p. 914, and Index-Lexicon to the Old Testament, see word "BAR," p. 7

19.Frye, Richard, The Heritage of Persia, pp. 58, 213, 220, and 238

20.Rawlinson, The Sixth Great Oriental Monarchy, p. 159

21.Young's Analytical Concordance to the Bible, Old Testament Hebrew Lexicon, word "Sur," p. 48

22.Ibid, word "Ayin (=En)", third meaning, p. 6

23.Alexander, Caroline, "Alexander the Conqueror," National Geographic, March, 2000, p. 72

24.Frye, The Heritage of Persia, p. 208; and Rawlinson, Parthia, p. 10

25.Rawlinson, The Sixth Great Oriental Monarchy, pp. 42-44; and Encyclopaedia Britannica, Vol. 17, Heading entitled "Parthia," p. 344

26.Frye, Richard, The Heritage of Persia, p. 198-199

27.Rawlinson, Henry, Bactria, p. 12

28.Ragozin, Media, pp. 57-60, and map before p. 1

29.Encyclopaedia Britannica, Vol. 24, Index Section, see "Eran," p. 580

30.Ragozin, Media, p. 20-22

31.Encyclopaedia Britannica, Vol. 17, Heading entitled "Pahlavi or Pehlevi," p. 30

32.Frye, p. 201; and Encyclopaedia Britannica, Vol. 17, Heading entitled "Persia," p. 577

33.Rawlinson, Sixth Great Oriental Monarchy, pp. 231-233, 263, 320-321

34.Strabo, Geography, 11, 3, 3

35.Gawler, Our Scythian Ancestors Identified With Israel, p. 9

36.Culican, The Medes and Persians, p. 50

37.Frye, p. 211; and Encyclopaedia Britannica, Vol. 17, Heading entitled "Parthia," pp. 344-345

38.Strabo, Geography, 15, 1, 27

39.Frye, p. 210; and Encyclopaedia Britannica, Vol. 17, Heading entitled "Parthia," p. 345

40.Rawlinson, Ancient History, p. 474

41.Ibid, p. 475

42.Rawlinson, The Sixth Great Oriental Monarchy, pp. 297 and 318

43.Ibid, pp. 63, 69, 91, 220, 228, 250, 269, 294, 296 and 320

44.Eusebius, The History of the Church, III, 1

45.Frye, p. 201; and Encyclopaedia Britannica, Vol. 17, Heading entitled "Persia," p. 577

46.Waddell, pp. 52-59

47.Ibid, pp. 53-54

48.Encyclopaedia Britannica, Vol. 12, see "Ireland," p. 598

49.Sammes, Aylett, Britannia (Antiquities of Ancient Britain), p. 49

50.Waddell, Appendix 1, p. 387

51.Fell, America BC, pp. 41-42

52.Josephus, Antiquities of the Jews, XI, V, 2

53.Rawlinson, Ancient History, p. 472

Chapter 2
PARTHIA:
The Forgotten Ancient Superpower

The lack of awareness concerning Parthia's power and influence in the ancient world was briefly mentioned in the previous chapter. In this chapter, the reader will learn the history of the Parthian Empire, an ancient "superpower" whose history has been forgotten and ignored in the modern world. A quote by the nineteenth century British historian, George Rawlinson, lamenting the widespread lack of awareness about Parthia, opened the preceding chapter. This chapter will begin with an expanded version of his quote:

> "**the picture of the world during the Roman period...put before students in 'Histories of Rome,' was defective, not to say false, in its omission to recognize the real position of Parthia**...as a counterpoise to the power of Rome...**a rival state dividing with Rome the attention of mankind and the sovereignty of the known earth**. Writers of Roman history have been too much in the habit of representing [Rome]...as a Universal Monarchy...having no other limits than those of the civilised world...the truth seems to be that...**from first to last...there was always in the world a Second Power...which in a true sense balanced Rome, acted as a counterpoise and a check...This power for nearly three centuries (B.C. 64-A.D. 225) was Parthia**...In the hope of gradually vindicating to Parthia her true place in the world's history, the author has...placed the Parthians alongside of the Romans."[1] *(Emphasis added)*

George Rawlinson is not the only historian to note that Parthia was a world empire equivalent to Rome. James Strong, the author of *Strong's Concordance*, a famous biblical resource book, co-authored with John McClintock the *McClintock and Strong Cyclopedia of Biblical, Theological, and Ecclesiastical Literature*. First published in the 19th century, they wrote:

> "Parthia was a power almost rivaling Rome — the only existing power which had tried its strength against Rome and had not been worsted in the encounter."[2]

In neglecting the history of the Parthian Empire, modern writers have committed a grievous omission and done a great disservice to modern students of history. To grasp the scale of this omission, consider this analogy. If historians two millennia in the future wrote the history of the 20th century entirely from the standpoint of Russia, and mentioned the United States as a mere footnote, it would yield a grossly inaccurate perception of the 20th century. Yet that is the scale of historical inaccuracy which results when historians focus only on Rome and scarcely mention the Parthian Empire. This chapter will reveal the true role of Parthia in world history.

Even though much is known about Parthia, very little about Parthia is ever taught in modern history texts. Rawlinson's books about Parthia are based on the histories of the Greco-Roman classical writers — Justin, Dio Cassius, Strabo, Plutarch, and others — who wrote extensively about Parthia. It is very odd that although Roman writers deemed Parthia worthy of a great deal of attention, modern history texts virtually ignore this ancient world empire. As the previous chapter has demonstrated, Parthia was an Asian Empire dominated by the ten tribes of Israel who had been transplanted into the region of Asia formerly ruled by Assyria and Medo-Persia. If the history of Parthia had been consistently taught to students, the myth that the ten tribes of Israel were "lost" would never have existed.

Parthian-Seleucid Greek Wars

Rawlinson began his discussion of Parthia at a time when it was "Rome's equal" in 64 B.C. In fact, Parthia possessed a large

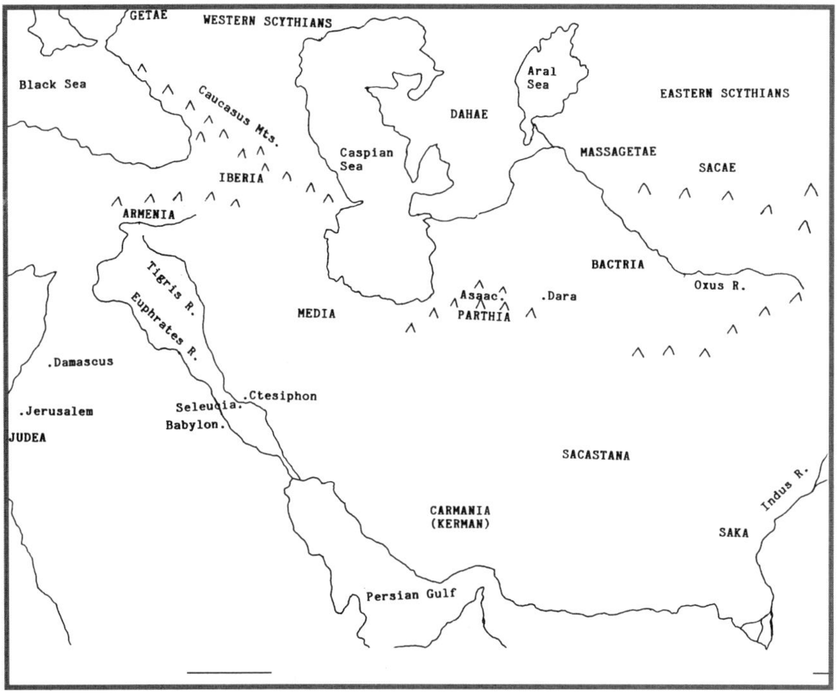

empire long before that date, but had little contact with Rome in its early period. Parthia's first great opponent was the Seleucid Greek Empire, which was heir to most of the Asian conquests of Alexander the Great. The Parthians had become a province of the Seleucid Greek Empire after Alexander the Great destroyed the Persian Empire.

Parthia was located southeast of the Caspian Sea and declared its independence from the Seleucid Greek Empire in 256-250 B.C. To help modern readers put their action in perspective, the Parthian action was similar to that of the American colonies in 1776 who declared their independence from the British Empire. Just as the American colonies had been ruled by the large and powerful British Empire, the Parthians had been ruled by the large and powerful Seleucid Greek Empire. Like the Americans, the Parthians had to fight for their independence before it became a reality.

The first independent king of Parthia was known as Arsaces, and history records that he came to Parthia from Scythia or Bactria. As discussed in the first chapter, the "Bactrians" were very likely the "Bachrites" of the tribe of Ephraim *(Numbers 26:35)*, a related Scythian "Sacae" tribe. Arsaces, therefore, came to Parthia from another region inhabited by the ten tribes of Israel. Ar**sac**es (whose name included the root word: "**Isaac**") began a dynasty that ruled Parthia throughout its history. Since Genesis 49:10 promised that dynasties of kings would proceed from the tribe of Judah, it suggests that Arsaces was a member of the tribe of Judah. As Israelites, the Parthian people would understandably have been receptive to being ruled by a member of the royal dynasty which had previously led the Israelites to their greatest glory under Kings David and Solomon. As the previous chapter also noted, the Davidic origin of Parthia's kings is indicated by the root word, Phares, an ancestor of King David, in the names of Parthian kings. Also, since Jeremiah 33:17 promised that David's descendants would always serve on thrones over the ten tribes of Israel, Arsaces was surely a descendant of King David. As the first chapter noted, David's royal descendants were made vassal kings over parts of the Babylonian empire, and his descendants had become numerous in Asia.

Rawlinson comments that "the Parthian kingdom was thoroughly anti-Hellenic,"[3] and revolted from the Hellenic Seleucids at a time when the Seleucids were involved with their on-going rivalry with the Egyptian Ptolemies.

ALEXANDER TAMING BUCEPHALUS

Consider the political situation at the time of Parthia's "declaration of independence." After the death of Alexander the Great, his empire was divided into four separate kingdoms, the two strongest of which became the Seleucid Empire of Asia and the Ptolemaic Empire of Egypt. The four way division of Alexander's Empire was a fulfillment of Daniel's prophecy in Daniel 11:1-4 about a mighty Grecian king who would supplant the Persian Empire, die in his prime, and have his kingdom divided into four sections. According to Josephus, the Jewish High Priest personally showed this prophecy in the book of Daniel to Alexander when he was in Jerusalem.[4] Daniel's prophecy was given in the sixth century B.C., and Alexander the Great fulfilled it in the fourth century B.C. This is one more example that there is a Creator God who controls world events to ensure that His prophecies do come to pass.

The Greek Seleucids and the Egyptian Ptolemies fought a series of wars, making it possible for Parthia to revolt in approximately 250 B.C. With the Seleucids weakened by warfare, the Parthians were emboldened to annex another Seleucid province. The Seleucid king then attacked and initially routed the upstart Parthians, causing Arsaces to flee to his Scythian kinsmen to seek refuge and reinforcements. Throughout Parthia's history, Parthian kings sought refuge or military support from the Sacae Scythian tribes during times of crisis, underscoring their common heritage with the Sacae. The Sacae gave the Parthian king military assistance, as did the Bactrians. In 237 B.C., this alliance defeated the army of the Seleucid Empire in a critical battle which made the independence of the Parthians a reality. It was an historic turning point, and Rawlinson records that the Parthians long observed the anniversary of this battle as "a solemn festival."[5]

American readers can relate to the beginning of the Parthian nation. The traditional Parthian celebration of an "independence day" to commemorate their freedom from Seleucid rule is comparable to Americans celebrating their "Independence Day" on July 4th to commemorate their freedom from the British. Also, just as the Parthians needed outside help from the Scythians to obtain their independence, America needed outside help from France in order to realize its independence. There are a number of striking parallels between the Parthians of the ancient world and the Americans of the modern world. Since they do exist, these parallels will be noted periodically in this chapter.

Parthia's rise to power coincided with the gradual waning of Carthage in the second and third Punic Wars. However, during the first few decades of Parthia's rivalry with the Seleucid Greeks, Rome was fighting for its survival as Hannibal's Carthaginian army invaded Italy and almost conquered Rome. Eventually, Rome gained the advantage and while Carthage (an Israelite power in the Mediterranean) was in decline, Parthia (an Israelite power in Asia) was gradually rising to empire status. By the time Carthage fell, Parthia had already become an empire and was destined to become Rome's great enemy.

When Arsaces died, he was replaced by his brother Tiridates, who led the Parthians in their great victory over the Seleucids. He also built a fortress city named "Dara." Dara is a Hebrew name *(I Chronicles 2:6)*, and because Dara was the name of a patriarch of the tribe of Judah, King Tiridates' naming a city in honor of a Jewish patriarch supports the conclusion that the Arsacid dynasty was from the tribe of Judah. Since the early Parthian city of **Asaak,** named after Isaac, also bears a Hebrew name, the Israelite nature of the Parthian Empire was easily apparent from its inception. It needs to be stressed, however, that although the ruling dynasty of the Parthians were descendants of Judah's King David, the Parthians themselves were descendants of the ten tribes of Israel. This fulfilled the prophecy of Jeremiah 33:17 that David's descendants would rule over the non-Jewish descendants of the ten tribes of Israel, known as the "house of Israel."

Another war with the Seleucids occurred about three decades after Parthia's "declaration of independence." Although the more-powerful Seleucids temporarily captured Parthia's capital city, the war ended with a treaty calling for the Seleucids' withdrawal in about 206 B.C. and Parthia remaining independent.[6] This results in another striking parallel to the early history of the United States of America. Having won its freedom from Britain, America had to again fight the British in the War of 1812. In it, the British temporarily captured Washington, D.C., the American capital city, but the war ended with a peace treaty, in which the British withdrew and the Americans maintained their independence.

Just as America's War of 1812 was soon followed by a period of "manifest destiny" in which the young and vigorous American nation spread across North America, Parthia's second war with the Seleucids was followed by a period of great expansion which extended

Parthian rule over much of south central Asia. Phraates I of Parthia took control of the Caspian Gates, key mountain passes which control the east-west invasion routes across Persia.[7] Parthia's possession of the strategic Caspian Gates fulfilled another aspect of the Abrahamic Covenant which had been inherited by Isaac, Jacob, and the Israelite tribes of Ephraim and Manasseh *(Genesis 48).* God had promised Abraham that his "birthright" seed would "possess the gates of their enemies" *(Genesis 22:17).* Such "gates" are geographical chokepoints which control or limit access to military forces in wartime or key routes of commerce in peacetime.

The next Parthian monarch, Mithridates I, expanded Parthian power to true empire status. Rawlinson describes Mithridates, the brother of Phraates I, as:

> "...one of those rare individuals to whom it has been given to unite the powers which form the conqueror with those which constitute the successful organizer of a state. Brave and enterprising in war...yet...mild, clement, philanthropic, he conciliated those whom he subdued almost more easily than he subdued them, and by the efforts of a few years succeeded in welding together a dominion which lasted without suffering serious mutilation for nearly four centuries."[8]

By the time of his death, Mithridates I had placed Bactria, Media, Babylonia, Persia, and other regions under Parthian dominion, ruling "from the Hindu Kush to the Euphrates...a distance of 1500 miles from east to west."[9] On modern maps, the dominion of Mithradates I is roughly equivalent to the territory from northern Syria and eastern Turkey to western Pakistan, and from modern Uzbekistan and Tajikistan to the Persian Gulf. The Euphrates River, as early as the second century B.C., became the traditional western border of Parthia. Most of Parthia's expansion came at the expense of the Seleucid Greeks, whose emperor he defeated and captured. Mithridates I died in 136 B.C., leaving a large empire in the hands of his son, Phraates II. Although Mithridates I of Parthia was one of the ancient world's greatest conquerors and the builder of one of the ancient world's largest and most powerful empires, it would be difficult to find a modern history text which even mentions him.

In 129 B.C., the Seleucids attacked the new Parthian Empire with an army numbering approximately 300,000 while the Parthian army numbered only 120,000. Scythian troops reinforced the Parthians, but arrived too late to be decisive in the battles that followed.[10] However, this willingness on the part of Scythia to aid Parthia in its wars was an oft-repeated pattern in Parthian history. The western provinces of the Parthians revolted to the side of their old rulers, the Seleucids. Three battles were fought in which the outnumbered Parthians were defeated each time. The Parthians exhibited a dogged determination, however, and refused to capitulate even though the war so far favored their enemies. Winter set in, and the Seleucid army conducted itself so oppressively in the occupied provinces that their people privately sent word to the Parthians that they would again welcome Parthian rule if Parthia would liberate them from the oppressive Seleucids.

Even though the Seleucids were now in grave danger, they spurned a merciful offer of peace from Phraates with unacceptable demands of their own. The people of the captive provinces attacked the unsuspecting Seleucid troops within their garrison towns, and the Parthian regulars crushed the Seleucid monarch and his remaining troops in a final battle. Historians record that the Seleucid monarch, Antiochus, perished along with his army of 300,000.[11] This battle was another historic turning point in world history, because it broke the back of the Seleucid Empire, which withered away to nothing, trapped between the two growing powers of Rome on the west and Parthia on the east.

One result of Parthia's historic victory was that the Maccabees of Judea were able to assert their independence from the now mortally wounded Seleucids. Rawlinson comments on this fact in the following words:

> "The immediate result of the destruction of Antiochus and his host was the revolt of Judea."[12]

The Jews even conquered the Idumeans (Edomites), who submitted to circumcision and Jewish laws. Josephus records that these Edomites merged with the Jews and they became one people.[13] However, Judea (the house of Judah) was able to assert its independence from the Seleucids only because Parthia (part of the ten tribes of Israel) had crushed the Seleucids. The Parthians treated the conquered Seleucids mercifully and their royal households intermarried.

Herein lies another parallel between Parthia and modern America. Even as America has been a merciful conqueror — building up Japan and Germany after World War II, rescuing the German capital from a Russian blockade via the Berlin Airlift, and many other honorable deeds — Parthia was also a merciful ruler of the people it defeated in warfare. It is a clear commentary on the enlightened character of Parthian rule that the people in the contested provinces, after tasting both Parthian and Seleucid rule, actively fought the Seleucids in order to become Parthian subjects again!

At this juncture, Phraates II and the Parthians should have enjoyed their time of great triumph. However, a bizarre event occurred. Earlier it was noted that a Scythian army allied to the Parthians arrived too late to assist in the final battle of the war. The Scythians arrived just after Parthia had crushed the Seleucid army, and a battle between the Scythians and Parthians erupted when the Parthians refused to share any war booty with the Scythians. The Scythians likely suspected that the Parthians had "jumped the gun" on the war in order to deprive the Scythians of their share of the expected booty. The Parthians felt that since the Scythians did not participate in the fighting, they should not be paid. At any rate, Phraates II reneged on his promised payments to the Scythians, who had, after all, left their lands and families and marched hundreds of miles to hazard their lives at Parthia's request.

A Scythian Horseman. (From the sculptures at Kertch.)

In this bizarre battle between related tribesmen, the Scythian army was victorious, and the Parthian king died in the battle. Just after crushing the Seleucid Empire, the Parthians were themselves defeated by their Scythian allies who had marched out of the north to help Parthia. At that point in history, Scythia was still more powerful than Parthia. However, as one would expect between a battle of brothers, the victorious Scythians had no interest in annexing Parthia to their own tribal homelands. While the Parthians were motivated to conquer and hold an empire composed of different nations, the isolationist Scythians had no interest in taking advantage of this obvious opportunity for territorial gain.

The whole event is uncannily similar to a battle described in the Bible. *(Judges 11-12)* After winning a great victory over the Ammonites, Jephthah and an army of Gileadites — the tribes of Manasseh, Reuben and Gad — were confronted by an army of Ephraimites which was upset that it had not participated in the battle and missed out on the booty. The usually allied brother tribes of Ephraim and Manasseh then fought each other in a needless battle over war booty. The tribe of Manasseh defeated the Ephraimites in a battle costing 42,000 Ephraimite lives. The dominance of the tribe of Ephraim in the Parthian Empire and the dominance of Manasseh in the Scythian Empire has been discussed earlier, making this Parthian-Scythian battle a rerun of the war in Judges 12. Though Ephraim and Manasseh are brother tribes, even they can fight one another. Historically, whenever the "birthright" tribes of Ephraim and Manasseh came to blows, Manasseh usually won.

After the warfare the Scythians, satisfied by their possession of war booty and the death of the Parthian king who "cheated" them, returned to their own land. This confirms that the Scythians had no territorial designs against their Parthian kinsmen and were content simply "to teach the Parthians a lesson." That lesson was learned, as there is no record that the Parthians ever again reneged when the Scythians came to help them in a war.

Nevertheless, Parthia had now replaced the Seleucids as the dominant power in southern Asia, and it was only a matter of time before Rome and Parthia came in contact with each other. Before we discuss the epic struggles between Parthia and Rome, we will examine the governmental structure and policies of the Parthians to see what it was which made their dominion so preferable to that of the Seleucid Greeks.

Parthia's Feudalism, Magi and Moderate Rule

Although Parthia was ruled by a single dynasty, there was no custom of primogeniture, whereby the oldest son of the previous king automatically inherits the throne. Any male relative of the king could serve as the new monarch. The Parthians had a system of checks and balances upon the authority of the king, which predated the Magna Carta by more than a millennium. Strabo, a Greco-Roman who lived just prior to the time of Christ, wrote:

> "That the Council of the Parthians...consists of two groups, one that of the kinsmen, and the other that of the wise men and magi, from both of which groups the kings were appointed."[14]

Rawlinson refers to these two bodies as the "Royal House" and the "Senate." The Royal House contained the male members of the royal line, and the Senate consisted of the "Wise Men" (prominent secular leaders) and the "Magi" (the priestly caste). He observed that these two houses jointly constituted: "the Megistanes, the nobles...the privileged class which to a considerable extent checked and controlled the monarchy."[15] He also noted:

> "The King was permanently advised by [these] two councils...The monarchy was elective, but only in the house of the Arsacidae; and the concurrent vote of both councils was necessary in the appointment of a new king."[16]

This means that while kings were elected by a concurrent vote of the two houses, all new kings had to be members of the Royal House. The fact that the Parthians elected their kings via a bicameral vote may be one of the best-kept secrets of the ancient world. While only the members of the two houses of the Megistanes voted in royal elections, there are few examples of an elective process being involved in the

selection of ancient monarchs. The fact that the Megistanes were standing deliberative bodies also acted as a further check upon the power of Parthian kings. Even though Parthian monarchs could exercise autocratic powers once elected, the existence of this bicameral council provided some restraint upon them. Kings could even be "recalled" if they sufficiently offended Parthia's nobility and priests. Parthia's governmental structure manifested the beginnings of a "Parliament," and foreshadowed the Magna Charta of medieval England, which enabled the nobility to limit the power of English kings.

The Magi — subject of Christmas stories as the givers of "gold, frankincense, and myrrh" to Jesus — were a very influential part of Parthian society, and some of them served as members of Parthia's "Senate." Rawlinson states that the Magi:

> "were a powerful body, consisting of **an organized hierarchy which had come down from ancient times**, and was feared and venerated by all classes of people. Their numbers at the close of the Empire, counting males only, are reckoned at 80,000; they...**were the sole inhabitants of many large towns or villages, which they were permitted to govern as they pleased.**"[17] *(Emphasis added)*

The Magi paralleled the Levites of ancient Israel. The tribe of Levi had been the priestly tribe of the Israelites, and the Law of Moses *(Numbers 35:1-8)* required that the Levites dwell in their own independent cities. Joshua 21 records that the priestly Levites were given 48 independent cities to inhabit in the territory of ancient Palestine. The Parthians emulated the Israelite tradition of having independent cities for its priestly class. That the Parthian Magi were a hierarchy of priests that had descended "from ancient times" indicates that **the Magi were**

an hereditary body: an actual tribe of priests. Since the Israelite nature of the Parthians has already been shown, the Parthian Magi were likely a body of Levites, Israel's hereditary tribe of priests. A priest of the Parthian Magi is depicted on a bas-relief wearing a conical hat,[18] reminiscent of the miter worn by Israelite priests and the tall caps of Scythian leaders.

While the image of Rome's legions brutally enforcing obedience in Rome's conquered provinces is a common theme in history, what was Parthia's rule like? Parthia's king was the overall monarch of Parthia's empire, but provincial vassal kings and rulers were given considerable autonomy within the overall guidelines set by the Parthian king. Concerning the vassal kings, Rawlinson stated:

> "so long as they paid their tribute regularly to the Parthian monarchs, and aided them in their wars..., [they] were allowed to govern the people beneath their sway at their pleasure."[19]

While the Parthian kings retained sovereignty concerning such matters as taxes and national defense, Parthian provinces were largely self-governing regarding local matters. Parthia's system of vassal kings and subordinate nobles who were subject to an overall king will remind some readers of the feudal system utilized by the Europeans in the Middle Ages. Edward Gibbon, the prominent historian who authored *The Decline and Fall of the Roman Empire*, also noted the parallels between the feudal systems of the Parthians and Medieval Europe. Gibbon's observation about the similarity between the Parthian and European feudal systems is quoted by Rawlinson:

> "The remark has been made by...Gibbon, that the [Parthian] system...'**exhibited under other names, a lively image of the feudal system, which has since prevailed in Europe**'...the points of difference between the Parthian and the [European] feudal system being **probably** more numerous than those of resemblance, but **the points of resemblance being very main points, not few in number, and striking**."[20] *(Emphasis added)*

It is noteworthy that while the known parallels between the Parthian and European feudal systems are "very main points" and "striking," their differences were only assumed to exist, as one can see by the use of the word "probably" in the above quote. It is as if Rawlinson could scarcely believe that the Parthian Empire in Asia represented such a remarkable forerunner of the society of medieval Europe. The *Encyclopaedia Britannica*, also commented on the feudal nature of Parthia's empire:

> "these nomads [the Scythians and Parthians] were the main pillar of the empire, and from them were obviously derived the great magnates, with their huge estates and hosts of serfs, who composed the imperial council, led the armies, governed the provinces and made and unmade the kings."[21]

As will be documented in the fourth book in this series on Israelite history, the "striking" similarities between the Parthians and Medieval Europe were no coincidence. It is also recorded that the Parthians pioneered the concept of municipal "home-rule" privileges for some of its cities. For example:

> "The Greek towns...in large numbers throughout the [Parthian] Empire, enjoyed a municipal government of their own, and in some cases were almost independent communities...Seleucia...its population was estimated in the first century after Christ at six hundred thousand...had its own... **municipal council...elected by the people** to rule them."[22] *(Emphasis added)*

The astounding fact that Parthia's Empire included large "home-ruled" cities that held municipal elections to elect city councils should be taught in every classroom in the modern western world! Cities in the modern western world have for centuries copied this ancient Parthian practice, and it is remarkable that an ancient empire allowed its citizens such freedoms. Most ancient empires, fearing dissent and revolts, ruled their subject peoples with an iron hand.

Josephus records a curious trait of the Parthians, which provides another uncanny parallel that modern Americans will readily understand. Josephus recorded that it was a Parthian custom to seal an agreement by "shaking hands." Josephus wrote:

> "This is of the greatest force there with all these [Parthians]...for none of them will deceive you **when once they have given you their right hands**, nor will any one doubt their fidelity, when it is

> once given...**The joining of the right hands was esteemed** among the Persians and Parthians, in particular, **a most inviolable obligation to fidelity**."[23] *(Emphasis added)*

When Parthians "shook hands on a deal," it meant that their entire honor was at stake in keeping whatever had been the subject of the agreement. This Parthian custom continues today among modern Americans, who have a long history that one's honor is at stake when they "shake hands on a deal." To renege on a deal after you had "shaken hands" over it, meant one's reputation would be permanently damaged.

There was also a substantial Jewish population in Parthia's empire. When the Jews were carried captive by the Assyrians and Babylonians into Asia, most never returned to Palestine. Only a small remnant of Jews returned to rebuild Jerusalem during the rule of the Medo-Persian Empire, as described in the Biblical books of Ezra and Nehemiah. Those returnees gave birth to the Jews who populated Judea during the time of Christ. However, far more Jews remained in Asia than the smaller number that returned to Judea. The book of Esther records that the Jews were numerous and present in the provinces of the Persian Empire "From India unto Ethiopia." *(Esther 8:9-17)*

Confluence of the Tigris and Euphrates Rivers

The Asian Jews in the Persian Empire eventually became subjects of the Parthian Empire. The policy of the Parthians toward the Jews was very magnanimous. Rawlinson records that: "there were also a certain number of places the inhabitants of which were wholly Jews, and these enjoyed similar privileges with the 'free towns' of the Greeks."[24]

> ***The book of Esther records that the Jews were numerous and present in the provinces of the Persian Empire "From India unto Ethiopia."*** *(Esther 8:9-17)*

Parthia's large Jewish population merits additional comment. Josephus wrote that the descendants of the ten tribes of Israel were very numerous, not subject to Rome, and were located "beyond Euphrates."[25] By referencing the Euphrates River — the border between the Roman and Parthian Empires — Josephus was indicating that Parthia was "Israelite territory." Since Josephus knew about the Israelite nature of the Parthians and Sacae, many other Jews surely did as well. Some Jews, tired of Rome's yoke in Palestine, may have emigrated to Parthia, which was dominated by the descendants of the ten tribes of Israel and allowed much personal liberty. However, the main reason for a substantial Jewish population in Asia is that most exiled Jews never did return to Palestine from their Babylonian captivity, and their descendants stayed in Asia, flourishing under Parthian rule.

While Rome imposed a "rule of iron" within its empire, Parthia permitted greater individual freedoms. This fact has strong parallels in the modern world, a discussion of which will enable the reader to relate to the struggles between Rome and Parthia.

Parthia and Rome were the two "superpowers" of their day. Parthia had the beginnings of a bicameral body with some checks and balances upon the power of the monarchy. It gave provinces and cities considerable local autonomy while maintaining "federal" control of foreign and military matters. Parthia was tolerant toward its subject people and allowed Greek and Jewish cities broad local freedoms. Rome, however, ruled its subject nations in a totalitarian, oppressive manner with Roman troops supporting Rome's tight controls over conquered nations.

In any comparison between (A) the ancient superpowers of Rome and Parthia and (B) the modern superpowers of the United States of America and the former Soviet Union, Parthia's freedoms would compare it to the United States while Rome's oppressiveness would make it an ancient counterpart of the Soviet Union. In one sense, this is too strong an assertion, for the Romans were a very religious people, worshipping many gods, unlike the godless atheism of the former Soviet Union. Yet the point to be made is that the whole western world is force-fed, almost exclusively, the history of Rome while Parthia's remarkable history is widely ignored. While this parallel may seem revolutionary to some, it is necessary to help undo the widespread myth that Rome was "civilized" while all the rest of the world was "barbarian." In the remainder of this chapter, and in the fourth book in this series on Israelite history, we will see that the social institutions of medieval and modern Europe developed from the Parthian system, not the Roman system.

Ancient Representation of a Scythian Family.

The Eastern Scythians Merge with Parthia

There is one important event in Parthian history that must be discussed before we examine its long, historic rivalry with Rome. After the Seleucid Empire had been defeated and absorbed by the Parthian Empire, the eastern part of Parthia's empire was "invaded" by a large number of Scythian "Sacae." In fact, this "invasion" gave the Parthians a major infusion of related Sacae (Scythian) kinsmen to bolster their empire. These Sacae entered the eastern portion of Parthia's empire in the first century B.C. after migrating southward from the Caspian Sea region. Besides bearing the name of Isaac, these Scythian tribes had tribal names that can be linked to the names of various Israelite tribes.

The principal Scythian tribe which migrated into the Parthian Empire was the Massagetae, the same Scythian tribe which crushed an invading Persian army under King Cyrus the Great, as discussed in the final chapter of the previous book in this series. The Massagetae were accompanied by allied tribes: the Dahae, the Tochari, the Asii, the Sacaruli, and other clans such as the Parni, Aparni, Chorasmii, etc.[26] George Rawlinson opined that this invasion was a "barbaric peril" from Asia; however, the facts do not support such a view. For example, the Parni and Aparni are frequently cited as being the original tribe of Arsaces, the first Parthian king.[27] Another Scythian tribe, the Dahae, aided the Parthians in various wars. These "invaders" were actually the Parthians' own Scythian kinsmen. History records that after some fighting over territories, the Scythian tribes became part of the Parthian Em-

1. A Scythian Footman; 2. A Scythian General.

pire, with their new homeland being named "**Sacastane** (land of the Saka or Scyths)."[28] The Scythians, who named their new territory in honor of Isaac, the Israelite patriarch, had a common racial and cultural heritage with the Parthians. In one of his maps, Rawlinson shows "Sacastana" in the eastern part of the Parthian Empire.[29]

The fact that Israelite tribes would fight among themselves is not surprising, given that they had to jostle one another to find territory to contain their large populations. Rawlinson proposed in his book that these migrating Scythians were themselves pushed into Parthia by the Huns of central Asia.[30]

Most Scythian names do not exactly reflect the names of Israelite tribes because they are the names which Greco-Roman historians gave them centuries after these tribes left Palestine. Even so, several names (besides their common name as "Sacae") have recognizable Israelite origins. The Massagetae, as explained in chapter six of the previous book, were the Israelite tribe of Manasseh. The Dahae may have been part of the tribe of Dan. The Tocahri likely descended from the Israelite tribe of Issachar as Tola was one of the clans of Issachar (Numbers 26:23). Combining syllables from the names "Tola" and "Issachar" results in the term "To-chari." The Chorasmii exhibit a name based on the root word of a clan of the tribe of Reuben (the Carmites of Numbers 26:6). On this specific case of ancient root words, I wish to acknowledge the help of the late-Dr. Charles Dorothy, a graduate of the Claremont Graduate School for pointing out that such a relationship is possible "since 'Carmite' of Numbers 26 uses the Hebrew caph, sometimes transliterated 'c,' 'ch,' 'k,' or 'kh.'" On the other hand, since Rawlinson records that the Chor-asmii were a clan of the Massagetae,[31] they may have been named after the Ma-chir-ites, a clan of the tribe of Manasseh (Numbers 26:29). The "Sacaruli" can not be identified with a particular tribe of Israel, but their Israelite origin is attested to by the fact that they are known by the name of "Isaac."

These tribes migrating into Parthia were the Scythians who had lived in the steppes east of the Caspian Sea. The Sacae Scythians who lived in the Black Sea and Caucasus Mountain regions were not involved in this migration.

While this large infusion of kinsmen into Parthia's empire greatly increased its strength, it needs to be understood that Parthia was not a monolithic Israelite empire consisting of just the tribes of Israel. There were many native populations who were not Israelites — Medes, Persians, Babylonians, Elamites, Assyrians, and others — even though they were located within the Parthian Empire.

Another large mass of people, the Yue-chi, was being pushed out of Asia toward Scythia and Parthia. Early Chinese chronicles record that the "**Ephthalites**" were one of the tribes of the Yue-chi.[32] The Ephthalites were also called "White Huns" because they were "fair-skinned," indicating a Semitic origin.[33] Byzantine writers also called them the "**Hephthalites**" or "**Nephthalites**," although the *Encyclopaedia Britannica* adds an editorial comment that "the initial N [of Nephthalite]...is believed to be a clerical error."[34] **It is easy for anyone with even a slight biblical knowledge to identify this tribe as the Israelite tribe of Naphtali**! The consonants of Ephthali (or Nephthali) precisely match the very unique name of Naphtali, one of the "lost ten tribes" of Israel.

It is amusing that the *Encyclopaedia Britannica* observed that the Byzantines who recorded that this tribe's name began with an "N" are "believed...[to have made] a clerical error." It offered no evidence indicating it was a clerical error, but it is "believed" to be one. Why? The "establishment" historians have a very strong bias against "finding" any of the "lost" ten tribes of Israel, for doing so would affirm the Bible and compel a dramatic pro-biblical shift in our view of world history. While many Israelite tribal names can be found in Asia, the similarity between the Asian "**Nephthalites**" and one of the "lost" tribes of Israel, the **Naphtalites**, is glaringly obvious. The presence of a tribe in Asia bearing an Israelite tribal name unchanged from biblical times is an academic "hot potato!" A "belief" that the "N" is an ancient "clerical error" helps obscure the Israelite nature of this tribe. Indeed, if establishment histories were to examine either Scythian or Parthian history in much depth at all, their identity as the ten tribes of Israel would be impossible to miss.

Saka-Scythian Soldier

The fact that the Ephthalites were "fair-skinned" — Semitic or Caucasian — further verifies their identification as Israelites, since the Israelites were all Semites. That the Ephthalites were called "White Huns" indicates that while they came out of Asia, they were differentiated from the other Huns who were not fair-or white-skinned. Indeed, the *Encyclopaedia Britannica* refers to the Sakas (or Sacae Scythians), the Yue-chi and the Ephthalites as related "Indo-Scythian" tribes.[35]

The Bible provides the answer why the tribes of Naphtali, the Machirite clan of Manasseh, and parts of Dan, Issachar, or Reuben (i.e. the Nephtalites, Massagetae, Chorasmi, Dahae, Tochari, etc.) would be located together as a group of allied tribes in Asia. II Kings 15:29 states that about twenty years prior to Samaria's fall, the Assyrians invaded Israel and carried captive the entire tribe of Naphtali, and those Israelites living in "Gilead and Galilee." This occurred in approximately 740 B.C. I Chronicles 5:26 reveals that "Gilead" included one-half the tribe of Mannasseh and the tribes of Reuben and Gad. Numbers 26:29 further shows us that the half-tribe of Manasseh, which lived in Gilead, was the Machirites. A look at a biblical atlas will confirm that the tribes of Issachar and Asher and a portion of Dan lived next to Naphtali in the region of Galilee, and portions of these tribes would have gone captive with the entire tribe of Naphtali.

The Assyrians relocated the tribes of Naphtali, Gad, Reuben, the half-tribe of Manasseh, and portions of other tribes eastward into their empire. Many of these Israelites migrated to the east of the Caspian Sea when the Assyrian Empire fell. The Massagetae and their allied tribes in that area annihilated the army of Cyrus the Great in 530-528 B.C. After living east of the Caspian Sea for half a millennium, they migrated southward into Parthia's Empire.

The Book of Tobit claims to tell the experiences of a family of Naphtalites *(Tobit 1:1-2)* after the Assyrians resettled them in Assyria and in the cities of the Medes. While Tobit is an apocryphal, non-canonized, book, its historical context makes it plausible reading for this time period. Tobit 1:21 parallels II Kings 19:37 in mentioning the death of the Assyrian King Sennacherib at the hands of his sons, who then fled to "Ararat" (Armenia) where they sought refuge. Tobit 14:12-15 states that Naphtalites lived in Ecbatana in Media when Nineveh fell. This is consistent with secular history as Ecbatana is named as a city of the "Scythians" who lived in Media during the fall of the Assyrian Empire.[36] The same people called "Naphtalites" in the book of Tobit, written from an Hebrew perspective, are called "Scythians" in secular accounts written from a non-Hebrew perspective.

Saka-Scythian soldiers and Caucasus Mountains

When the Assyrian Empire fell, many of their formerly subject peoples were suddenly free to migrate to new locations. One such people were the Israelites, including the tribe of Naphtali, and one group of them migrated to the steppes east of the Caspian Sea. The half-tribe of Manasseh stayed in that region, but the tribe of Naphtali went even further into Asia. However, they still bore their Israelite tribal name centuries later when they migrated out of Asia toward Parthia. The migration of the Massagetae and Nephtalites toward Parthia was not a coincidence. As they were pressured by other Asiatic tribes, they would logically retrace the historic routes their ancestors had followed into Asia.

The connection is clear. The Massagetae, the "Saka" (or Sacae) and the "Ephthalites" were related clans of the ten tribes of Israel who had been taken captive from Gilead and Galilee circa 740 B.C. While many settled in the eastern portion of the Parthian Empire, some Saka tribes founded a kingdom of their own in the region of the Indus River and historical accounts indicate that a large body of the Nephthalites apparently remained outside the borders of the Parthian Empire. It is likely that the tribe of Naphthali retained its exact Israelite name over many centuries because it was taken captive in one entire group. Other tribes, which left Palestine in a piecemeal fashion, came to be known by their appropriate clan names.

Since the Ephraimite role in the formation of Parthia was discussed earlier in this narrative, this infusion of Scythian Israelites meant that the Parthian empire came to include a large portion of the tribe of Ephraim, one-half the tribe of Manasseh, the tribes of Reuben and Gad and portions of the tribes of Issachar, Asher, Dan and Naphthali. While Gad is unnamed among the Scythians, it was likely present with the Massagetae as Gad migrated into Asia with the half-tribe of Manasseh and the tribe of Reuben. Since many Jews of the house of Judah had lived in the region of the Parthian Empire from the time of the Assyrian and Medo-Persian Empires, the tribes of Judah and Benjamin were present as well. The tribe of Levi was also in Parthia because there were Levites among the Jews *(Ezra 1:5)* and the Parthian priestly tribe, the Magi, may have been the hereditary Levites. Not all the tribes of Israel lived in Parthia. The Black Sea Scythians and the Iberians of the Caucasus region were large bodies of independent Israelites led by the other half of the tribe of Manasseh, the main bodies of the tribes of Asher, Issachar, Simeon and contingents of other tribes. A large body of the tribe of Dan was also present among the Black Sea Scythians as the rivers emptying into the Black Sea were all renamed after the tribe of Dan when the Scythians occupied that region after the fall of the kingdom of Israel. This was discussed in greater detail in the previous book in this series. However, at this time, there were even more scattered Israelites in the world. The Israelite-Phoenician and Carthaginian Empires had various colonies in Spain, the British Isles and Europe. When those empires fell, the survivors in their scattered colonies became independent, and where afterwards known as Celts, as was discussed in the previous book in this series.

The Israelite character of the Parthian Empire is well documented. The wars between the Roman and Parthian Empires will be much more interesting to read when it is realized that the Parthian Empire was dominated by the reunited and revitalized tribes of Israel ruling over native populations who had previously been Israel's captors.

Parthian bas-relief of a Magus (after Flandin and Coste).

The Roman-Parthian Wars

Rome and Parthia did not initially come into contact with each other as enemies. For several centuries the Seleucid Greek Empire had separated them. When Parthia replaced the Seleucids as the dominant Asian Empire, Rome seized the western portion of the Seleucid Empire. The kingdom of Armenia, which then had a large domain in Asia Minor, still served as a buffer state between the Roman and Parthian Empires. Rome became embroiled in a war with Armenia while Parthia tried to remain neutral. Parthia's neutral policy finally became untenable, and the Parthians entered the war on the side of the Romans. Rome, in the person of Pompey, offered Parthia an alliance with the promise that Rome would respect Parthia's right to have certain territories as her portion for assisting the Romans.

After the war was over, the Romans reneged on their word, and resisted the Parthians when they tried to occupy their promised portion of the conquered territory. Pompey also insulted the Parthian monarch, Phraates III, by refusing to address him by the customary Parthian title of "King of Kings." Rawlinson comments on this episode that: "Phraates learnt what Roman promises were worth."[37] Note that this Parthian king (Phraates) had a name that included the Hebrew root word for Phares, the dynastic line of David and the kings of Judah. From this very first Parthian-Roman contact, about 62 B.C., the Euphrates River became the border between their two empires.[38]

Earlier, we noted that binding one's word with a "hand shake" was viewed as a sacred bond of commitment among Parthians. Being true to one's word was critically important in Parthian society. Once a Parthian King offered to meet with two rebels under a guarantee of security that included "sending his right hand" to them via an ambassador.[39] This signified that even the Parthian King was bound to observe any agreement that involved "shaking hands." Indeed, offering "his right hand" to the rebels was the highest degree of security he could give them! Because honoring one's word was so high a value in Parthian society, the ease with which the Romans "broke their word" caused the Parthians to see the Romans as an untrustworthy, "barbarian" society.

MAP TO ILLUSTRATE EASTERN GEOGRAPHY OF THE BIBLE.

Phraates III was assassinated by his sons, Mithridates and Orodes, with the former then banishing the latter. The Parthian nobles — the "Wise Men" and Magi — later deposed Mithridates because of his harsh rule, and recalled Orodes from banishment to be the new king.[40] The Wise Men and Magi were powerful enough at this time, circa 56 B.C., to dethrone a monarch they disliked.

There is another parallel to modern American and European societies in the fact that a Parthian Emperor could be "recalled" by the Megistanes, the bicameral body of the king's kinsmen and the "Senate" of the Magi and nobility. American Presidents can be "impeached" by the U.S. House of Representatives and tried by the Senate, as happened to President Clinton. European governments having a parliamentary system can also be overturned by the government losing a "no confidence" vote in Parliament. It is a remarkable fact of ancient Parthia that its monarchs could be removed from office by the very people who put the monarchs in office!

The first Roman-Parthian war resulted from Roman aggression. Crassus, who ruled Rome in a triumvirate with Julius Caesar and

Pompey, sought wealth and fame by attempting to subjugate Parthia. The Greco-Roman biographer, Plutarch, recorded that Crassus invaded Parthia because he was envious of Julius Caesar's war record and wanted to be honored like Caesar.[41] Plutarch also records that Julius Caesar "wrote to [Crassus] from Gaul expressing his approval of the project and encouraging him to enter upon the war."[42] Plutarch recorded that Julius Caesar even detached 1,000 cavalrymen from his own forces to Crassus for his invasion of Parthia.[43]

To help modern readers gain a perspective on Crassus, he was the Roman general who defeated the slave army of Spartacus, a gladiator who revolted against Rome; this revolt is the subject of the epic movie "Spartacus." Crassus, flush with victory, marched eastward toward Parthia in search of glory and plunder. In the words of the *Encyclopedia Britannica*:

> "Crassus, greedy of wealth and jealous of...military renown, set out for the east, **determined to make war on the Parthians, although they had given Rome no provocation**."[44] *(Emphasis added)*

The Parthians were simply "minding their own business" when the Romans charged into their territory looking for plunder to satisfy Crassus' pride and avarice. Readers might ask themselves: "Who were the real 'barbarians' in this war?" Obviously, it was the Romans who acted in a "barbarian" fashion, and the Parthians played the "civilized" role.

The campaign of Crassus was the first of many Roman-Parthian wars that typically occurred as a result of Roman aggression against Parthia. The *Britannica* makes this further comment about this initial war and the whole history of the Parthian-Roman wars:

> "Thus **the wars between Parthia and Rome proceeded, not from the Parthians...but from Rome herself**."[45] *(Emphasis added)*

Parthia was forewarned of this invasion, and made preparations to defend itself. After defeating some weak buffer kingdoms, Crassus turned to looting the wealth of the Middle East. Full of avarice, he stole all the gold and treasure that he could find. He even looted the Temple of God in Jerusalem, stealing an immense amount of gold, the largest piece being (according to Josephus) a solid gold beam of 750 pounds.[46] The Jewish High Priest had offered Crassus this beam of gold in exchange for Crassus sparing the rest of the Temple's treasures. Crassus agreed, but in typical Roman fashion, "broke his oath, and carried away all the gold that was in the temple."[47] This was the greatest sacrilege in the Temple of God since Antiochus Epiphanes offered swine's blood in the Temple to profane it. The reader may choose to see divine justice in what transpired next. Soon after Crassus' sacrilege in violating the Temple of God in Jerusalem, he lost his life in one of the greatest military defeats in Rome's history. Parthia, the Asian empire of the ten tribes of Israel, the "birthright" tribes of the very God whose Temple in Jerusalem had been violated, would administer "poetic justice" to the Roman Triumvir, Crassus.

Crassus was more interested in looting the weak than in seriously invading Parthia. Parthia, now well prepared for war and eager to teach the Romans a lesson, taunted Crassus with a message that was intended to so inflame his vanity that he would seek a battle. The Parthians sent Crassus this provocative message:

> "'If the war...was really waged by Rome, it must be fought to the bitter end. But, if, as they had good reason to believe, Crassus...had attacked Parthia and seized her territory for his own private gain, Arsaces [the Parthian king]...would have pity on the advanced years of the proconsul [Crassus was a sexagenarian], and would give the Romans back those men of theirs, who were not so much keeping watch in Mesopotamia as having watch kept on them.' Crassus, stung with the taunt, exclaimed 'he would return the ambassadors an answer in Seleucia [a large city near the Parthian capital].' Wagises, the chief [Parthian] ambassador...glad to heap taunt on taunt, replied, striking the palm of one hand with the fingers of the other: 'hairs will grow here, Crassus, before you see Seleucia.'"[48]

Infuriated by these insults, Crassus drove his army toward the Parthian forces, but he was deceived into thinking the Parthians were fearful and retreating. In reality, a powerful force of Parthian cavalry awaited the Romans. Parthia's cavalry was commanded by Surenas, a noble of the Suren family that crowned Parthian monarchs. The

Roman invaders consisted of 39,000 infantry and 4,000 cavalry.[49] Sending so small an army to invade an empire the size of Parthia confirms Crassus had seriously underestimated the Parthians.

To understand what the Romans were up against, one must realize the fearsome nature of the Parthian cavalry. This was no wild mob from the steppes, but a disciplined and well-prepared military force. Indeed, the Romans were warned about the Parthians' capabilities. Plutarch wrote that Crassus received this warning:

> "...their armoured cavalry has weapons...which will cut through everything and defensive equipment which will stand up to any blow."[50]

The Parthians had both a heavy cavalry and a light cavalry. The light cavalry was composed of fleet horses with riders armed with bows and arrows. These horsemen could rain down upon an enemy a continuous barrage of arrows while riding in shifts, with each troop resupplying itself from camel-borne arrow carriers when their supply became exhausted in battle.[51]

The heavy cavalry must have been truly frightening to the Roman legionnaires. Rawlinson describes them in the following manner:

> "The strong horses selected for this service were **clad almost wholly in mail. Their head, neck, chest, even their sides and flanks, were protected by scale-armour of brass or iron...Their riders had cuirasses and cuisses** [breastplates and leg armor] **of the same materials, and helmets of burnished iron.** For an offensive weapon they carried a long and strong spear or pike. They formed a serried line in battle, bearing down with great weight on the enemy whom they charged, and standing firm as an iron wall against the charges that were made against them."[52] *(Emphasis added)*

The Romans were opposed by a phalanx of armored Parthian cavalry. With their armored mounts, body armor, and long spears, the Parthian heavy cavalry must have looked like mounted knights from Europe's medieval period! Again we see another parallel between the ancient Parthians and the Europeans of the feudal period. The Parthian heavy cavalry was like a huge formation of feudal knights armed for combat. Indeed, the *Encyclopaedia Britannica* even described the Parthian heavy cavalry as "knights."[53]

Having a mail-clad army was a trait of several ancient Mideast peoples, including the Israelites. In II Chronicles 26:14, Judah's King Uzziah (of the lineage of Phares and David as well as an ancestor of the Arsacid kings of Parthia), equipped his army with "shields, spears and helmets, coats of mail [and] bows..." *(RSV)* Put Uzziah's armored Israelite troops on mounts, and you have a good forerunner of the Parthian cavalry.

Rome's own writers acknowledge that the Roman commander, Crassus, was driven by greed and ambition to invade Parthia. What do we know about the Parthian commander? Plutarch, the famous Greek biographer of Roman leaders, writes this about Surenas (or Surena), the Parthian leader who opposed Crassus.

ROMAN STANDARDS.

Roman attack on a fortified city

> "Surena...in wealth, birth, and in the honor paid to him ranked next after the King...when he traveled about the country on his own affairs **he was always accompanied by a baggage train of 1,000 camels; 200 wagons carried his harem; 1,000 armored cavalry and still more light armed cavalry acted as his escort. The total number of his cavalry, his vassals, and his slaves came to at least 10,000 men**. He had, as an ancient privilege of his family, the right to be the first to set the crown on the head of a King of Parthia at the coronation."[54] *(Emphasis added)*

Surenas, a high-ranking member of Parthia's nobility, did not "travel light." The huge size of his entourage was not just what he took to war, but was what he "always" took with him "on his own affairs." This precedent that members of the Parthian nobility routinely traveled with immense entourages and large bodies of armored cavalry will become of vital importance in the next chapter when we examine the travelling entourage of the Magi, who were also part of Parthia's noble classes.

The invading Romans met the Parthian defenders at the battle of Carrhae in 53 B.C., near the modern border of Syria and Turkey. The overconfident Romans invaded Parthia thinking they would easily defeat the "barbarian" Parthians. The well-prepared Parthians knew they were going to win. In fact, the Parthians were so certain of victory that they split their forces and only sent the cavalry to engage Crassus. The Parthian King took his infantry into the mountainous region of Armenia to prevent its king from joining the Romans. The

Parthians waged an expert "disinformation" campaign against the Romans. They used a friendly Arab chieftain to "confide" to Crassus that the Parthians were so afraid of the Romans that they were retreating to "the depths of Scythia."[55] The Romans took the bait and advanced to their deaths. The ruse that the Parthians were retreating all the way "to Scythia" is further evidence that the close relationship between the Parthians and the Scythians was well-known to all the people of that time, whether they were friends or enemies of Parthia. If the Parthians were truly terrified of the Romans, they would logically have sought refuge with their brother tribes in Scythia. However, Crassus would soon learn that Parthia so discounted Roman fighting abilities that it had seen no need to call in Scythian allies for this war.

When the forces finally met, the Parthians "suckered" the Romans into thinking the Parthians were a rag-tag barbarian force. Plutarch gives this account of the battle's opening act:

> "Surena had hidden his main force behind the front ranks and had ordered them to cover themselves with coats and skins so as to conceal the glittering of their armor...the Parthians...make use of hollow drums...they beat on these drums all at once in many different parts of the field and the sound produced is most eerie and terrifying..."[56]

The Parthians knew how to wage "psychological war" on the Romans as well, first preying on their emotions via the sense of hearing. The Parthians next disheartened the Romans via the sense of sight. Plutarch continues:

> "Before the Romans had recovered from their consternation at this din, the [Parthians] suddenly dropped the coverings of their armor. Now they could be seen clearly, their helmets and breastplates blazing like fire, their...steel glittering keen and bright, their horses armored with plates of bronze and steel."[57]

This had a very negative effect on Roman morale. When the battle began, it turned into a massacre of the seven Roman legions that were with Crassus. The Parthians astounded the Romans with the force of their arrows, which penetrated Roman shields and armor. Plutarch recorded the Parthians increased their arrows' velocity by using specially curved, great bows.[58] The Parthians apparently had re-curved bows, which modern archers will understand as a design increasing the penetrating power of arrows. The Romans tried to pull the Parthian "knights" off their horses, as they could not fight well on the ground, encumbered by their heavy armor.[59]

Crassus had a chance to save his own life. At a brief conference between the two commanders, Surena "held out his right hand to Crassus" and demanded that the terms of a peace treaty be put into writing, saying: "We find...that you Romans have not got very good memories about the terms of treaties."[60] Plutarch does not indicate that Crassus accepted the offer of a "hand shake" with Surena, and the Parthians would have seen this as a severe insult by Crassus. The fighting soon resumed.

The Romans suffered one of the worst defeats in the history of the Roman Empire; half the 40,000-man army perished, a quarter fled, and 10,000 Romans were captured. Crassus, a member of the triumvirate ruling the Roman Empire, was slain and the head and right hand of his corpse were cut off.[61] Cutting off Crassus' right hand symbolized Parthia's view that Rome could not be trusted to keep its word, since shaking right hands was like an inviolable oath with the Parthians.The Parthians also captured the imperial standards of the vanquished Roman legions, a de facto testimony to Parthian supremacy over Rome which was particularly galling to the Romans.

Parthia's treatment of captured Romans was unusually magnanimous, especially considering the fact that the Romans were the aggressors. The 10,000 captured Romans were resettled east of the Caspian Sea, given wives, and later even served as Parthian soldiers.[62] This would place the resettled Roman captives in the northern portion of Parthia's empire (roughly the modern nation of Turkmenistan). Indeed, the modern Saparmurat Turkmenbashy National Museum of Turkmenistan in Ashgabat, Turkmenistan contains an exhibit of Parthian artifacts excavated from the ancient Parthian city of Nisa. The exhibit includes a clay statue of the head of a Parthian warrior

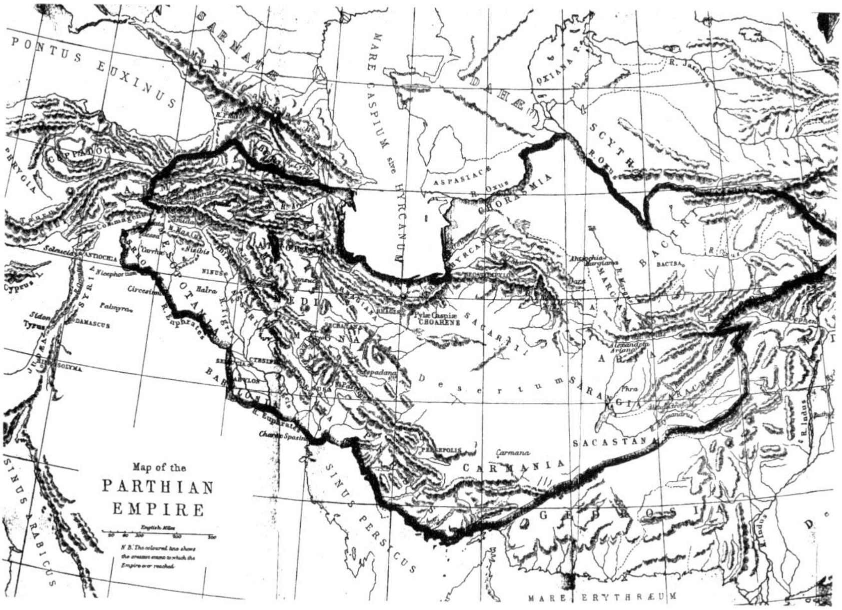

with obvious Caucasian-European (i.e. "Semitic") features, as well as the armored helmet about which Plutarch and other historians wrote. Readers with internet access may view the Parthian warrior at: "unesco.freenet.kz/heritagenet/tm/turkm_muz/index." Once at the site, click the link entitled "Antiquity Hall" and view the "Parthian warrior, Fragment of clay statue, Old Nisa, 2nd cent. BC." This site was accessible in January, 2002.

Rawlinson comments that at Carrhae, the Parthians:

> "acquired by their use of the bow a fame like...English archers...at Crecy and Agincourt. They forced the arrogant Romans to...allow that there was at least one nation in the world which could meet them on equal terms...**They henceforth obtained recognition from the Graeco-Roman writers...as the second Power in the world, the admitted rival of Rome**."[63] *(Emphasis added)*

Although the Greco-Roman writers acknowledged that Parthia was a "second superpower" which equaled Rome, modern history accounts generally omit that important fact. However, Richard Frye's *Heritage of Persia* does note that, after the battle of Carrhae: "the world was divided between Rome and Parthia according to Greek and Latin authors."[64] The two empires divided the known world into Parthian and Roman "spheres of influence," much like the modern world was divided during the Cold War into American and Russian spheres of influence.

Crassus was given a final, grisly insult by the Parthians. Surenas sent the head and hand of Crassus to Armenia where the Parthian king was visiting. Armenia had made peace with the Parthian king. The Parthians, mindful of Crassus' avarice, poured molten gold into the mouth of Crassus' decapitated head. This was done to impress upon the Armenian rulers the utter superiority of the Parthians over the Romans. Parthian rulers were well educated and multi-lingual. When Crassus' body parts arrived, the Parthian and Armenian kings were enjoying a Greek theatrical performance, and the actors even contemptuously utilized Crassus' head as a prop in the play.[65]

The first Parthian-Roman war was an absolute Parthian victory. In terms of both tactics and technology, Rome was no match for Parthia. Rome would not underestimate Parthia again, but it is possible that Rome never really grasped the true size and power of the Parthian Empire. Maps of the Parthian Empire do not show its borders extending into India, but Parthia's eastern border is a matter of some conjecture. The *Encyclopedia Britannica* records that kings with Parthian names (i.e. "Gondophares") reigned in the Punjab region of India and that the "great commercial town of Minnagar in the Indus Delta was under Parthian kings."[66]

Perhaps fearing that the great victory of Surenas would make him a rival, Orodes, the Parthian king, had his loyal commander killed. This illustrates a paradox in Parthian history. Although Parthian rule over its subjects was generally wise and temperate, the Parthian royalty had a history of murderous, internecine struggles. Since any male Arsacid could be king, there was always a host of pretenders and schemers with royal ambitions, causing many Arsacids to kill each other to eliminate rivals. This violent family history fulfilled a biblical prophecy (II Samuel 12:10) that the "sword [violent deaths] would never depart" from David's progeny because of David's murder of his own loyal military commander, Uriah.

Ancient Parthian Horseman.

Parthia soon retaliated for Rome's invasion by crossing the Euphrates River and attacking Rome's eastern provinces. Pacorus, the son of the Parthian Emperor, Orodes, led a large Parthian army. King Orodes sent an experienced military commander named "Osaces" to help Pacorus in his campaign. Note that the name of the Parthian commander, **Osac**es, is based on the Hebrew name, "**Isaac**," after whom all the Scythian "**Sacae**" were named. This invasion was short-lived, and Parthia withdrew its forces to its own side of the Euphrates River in 50 B.C.

In 40 B.C., the Parthians attacked Rome in considerable power. The Roman Empire buckled under the force of the attack. The Parthians conquered Syria, Judea and even pushed the Romans out of Asia Minor. Emboldened by Parthian successes, the Jews asserted their independence from Rome and a Jewish prince, Antigonus, ruled Palestine as a Parthian Satrap until 37 B.C.[37] Rawlinson wrote the following about Parthia's conquest of Rome's Asian provinces.

> "the Parthians...were in possession of Asia to the shores of the Hellespont. It may be said that for a full year Western Asia switched masters; the rule and authority of Rome disappeared; and the Parthians were recognized as the dominant power."[68]

This marked the greatest size of the Parthian Empire. Parthian rule extended from the Indus River to the shores of the Aegean Sea, and their armies had defeated the Romans with relative ease. At this point in history, all the nations within the Roman and Parthian spheres of influence realized that the Parthians had the Roman Empire "on the run." The *McClintock and Strong Cyclopedia* notes the following about the Parthians:

> "From the time of Crassus to that of Trajan they were an enemy whom Rome especially dreaded."[69]

Up to this point, Parthia had little reason to respect either Rome's words or its military abilities. However, at this point of supreme Parthian accomplishment against Rome, the Parthians would now learn that the Roman Empire could be a powerful foe after all. Parthia had overextended itself, and the Romans had been crippled by civil wars and leadership struggles, which prevented it from mounting an effective defense of its eastern provinces. However, at this juncture it was critical that the Romans recover their eastern provinces from the Parthians. If they did not do so, not only would Roman honor and pride be permanently damaged, but such apparent Roman weakness could embolden other Roman provinces to revolt in an effort to break free of Roman rule.

The Romans counterattacked with great determination, recovered their lost territories, and reestablished the Euphrates River as the border between the two empires. Rawlinson records that the short Parthian rule of the conquered Roman provinces was "mild and just,"[70] and many of the natives preferred Parthian to Roman rule. Indeed, Antigonus, the Parthian-sponsored ruler of Judea, resisted King Herod, his Roman-sponsored replacement for a time.

In the previous book in this series, it was shown that when the Scythian Israelites conquered Judea around 620 B.C., it resulted in the descendants of the ten tribes of Israel again briefly ruling Palestine. They stayed only a few years, and left voluntarily. When the Parthians controlled Palestine from 40-37 B.C., it was a second instance when the ten tribes of Israel again dominated their ancient homeland. Again, it lasted only a few years.

During the three years of Parthian rule over Palestine, there would have been a large exchange of information between the Jews and the Parthians. The Jews would have become aware, if they did not already know, that the Parthians were descendants of the ten tribes of Israel, their "brother" tribes. Under Parthian rule the Jews would have enjoyed unhindered contacts with the large Jewish communities living in the Parthian Empire. Josephus, a prominent Jewish historian, likely

Parthian bas-relief (after Flandin and Coste).

drew on this knowledge when he later designated the Parthian Empire — the land "beyond the Euphrates" — as the region inhabited by the numerous descendants of the ten tribes of Israel.[71]

The next Parthian king, Phraates IV, killed his brothers, his father, King Orodes, who had abdicated in his son's favor, and even some of the Parthian nobility, again fulfilling the curse of II Samuel 12:10 about "the sword" abiding among David's progeny. At this time of internal chaos, the Romans again invaded Parthia in a new war of imperial aggression. This time, Rome's aggression was led by Mark Antony, the famous consort of Cleopatra, the Queen of Egypt. Antony invaded Parthia in 37 B.C. with sixteen legions and an army of 113,000 men.[72] The Romans now had more respect for Parthian power, and Antony invaded Parthia with an army almost three times the size of Crassus' ill-fated expedition. Rome keenly felt dishonored that the standards of Crassus' seven legions had been captured by the Parthians at the battle of Carrhae. Antony was to try to recover them as one objective of the war. As events unfolded, Antony was fortunate to get out of Parthia with his own life and standards intact.

Bas-relief of Gotarzes (after Flandin and Coste).

Antony's army besieged a Parthian provincial capital in Media, modern northwest Iran, but could not subdue it. Parthia's own army arrived, and wiped out Antony's supply columns, killing 10,000 Romans. With winter imminent, Antony had to admit defeat, and led his beaten and retreating army ignominiously through Armenia, fighting the terrain, the weather, hunger and the Parthians the whole way. Considering the hardships faced, Mark Antony did well to salvage 60-70,000 Romans soldiers from his disastrous campaign, as he almost lost his whole army and his own life.

Mark Antony and the retreating Romans acted cruelly toward the Armenians, creating a lasting impression among the Armenians that Parthian rule was preferable to Roman rule. Once again, a Roman invasion of Parthia turned into a complete Parthian victory.

A peaceful period of "détente" then occurred between Parthia and Rome which lasted almost a century, from 36 B.C. to 58 A.D.[73] Parthia and Rome had learned that they were equal "superpowers" in the ancient world, with the Euphrates River serving as a mutually accepted border. While Parthia had crushed two Roman attempts to invade the Parthian Empire, Rome had successfully pushed Parthian armies back across the Euphrates after Parthia occupied Rome's eastern provinces for three years. Phraates IV, the emperor of Parthia who had killed his brothers and father after ascending to the throne, lived to "reap what he had sown." After a thirty-five year reign, he was assassinated by his wife and son in 2 B.C. It is also quite significant that a delegation of Parthia's nobility, the "Wise Men" or "Magi" of Matthew 2:1-12, had come to worship the "Christ-child" at about this same time, as this confirms that God was very personally involved with the Parthian leadership and had even revealed Jesus Christ's divinity to them.

In 1 A.D., when another Roman invasion seemed imminent, Parthia and Rome avoided hostilities via a "summit conference." Roman writers recorded that the respective armies of the Roman and Parthian empires lined up on each side of the Euphrates River while the negotiators met on neutral territory, an island in the river. Parthia's emperor, Phraataces, met with Caius Caesar, the grandson of Augustus Caesar as they negotiated an agreement.[74] While war was averted, the Romans seem to have won a slight victory at the conference table. While the Romans agreed to withdraw their armies from Parthia's borders, the Parthians agreed to accept Armenia as being within Rome's sphere of influence. This Parthian-Roman summit conference prolonged the period of peace between the two great empires. It was during this time that Jesus Christ was born, conducted His ministry, and was crucified. Jesus Christ himself was personally involved in the geopolitics of Parthian-Roman relations, as we shall document in the next chapter. Indeed, if this period of peaceful relations had not occurred, some critical events in Jesus' life could never have happened.

The internecine conflicts of the Arsacid family members became so great that Parthia even sent members of its royal family to Rome during this period of detente. They were safer there than in Parthia due to the assassinations among the Arsacid family in Parthia. However, when Parthian royalty were summoned to Parthia from Rome, they alienated the Parthians with their foreign ways. Several times the

Scythians became arbiters of who should be the Parthian king by their military intervention in behalf of specific Arsacid princes.

Given the turmoil within the royal house of the Arsacids, it is remarkable that this one dynasty maintained its rule over Parthia throughout its existence. The prophecy of Jeremiah 33:17, that David's descendants would continually rule over the ten tribes of Israel, was kept unbroken during Parthia's existence. While many Parthian monarchs were corrupt in their personal lives, a few were devout.

One Parthian provincial king adopted Judaism and had his remains buried near Jerusalem.[75] The presence of Parthian pilgrims at a Pentecost (Feast of Weeks) celebration in Jerusalem *(Acts 2:9)* confirms that some Parthians served the God of Israel. The events of Acts 2 occurred during the "détente" period between Rome and Parthia when Parthians were free to travel to Jerusalem and participate in the biblical Holy Days of God.

Seal

לקניו

(From Clermont-Ganneau, in "Archéologie Orientale.")

While Parthian-Roman affairs were calm, Parthia fought and lost a war in the region of Armenia to an alliance of Iberians and Scythians headed by king Pharasmanes of Iberia.[76] This war of 35-36 A.D. pitted two alliances of the tribes of Israel against each other. The previous book in this series documented that the Israelites who escaped the Assyrians by fleeing to the Black Sea region north of Armenia had established Iberian and Scythian kingdoms. King **Pharasmanes** bore the name of the Judaic line of

Phares, and "Iberia" was named after "Eber," the Hebrew patriarch. Parthian King Artabanus lost this war, and he fled to the Scythians living by the Caspian Sea for sanctuary.

The Parthian Arsacids were severely reduced in numbers by 51 A.D. because an extraordinarily cruel emperor, Gotarzes, had sought to eliminate all rivals to the throne in the usual way by murdering all his close and distant male relatives. He even killed Arsacid children and pregnant women in the royal families.[77]

In 51 A.D., a remarkable amity occurred between three brothers who were eligible for the Parthian throne. One, Volagases I, became the Parthian emperor, a second, Pacorus, became vassal-king of Media, and the third, Tiridates, was appointed king of Armenia. This latter choice caused severe political problems, because Armenia was again claimed by both the Romans and the Parthians. Also, a king with a Parthian name, Mithridates, who was also the brother of King Pharasmanes of Iberia, already ruled Armenia. To assert Parthian rule over Armenia would surely result in war, but an external war was likely preferable to the internal civil war which could have occurred within Parthia had not the third royal brother been awarded a prominent province.

This Parthian action resulted in a desultory Parthian-Roman conflict over Armenia until 62 A.D. when Nero, Rome's emperor, sent a Roman army to fight the Parthians. The Romans were shocked when Parthia launched a winter offensive against them, and the Romans suffered another crushing defeat that left Armenia firmly in Parthian hands. During this time the Armenians fought to be under Parthian rulership.[78] This was understandable since Parthian rule was typically milder than Roman rule.

A strange peace settlement occurred in which Parthia kept control of Armenia and Rome won a "concession" to her imperial vanity at great cost to Rome. The agreement left Tiridates, the brother of the Parthian king, as the undisputed ruler of Armenia, recognizing Parthia's victory on the battlefield. However, to assuage Rome's pride, Tiridates agreed to travel to Rome to receive his crown from Nero to preserve a facade that Rome "gave" rulership of Armenia to Tiridates. Tiridates traveled to Rome, escorted by 3000 Parthian cavalry troops. Rome paid all Parthian travel expenses, and classical writers recorded that it cost the Roman treasury 800,000 sesterces a day for nine months![79]

This treaty gave the Parthians control over Armenia, and the Romans "won" the right to reward 3000 Parthians with an all-expense-paid trip to Rome so Tiridates could cooperate in Nero's facade. At any rate, both parties were satisfied, and Parthian-Roman relations were amicable for several decades. This was the only time that thousands of Parthia's famous armored cavalry force actually made it to Rome; however, they were there as Rome's guests.

Toward the end of the first century B.C., the Parthians established friendly relations with the Dacians, a people living in Eastern Europe along the Danube River, who also disliked the Romans.[80] The establishment of Parthian good will with the Dacians, called "Getae" by the Greeks,[81] will become significant in the next book in this series so it is mentioned at this juncture.

In the reign of Mithridates IV (107-113 A.D.), the Parthians began placing Semitic inscriptions on their coins; previous coins had simply continued the Seleucid practice of using Hellenistic inscriptions.[82] The switch was consistent with the fact that the Parthians utilized a Semitic alphabet. The *Encyclopaedia Britannica* notes the following regarding Parthia's language:

> "**The alphabets** in use in Persia, at least from the time of the Arsacid dynasty onward [i.e. the time of the Parthian Empire] **are based upon the Aramaic**."[83] *(Emphasis added)*

The Parthian use of an alphabet based on Aramaic, a language closely related to Hebrew, furthers affirms that the Parthians were the descendants of the ten tribes of Israel. If the Parthians and Scythians had originated in northern Asia, their alphabet and language would not have been Semitic in nature. The very fact that the Parthians utilized an eastern Mediterranean alphabet confirms that Parthian origins were in the eastern Mediterranean, the former homeland of the ten tribes of Israel.

Parthian horsemen
From the Triumphal Arch of Septimus Severus in Rome

George Rawlinson translates the legend on the coins of Mithridates IV as "Mitradat malcha"[84] Richard Frye's book, *The Heritage of Persia*, makes this observation about the Parthian coins:

> "After the Parthian conquest of western Iran the coins change to resemble Parthian prototypes and **the title MLK, 'king,' appears**."[85] *(Emphasis added)*

The Hebrew-Aramaic word for king is "melek;" the consonants being "MLK." Frye lists the Parthian word for "king" as being the Hebrew-Semitic word "M-L-K," and Rawlinson renders the consonants as "M-L-CH." This linguistic evidence further confirms the Hebrew-Semitic origin of the Parthians.

Around 114 A.D., the Romans again broke their treaties and war resulted. Rome's Emperor Trajan, by subterfuge, had a nephew of the Parthian monarch killed who had come to him as a diplomat. In noting Trajan's deceitfulness, Rawlinson describes Trajan's actions as "disgraceful" and "base."[86] Filled with arrogance and pride, Trajan set out to conquer Asia like a new Alexander the Great.

While wintering in Antioch of Syria, Trajan barely escaped with his life when he was almost killed in a destructive earthquake, which was "of a violence and duration unexampled in ancient times...many Romans of the highest rank perished."[87] Besides leveling Antioch, it destroyed nine other cities in Roman provinces in Asia Minor and Greece. Was it a portent of things to come? Rawlinson wrote.

> "it seemed as if Providence had determined that the new glories which Rome was gaining by the triumphs of her arms should be obscured by calamities of a kind that no human power could avert or control...that [the reign of Trajan]...should go down to posterity as one of gloom, suffering, and disaster."[88]

If the earthquakes were a divine warning, Trajan paid no heed. He resumed his invasion of Parthia's western provinces, and was almost unopposed as he marched through Mesopotamia, advancing as far as the Persian Gulf. Trajan then indulged in sheer egomania, viewing himself as "another Alexander," taking a "pleasure voyage" down the Tigris River, and regretting "that his advanced years prevented him

Parthian Warriors

from making India the term of his labours."[89] The Bible states in Proverbs 16:18 that: "Pride goeth before destruction and a haughty spirit before a fall." Trajan was about to become a living example of the truth of that proverb.

The Parthians had not yet fought a serious, pitched battle to oppose the invasion of Trajan's Roman army. Either they were caught unprepared by Trajan's campaign or they had another strategy. As Trajan was indulging his ego on the Persian Gulf, the Parthian provinces recently occupied by the Romans rebelled on a massive scale. Although the Romans burned Seleucia and other cities, the natives exacted a heavy toll on the Romans, and even exterminated an entire Roman army. The Parthians, meanwhile, risked little as their former subjects did the fighting to remove the hated Romans. History was repeating itself. The ancestors of these same native populations had once fought the Seleucid Greeks in order to return to Parthian rule. Now their descendants were fighting the Romans to return to Parthian rule.

Trajan was in a dangerous situation as his line of retreat was full of hostile nations. Additionally, nature itself became a Parthian ally. It is recorded that the Romans:

> "**suffered from the heat, from**...**swarms of flies** which disputed with them every morsel of their food and every drop of their drink, and finally **from violent hail and thunderstorms**."[90] *(Emphasis added)*

Perhaps it was no coincidence. There is a strong likelihood that God periodically involved Himself in the affairs of the Parthian Empire. It was God who conveyed upon the Parthians the "birthright" benefits of the Abrahamic Covenant. God was involved with keeping his biblical promises by placing the descendants of King David on the thrones ruling the ten tribes of Israel in Parthia, Scythia, and Iberia, and even by ensuring that David's own progeny were often slain by the sword via intrigues and plots within the royal family. God has prophesied that he would remain involved with the ten tribes of Israel after the kingdom of Israel fell and they either fled to or were carried as captives into Asia. Hosea 1:4-10 contains a prophecy that God would control the fates of Israel's tribes in such a way that they would be vastly increased in population *after* they were placed in Asia. Josephus' writings, cited earlier, records that this prophecy had been fulfilled by his lifetime. As will be discussed in considerable detail in the next chapter, God had to be involved personally with the Parthian Magi to bring them to worship the "Christ child" soon after he was born in Judea. There were worshippers of the God of Israel from many provinces of the Parthian Empire who made pilgrimages to Jerusalem for one of God's Holy Days (*Acts 2:9-11)*. There were many devout Jews in Parthia who served the God of Israel as well.

At least one Parthian provincial king worshipped Israel's God in the apostolic era, and the Parthians were placing Semitic inscriptions on their coinage. The last fact argues that the Parthians were openly and officially identifying with their Semitic (i.e., Israelite) roots. Given all the above facts, there is every reason to believe that God took as much interest in the national affairs and destiny of the Parthians as he had in the affairs of the ancient kingdoms of Israel and Judah.

Roman Army Crosses the Tigris

Therefore, it is possible that God Himself caused the earthquakes, plagues of flies, hail, etc., to punish the arrogant Trajan. The Bible records many instances where God intervened in similar fashion in behalf of the Israelite tribes when they were in a state of reliance upon him. Also, while God gives humans a "lot of rope," the Bible has many accounts of God acting to punish nations and national leaders when they become too vain.

Most unusual at this time was the lack of any major Parthian military action against the Romans. In the past they quickly clashed with invading Romans, generally routing them on the battlefield. Why did they not confront Trajan? Were they internally weakened, or had the Parthians been told by an unnamed prophet of God **not** to fight because "the battle was the Lord's?"

The Parthians won a bloodless victory by reoccupying their territories as the retreating Romans abandoned them. Trajan died soon after his humiliating retreat, and the new Roman emperor (Hadrian) unilaterally gave back to Parthia all territory taken by Trajan, and recalled all Roman forces back on Rome's side of the Euphrates River. It was very uncharacteristic of Rome to yield large amounts of territory under any circumstance, and it was unprecedented for Rome to cede so much territory absent any military threat. Since the Parthians had done nothing militarily to warrant such action, it is likely that the polytheistic Romans feared Parthia's God, and viewed the many natural disasters visited upon the Romans who invaded Parthia to be divine punishment. Nothing else explains Rome's very unusual behavior.

Stung by the disasters that struck Trajan from the heavens, Rome avoided Parthian wars for another half-century. When hostilities did seem imminent at one time, peace ensued after another "Summit Conference" in 122 A.D. when the Roman Emperor, Hadrian and the Parthian Emperor, Chosroes, had a face-to-face encounter.[91]

The next Parthian emperor, Vologases, continued the use of Semitic inscriptions ("Volgasa Malcha") on his coins.[92] This prolonged Parthian use of the Semitic word "Malcha" for king is significant, and merits further comment. John 18:10 shows us that "Malchus" (the same root word) was being used as a Hebrew proper name in the first century A.D. The Hebrew word for king is represented by the consonants M-L-K,[93] and the Parthians used the consonants M-L-CH (or M-L-K) to designate the Semitic word "king" on their coins. When one considers that the "CH" symbol can represent the same phonetic sound as a "K," the Hebrew-Aramaic origin of this word is clear. Rawlinson noted that Semitic legends "are frequent on the coins of the later Parthian kings."[94] On this specific issue, I again acknowledge the help of the late Dr. Charles Dorothy, a graduate of the Claremont Graduate School, who noted to this author that the Hebrew caph may be transliterated as either "ch" or "k."

The prolonged Parthian switch to Semitic inscriptions on their coins is evidence that they were aware of their Semitic origins. This was a watershed event, and it is evidence of a major change in Parthian society. The Apostolic Christian Church had evangelized Parthia during the first century A.D. Eusebius wrote that the Apostle Thomas was sent to the Parthians and that Andrew went to Scythia."[95] I Peter 5:13 records that the Apostle Peter was inside the Parthian Empire (the city of Babylon) when he wrote his first epistle. Some mistakenly assume Peter figuratively meant "Rome" when he wrote "Babylon" as the city from whence he authored I Peter. However, Rome was gentile, and it was Paul, the apostle "sent to the gentiles"

A Charge Of the Parthian Cavalry

(Ephesians 3:8, II Timothy 1:11), who went to Rome. Peter was a simple "fisherman" who was not accustomed to using the literary devices of a highly-educated Jew like the Apostle Paul. Peter even wrote that Paul's epistles were "hard to be understood" *(II Peter 3:15-16)*. Peter wrote "Babylon" because he literally meant the city of Babylon located within Parthia's Empire.

Matthew 10:6 states that Jesus specifically told His twelve apostles to go to "the lost sheep of the House of Israel," the ten tribes of Israel. Peter's presence in the Mesopotamian city of Babylon, located in Parthia's empire, confirms he followed Jesus Christ's instructions. The presence of at least three apostles in Parthia and Scythia confirms that they were obeying Christ's instructions by evangelizing the ten tribes of Israel located in those regions. Their message surely included the theme: "you Parthians (or Scythians) are the ten tribes of Israel, and the Messiah (Jesus) has sent us to you!" Since some of Parthia's elites, the Magi, had worshipped Jesus Christ before the apostles were even called, they were assured of a warmer reception for their message in Parthia than in Roman domains.

The above reveals that Parthian-Roman events of this period must be understood in the context of what was clearly a significant penetration of the Christian religion into the Parthian Empire, including its ruling classes. The *Encyclopaedia Britannica* states the following regarding this period in Parthia's history:

> "...Greek culture practically vanishes and gives place to Aramaic; it is significant that in [the] future the Kings of Mesene stamped their coinage with Aramaic legends. **This Aramaic victory was powerfully aided by the ever-increasing progress of Christianity**...[and mentions] Edessa, a city in which the last king of Osroene, Abgar IX (179-214 A.D.), had been converted to the faith."[96] *(Emphasis added)*

According to *Harper's Bible Dictionary*, Aramaic was:

> "a Semitic language closely related to Hebrew... several passages in the OT are written in Official Aramaic [cited are texts in Ezra, Daniel, Jeremiah and Genesis]. Jesus probably spoke a dialect of Western Aramaic and some words in the NT come from Aramaic, e.g., 'Talitha Cumi,' 'Maranatha,' and 'Golgotha.'"[97]

The prominence of Aramaic in Parthian life during the apostolic and post-apostolic period was concurrent with the spread of Christianity into Parthia from Palestine. Whether the reader wishes to conclude that the Parthians were aided by divine action against the Romans or not, the fact remains that nature itself did wage war against Rome at a time when Christianity had many converts in Parthia and when Parthia had recognized its Semitic origins.

The reign of Volagases II, Parthia's emperor for 19 years (130-149 A.D.), is characterized as having "a general character of tranquility."[98] This tranquility within Parthia's ruling house stands in stark contrast to the murderous internal struggles of the Arsacids prior to the Christian Apostolic Period. As Christianity penetrated the Parthian Empire, it would seem that its benign doctrines influenced the conduct of Parthia's rulers as well.

Roman Captain or Centurion.

Predictably, the Romans eventually reneged on their treaty with Parthia. During Trajan's invasion, the Romans had captured a "golden throne" of the Parthians and the Roman Emperor, Hadrian, had promised to return it as part of a peace settlement. After attempts to secure Roman compliance with the treaty failed, Parthia went to war.[99] Under Volagases III, Parthia again conquered Armenia, and restored a native ruler as king of Armenia. A Roman legion crossed the Euphrates and was annihilated by the Parthians. The Parthians then crossed the Euphrates into Roman territory, but their success was short-lived. A Roman army led by Avidius Cassius won a major battle against the Parthians, who retreated to the Parthian side of the Euphrates River.

Avidius Cassius then led his army across the Euphrates, and reconquered Parthia's western provinces occupied briefly during Trajan's invasion. Cassius burned Seleucia, having then 400,000 residents, and captured Ctesiphon, Parthia's western capital. The Romans marched at will through Parthia's western provinces, and the Parthians seemed powerless to resist. Just when the Romans seemed invincible; however, they were driven from Parthia, not by a Parthian army but by a terrible plague. Again, it was "nature" which waged war against the Romans.

One wonders if the arrogant Romans, who knew of Trajan's disasters decades previous to this time, taunted the heavens with words like: "Parthia's God can't protect them from us!" Whether such an attitude provoked a divine response as it did in the time of King Hezekiah of ancient Judah *(II Kings 18-19)* or not, the plagues came with a terrible force upon the Romans and it eventually devastated the entire Roman Empire. This plague was so unprecedented that there was no doubt in the Roman minds that the plague was supernatural in origin. The polytheistic Romans attributed the divine plague to "spells of the Chaldeans" unleashed because of Roman excesses in looting a temple of Apollo.[100]

The Euphrates River and Plain of Chaldea

The plague, of a "strange and terrible character,"[101] was so contagious that Rawlinson refers to the return of this army to Rome as "a march of death through the provinces" as it spread the disease throughout the Roman Empire. Rawlinson cites Roman historians in stating:

> "the pestilence raged with special force throughout Italy, and spread as far as the Rhine and Atlantic Ocean. According to one writer, more than one-half of the entire population, and almost the whole Roman army, was carried off by it."[102]

This plague was responsible for severely reducing the native Latin population. It also had a permanent effect on the character and composition of both the Roman Empire and its army. In the centuries after this plague, the major die-off of Rome's Latin population resulted in a transformed "Roman" army. After this catastrophy, Roman armies were increasingly recruited from Gauls, Germans and other subject populations who were willing to serve under Rome's imperial standards for pay, booty or future Roman citizenship.

Significantly, while this plague devastated the whole Roman Empire, there is no mention of it affecting Parthia. That this plague rescued Parthia and devastated their Roman invaders does support a belief that the plague was a severe divine judgement of God against Rome.

The Romans, after two of their armies were expelled from Parthia by "divine action," developed a belief that the previous return of Parthian territory by the Emperor Hadrian "sprang more from prudence than from generosity."[103] While modern man may scoff at the thought of divine intervention in the affairs of nations, the ancient Romans accepted a divine origin for the terrible natural disasters and plagues that had driven them from Parthia. One such occurrence could be a random event, but two such occurrences in a row argued against any "coincidence."

Decades later, another major Roman-Parthian war was fought in approximately 194-200 A.D in which Mesopotamian natives massacred Roman garrisons, aided by Parthian vassal kings. This led to a Roman-Parthian war when Severus, Rome's emperor, led an army across the Euphrates. Diverted by internal problems, Severus returned to Rome. The Parthians attacked, routed the Romans armies, besieged Nisibis, a Roman headquarters, and crossed the Euphrates into Roman territory. Severus returned to the Middle East, and fought his way to Ctesiphon, Parthia's western capital on the Tigris River. The Roman army captured Ctesiphon and perpetrated an orgy of violence, killing Parthian males, and making slaves of about 100,000 women and children.[104] The Romans withdrew, but this time retained control of much of Mesopotamia. Parthia seemed inert, indicating a state of crisis within Parthia. Furthermore, if the previous defeats of Roman armies under Trajan and Avidius Cassius were the result of divine action, the lack of divine assistance in repulsing this Roman attack speaks volumes. Since God's assistance is dependent on obedience to God's laws, the lack of any help from "nature" indicated that Parthia was in a state of internal decline.

A ROMAN EMPEROR CELEBRATING A TRIUMPH

The Last Roman-Parthian War

The final Roman-Parthian war began with immense treachery on the part of the Romans. In 215 A.D., the Emperor Caracallus, launched a "disinformation campaign" to dupe the Parthians into letting down their defenses. He masqueraded as a peacemaker, and even offered to marry a daughter of the Parthian monarch. The deceitful Romans even proposed a political and economic union between Parthia and Rome.[105]

Even though Rome had a long record of breaking its promises and treaties, the Parthians believed Rome's phony "peace initiative," and allowed the Roman Emperor, escorted by a huge army, to proceed to the Parthian capital for the "wedding." It is a testimony to the human capacity for self-delusion that the gullible Parthians were so willing to trust Rome in spite of the fact that every historical precedent warned that such an offer could not be genuine. They continued in a state of denial even as Caracallus marched his army to Ctesiphon, Parthia's western capital. Parthia so wanted to believe that Caracallus was a reformer, an enlightened man of peace, different from the warlike Romans of the past. The Parthians received the Romans with genuine hospitality, certain that a "New World Order" [to borrow a modern phrase] of universal peace and harmony was beginning.

According to a classical author, Herodian, the Parthians "were transported with joy at the prospect of an eternal peace...and were keeping holiday"[106] as Caracallus and his army arrived. Finally, the Romans dropped their pretense of peace and began slaughtering the gullible Parthians. The Parthian monarch barely escaped with his life. Not content with his already heinous betrayal of Parthian trust, the Romans then added massive insult to massive injury by desecrating the Parthian royal cemetery at Arbela, the same area where Alexander the Great had defeated Darius of Persia in the battle of Gaugamela. The Romans scattered the remains of the deceased Parthian kings.[107] The Romans were desecrating the graves of the progeny of King David of ancient Israel, the progenitor of the dynastic line of "Phares" which ruled Parthia. The Romans would come to deeply regret this needless act of sacrilege against the deceased Parthian kings because that single act mobilized the entire Parthian Empire against Rome.

COIN OF ARTABANUS I.

Outraged beyond words, the Parthians assembled a vast military force to take vengeance on the Romans. Based on accounts and subsequent events, it may have been the largest army Parthia ever assembled against Rome. While Rome's armies had invaded the westernmost provinces of Parthia's empire, those provinces were inhabited by native populations subject to the Parthians. Rome's armies had never penetrated, or even threatened, the Parthian homelands near the Caspian Sea. Since Parthia's central, northern and eastern provinces had never been bothered by Roman invasions, Parthians in those undisturbed areas may have been growing increasingly resistant about furnishing soldiers to imperiled vassal kings in Parthia's western provinces.

Ctesiphon, the Parthian "capital" known to the Romans, was nowhere near the actual homeland of the Parthians. It is possible that Ctesiphon was an administrative center for governing Parthia's western provinces, and that other regional "capitals" existed elsewhere in Parthia's empire. H.G. Rawlinson's book, *Intercourse Between India and the Western World*, has a different perspective on the "capitals" of Parthia's empire. He wrote that Ctesiphon was only the "winter capital" of Parthia.[108] He also wrote the following about the role of the Parthian cities of Ctesiphon and Hecatomopylus in the great overland Silk Route across Parthia which connected China and India with the Mediterranean World.

> "Great cities sprang up, created by this traffic. One of the chief roads—the one which ran from the Parthian capital at

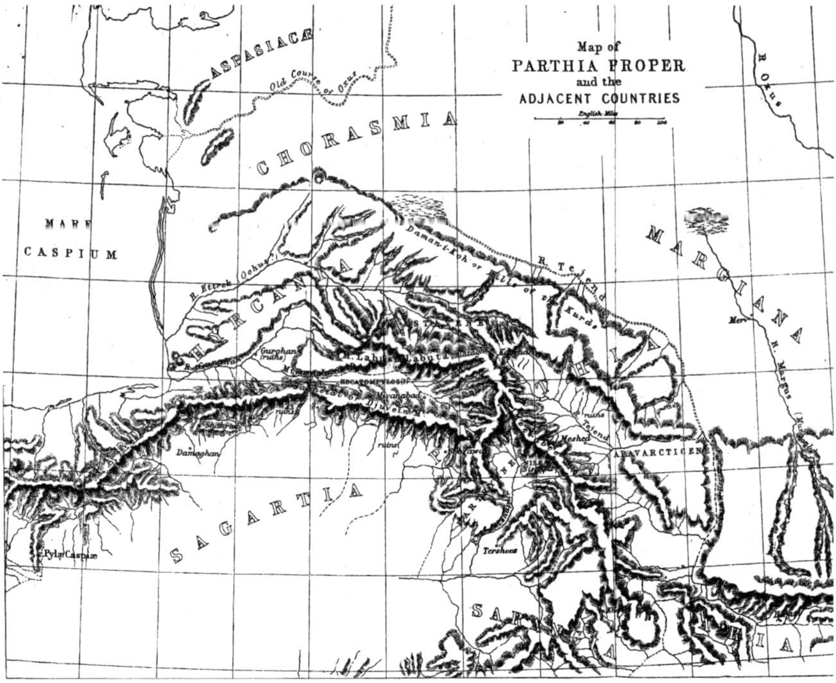

> Hekatompylus—passed through Ekbatana and Ktesiphon. At Ktesiphon it branched off in several directions, the main track running across Mesopotamia...and ending at Antioch. Another important branch of the road ran to Palmyra, and then to Damascus, Gaza, Tyre, and Sidon, and joined the network of highways which converged at Petra."[109]

H.G. Rawlinson favors the use of the consonant "k" instead of a "c" in his place names. However, he asserts that the city of Hecatompylus was actually the true capital of the entire Parthian Empire. Hecatompylus was a city located in the heartland of Parthia, near the southeast coast of the Caspian Sea. No Roman army ever got anywhere near Hecatompylus or the Parthian homeland in which it was located. Ctesiphon was apparently an important western administrative center due to its location at which the trade routes of the great Silk Road came together. Ctesiphon perhaps hosted the Parthian Emperor and his court during winters, when they moved south to avoid the harsher winters in Parthia's homeland. The Romans would have regarded Ctesiphon as Parthia's "capital" as it was the only Parthian city with which they associated the Parthian Emperor and his court.

No matter how remote they were from the site of Rome's sacrilege, all Parthians throughout the empire were outraged by the violations of the tombs and corpses of their dead emperors! That was an offense they could all fight to avenge.

The Scythian nature of the Parthians is well documented, and the Scythian reverence for the dead was a long-known historic fact. When Darius of Persia attacked the Scythians many centuries earlier near the Black Sea, he was warned that Scythia's retribution would be most dire if he desecrated Scythian cemeteries.[110] Given the historic relationship between Parthia and their Scythian kinsmen, it is possible that Scythian tribes furnished troops for this climactic battle against Rome. In the words of George Rawlinson:

> "...the passions of the Parthians had been roused. Artabanus...was determined to exact a heavy retribution for the treacherous massacre of Ctesiphon and the wanton impiety of Arbela."[111]

The Parthian army was assembled over the winter months, as it took considerable time to gather Parthia's enormous resources into one massive, military command. Parthian troops could have come from as far away as the Saka kingdoms in India. Rome also had time to reinforce its army with additional troops from throughout its empire. Roman sources record that the Romans even brought in a "powerful body of Mauritanian cavalry" from western Africa.[112] The tension throughout the Roman and Parthian Empires must have rose to a fever pitch as everyone knew that the two mightiest empires on earth were gathering their strengths for a titanic struggle. Because Rome and Parthia were both reinforcing their armies by drawing in additional forces from their respective vassal states throughout the Mediterranean and Asian worlds, the impending conflict was going to be an ancient "World War."

The Roman headquarters in the area was at Nisibis, near the modern border of Syria and Turkey. The enraged Parthian army headed for Nisibis thirsting for revenge. The Romans assassinated Caracallus, and the new Roman emperor, Macrinus, tried to appease the Parthians by offering to return Parthian captives as part of a peace treaty. The Parthian emperor, Artabanus IV, spurned the offer as the Parthians were coming toward the Romans to exact vengeance and spill as much Roman blood as possible. Nothing could have deterred the bloodletting that was about to happen.

Artabanus IV, the emperor of Parthia, personally led the Parthian army. Macrinus, the emperor of Rome, personally led the Roman army. These great armies clashed in what must have been one of the fiercest (and bloodiest) battles ever fought anywhere in the ancient world. Indeed, because nations from Western Africa to India were contributing forces to the two clashing armies, this may have been the greatest battle ever fought in the ancient world. What occurred in 217 A.D. was not merely a battle, but the death struggle of two huge, powerful, and well-established empires. Citing the classical Roman writers, Rawlinson states:

> "The battle of Nisibis, which terminated the long contest between Rome and Parthia, was the fiercest and best-contested which was ever fought between the rival powers. It lasted...three days. The army of Artabanus was numerous and well-appointed: like almost every Parthian force, it was strong in cavalry and archers; and it had...a novel addition of...soldiers, clad in complete armour, and carrying long spears or lances, who were mounted on camels...The Romans suffered greatly from the bows of the horse-archers, and from the lances of the corps mounted on camels; and...as they retired, they strewed the ground with spiked balls and other contrivances for injuring the feet of animals."[113]

This kind of fighting went on for three full days. The armor-clad Parthians must have looked like medieval knights mounted on camels as they charged the Romans with leveled lances. The Romans were ingenious in countering these assaults by devising methods to maim the feet of the Parthian mounts. The killing was awesome. The Roman historian, Herodian, recorded that:

> "...the heaps of dead [were] piled to such a height that the manoeuvres of the troops were impeded by them, and at last the two contending hosts could scarcely see one another!"[114]

At the point of mutual exhaustion, the battle ended with a decisive Parthian victory. Macrinus, the Roman emperor, fled the scene and afterward agreed to repatriate all Parthian captives and pay a large war indemnity to Parthia.[115] In his book, *Persia*, published in 1888, historian S.G.W. Benjamin writes of this event:

> "Macrinus, the Roman emperor, suffered two crushing defeats from Artabanus and was obliged to...pay an indemnity of 50,000,000 denarii...to the great rival of Rome almost in the very hour when the doom of Parthia was sounding on the great bell of time. The hero [Artabanus IV of Parthia] who wrested a war indemnity from a Roman emperor was also the last... [Parthian emperor]. Is there any event more dramatic in the record of the nations!"[116]

Given the significance of the great struggle at Nisibis, why has this titanic battle of two ancient "superpowers" been virtually censored out of the history texts? What is it about Parthia that causes its history to be ignored even though it was one of the world's largest and most powerful empires? Would any modern historian even realize that an event involving Parthia could be one of the most dramatic events "in the record of the nations?" The classical Greco-Roman historians wrote copiously about Scythian and Parthian history. As recently as the late 19th century, historians such as George Rawlinson and S.G.W. Benjamin could still recognize the immense battle at Nisibis between Rome and Parthia as one of the greatest events of world history. Yet today, the important histories of Scythia and Parthia have been virtually erased from history texts. Why does this glaring omission exist?

DATE PALM OF THE LOWER EUPHRATES.

Is it only a "coincidence" that history books generally de-emphasize or omit the histories of the great empires founded by the ten tribes of Israel — Phoenicia, Carthage, Scythia and Parthia — while waxing eloquent about the histories of the non-Israelite empires? In the late 19th and 20th centuries, the dogma of evolution became the new religion of a secularized world. It is now "politically incorrect" for academia to publicize anything which verifies the Bible or supports a belief in the God of Israel. Those in secular academia must now "bow down" to the new intellectual idol of evolution if they want to safeguard their educational careers.

Eastern Frankincense Tree

It hardly seems coincidental that the world's awareness of the empires of the ten tribes of Israel dramatically declined when evolution became the new "god" of modern academia. Because the historical truths of Phoenicia, Carthage, Scythia and Parthia, if told, would greatly affirm biblical accounts and verify that the God of the Bible really does guide and direct world events, the adherents of evolution have "held back the truth" about world history. This series of books on Israelite history is an effort to restore a balanced perspective on world history by restoring the Israelite empires to the prominence given them by classical Greco-Roman writers and other historians who pre-dated Darwinism.

The Fall of Parthia

At Nisibis, the Parthian Empire achieved perhaps its greatest victory over the Roman Empire. However, this triumph was the last Parthian military success. The end of its empire was at hand. It is recorded that Artabanus IV, Parthia's emperor, sought to the occult for guidance and was told Parthia's empire was about to end.[117] This account eerily echoes that of King Saul, the first Israelite king, whose efforts to seek occult guidance led to his own defeat and death. *(I Samuel 28:7-25)* Based on biblical precedent, it is a symptom of terminal moral decay when a society's leaders seek to occult mediums ("channelers") for guidance. Being a great idolatry, such actions not only forfeit God's favor, but also invite his direct punishment. If God had, indeed, divinely favored and protected Parthia in earlier decades, this sin of Artabanus was especially grievous. Even though Parthia had won a supreme victory over Rome, it collapsed soon after its emperor's seance.

In 220 A.D., the province of Persia revolted. A series of three battles was fought which resulted in a Persian victory in 227 A.D., costing Artabanus IV his life and effectively ending the Parthian Empire. The Sassanian Persian Empire replaced the Parthian Empire, and the Parthians were forced to migrate out of their old empire to flee the Persians. Many histories discuss Parthian history as part of

"Persian" history, but this is misleading. Although the Parthians ruled the territory of the former Persian Empire, the Parthians and Persians were separate and distinct people living in the same region of the world. The Parthians had been the subjects of the Persians during the reigns of Cyrus and Darius centuries previous to this time. For five centuries, the Parthians ruled an empire in which the Persians were a subject nation.

In 220-227 A.D., the Persians threw off Parthian rule and drove the Parthians out of the region. Where the Parthians went and the new names by which they came to be known will be discussed in book four of this series on Israelite history. When one of the greatest empires in the world collapses and its millions of people migrate elsewhere, it causes severe dislocations for many nations and regions of the earth. The migrations and dislocations of nations which followed the collapse of Parthia has been well-documented in secular history, and these accounts will be examined in the following book, which will trace the Israelites' descendants into the modern world. While the migrations and national dislocations which followed the collapse of the vast Parthian empire have been amply discussed and documented in secular histories of the world, those same secular histories have never realized or acknowledged that it was the collapse of Parthia, the great Asian Empire, which caused the great migrations and national dislocations which began in the 3rd century A.D.

This examination of Parthia's history has so far been dominated by events in its western provinces that bordered the Roman Empire. This is unavoidable since classical Greek and Roman writings are the basis for much of what we know about Parthia. Naturally, these ancient writers wrote about the events that occurred in the western areas of Parthia where Rome and Parthia's spheres of influence overlapped. The wars and events detailed so far took place within the territories of modern Syria, Israel, Turkey and Iraq. Parthia's Empire also included modern Iran, Afghanistan, part of Pakistan, and the southern regions of the former Soviet Union. No Roman army ever threatened these regions of Parthia, and less is known of their history.

Besides Parthia, portions of the ten tribes of Israel also ruled "Saka" kingdoms to the east of Parthia in the region of modern Pakistan and India. Various Saka (or "Sacae") kings began ruling in Pakistan and Northwest India during the first century B.C.[118] There were also "Pahlava" or "Indo-Parthian" rulers in that region who had names like the Parthian Arsacids. Among these rulers was Gondo**phares**, who exhibited the name of the Davidic royal line ("Phares") of the kingdom of Judah. The *Encyclopedia Britannica* states "the name [Pahlavi]...means Parthian, and adds that "the great commercial town of Minnagar in the Indus Delta was under Parthian kings."[119] The "Saka" kingdoms bore the name of "Isaac," and their kings had Parthian names. We know little about the extent to which the Parthian emperors and the Saka kings either cooperated or competed. Richard Frye writes the following concerning Parthian-Saka affairs:

> "Indian sources imply that the Sakas and the Pahlavas [Parthians] were allies in their Indian conquests and this would seem to be corroborated by the coins with both Saka and Parthian names. The adoption of the title 'king of kings' by Gondophares...would imply that these Indo-Parthian kings were completely independent of the Parthian rulers."[120]

The title "king of kings" was the standard title of Parthian Emperors, and the Indo-Parthian use of the same term confirms their affinity with Parthia even if they constituted separate kingdoms. While little is known of Parthia's eastern affairs, we do know that Parthian dominance and/or influence extended into modern India. When the Parthian Empire collapsed, some of the Saka and Indo-Parthian kingdoms on its eastern border continued to exist.

How far did Parthian contacts and influence extend to the east? Shahab Setudeh-Nejad, writing in the *Asian Culture Quarterly*, noted the following:

> "History of contacts between the Persian world and the Far East dates from the reign of Mithradates II (123 B.C.-87 B.C.), when in 115 B.C., this monarch of the Parthian Dynasty...received an envoy from the emperor of China...
>
> By the third century A.D., [the] Parthian Empire's trade routes were extended in the maritime ports of Southeast Asia as far as

Inscription on Column Discovered Near Amwâs by Clermont-Ganneau.

> the Malay Peninsula's international port of Tun-sun, where the...merchants had established settlements with no less than 500 residents. Their activities extended to the the Indo-Chinese port of Tonking as such accounts on sea trade activities of the Parthians were recorded by K'ang T'ai, Wu dynasty's envoy to the kingdom of Funan in the delta of the Mekong in the first period of the third century of the Christian era."[121]

The above is a remarkable account that Parthian trade and influence extended far eastward into Asia. Southeast Asia was so far from the Roman Empire that its writers knew nothing about Parthia's activities in that region. The above account indicates that Parthian contacts with China began early during the expansionary phase of the Parthian Empire. It also indicates Parthia's trade with the Far East Asia was extensive, requiring settlements of up to 500 Parthians in various Asian ports to handle the trading volume. The account that Parthian merchants were recorded in the Mekong delta region (modern Vietnam) in the third century A.D. shows how far Parthian influence had spread by the time its empire fell.

Parthia was strategically located in the middle of the famous "Silk Road" running from China across Asia to the Mediterranean and Roman world. No doubt, Parthia's government and its merchants used this fact to their advantage, charging transit fees for permission to ship Asian goods westward and Roman goods eastward across Parthian territory. During the peaceful period between Parthia and Rome from the first century B.C until later in the first century A.D., this traffic would have been quite extensive.

Boundary Inscription of the City of Gezer.
תחם גזר (Limit of Gezer).

A book by H.G. Rawlinson had the following description of the ancient Silk Route from Asia to the Mediterranean region:

> "Silk was destined to become an immensely important article of commerce. The expeditions of the Baktrian monarchs...had opened out the great trade route which runs from Balkh to the historic 'Stone Tower' of Sarikol. Some of the silk also found its way through Nepal to the Ganges and thence to the Malabar coast. Later on, it was taken straight from China to Rome, by the land-route from Sarikol to Balkh, Hekatomapylus, Ekbatana, Ktesiphon, Hira, and Charax, and then by sea to Petra, Tyre, and the Levant."[122]

H.G. Rawlinson's quote favors the use of the consonant "k" instead of the "c" used by most other writers for these place names. Using the more common "c," Hecatomopylus, Ecbatana and Ctesiphon were all major cities in the Parthian Empire. Obviously, when Parthia and Rome were at war, nothing traveled to or from Rome across this Silk Route. However, when Rome and Parthia had peaceful relations, Roman customers were eager for the goods of the Far East transported across Parthia's vast empire. The later period of the Parthian Empire witnessed frequent wars with Rome, which disrupted trade between Rome and China. In order to satisfy Roman demand for silk, Roman merchants initiated maritime traffic to Asia in 166 A.D., circumventing the Parthian-controlled Silk Route.[123]

The article from the *Asian Culture Quarterly* also recorded that China was concerned not only about Parthia's ability to block its trade Roman customers via the Silk Route, but also Parthia's growing merchant fleets in Asian waters.

> "China had been prevented by Parthia to receive envoys from Byzantium through Persian territory and was also denied direct access to the Mediterranean trade on geopolitical considerations. As such the Chinese in pursuit of an alternative trade route away from the Central-Asian overland routes under Parthian control were keeping an eye on Parthia's trade expansion on the maritime routes of Southeast Asia.[124]

Because Roman accounts about Parthia involved their relationships across the Eurasian land-mass, Rome had never directly witnessed Parthian naval capabilities. Parthian maritime skills would have been irrelevant in the wars fought with Rome on the western periphery of its empire. However, Parthian trade with ancient ports in Southeast Asia, the Malay Peninsula and Vietnam required maritime skills. Again, we are indebted to the article by Shahab Setudeh-Nejad for the following information:

> "Around this time [when Parthia traded with Southeast Asia], a technicalinnovation in the shipbuilding industry of the Persian Gulf resulted in the construction of vessels with a rig that accommodated the ships to sail nearerthe wind. The knowledge of this innovative development spread along the shores of the Indian Ocean and further East at a time when the Sasanian dynasty replaced the Parthians in Persia...
>
> ...Persian ships with up to seven sails carrying as many as 700 seamen and a 'thousand metric ton of cargo' were plying the Indian Ocean in the direction of the sea routes further East...[125]

At the time these maritime innovations developed, the Persian Gulf was dominated by Parthia. It is logical that Parthian ingenuity was the source of the maritime advances that facilitated trade between Parthia and the Far East. There is often some overlap in historical accounts involving the late-Parthian and early-Sassanian period in Persia. However, since it was Parthia which pioneered and expanded the maritime trade routes between the Persian Gulf and Far East Asia, it is likely that it was Parthian skill which led to these developments. The Sassanian Persian Empire, which supplanted

Early Hebrew inscription found in a cave at Arak el Emir *(Jewish Ency.)*

the Parthian Empire, would surely have also taken over the Parthian sea commerce with Asia and expanded it even further.

Consider the maritime technology that permitted the construction of ships "with seven sail" and crewed by 700 sailors! Given its huge complement of sailors, the phrase "seven sail" likely means these immense trade ships had seven masts. The Parthian merchant vessels had been sailing to East Asian ports for approximately three centuries by the time its empire collapsed. The Sassanians, eager to enrich their own coffers via trade with the Far East, surely would have assumed control of the Parthian trading vessels and maritime contacts. Contrast these Parthian leviathans with the relatively miniscule ships which Columbus sailed across the Atlantic Ocean in 1492 when he set out to "rediscover" America! It is a token of how far advanced was the culture of ancient Parthia that its sailing ships were vastly larger than the small sailing ships of medieval Europe in the 15th century A.D. when Europe was still emerging from the Dark Ages.

Parthian Culture and Science

We have already seen that the Parthians placed Semitic legends on their coins during the early Christian era. However, there is additional evidence that the Parthians had always spoken a Semitic language. Josephus observed that he originally wrote his *Wars of the Jews* in his native Semitic tongue so that the peoples of Parthia could understand the events of the Roman-Jewish war of the first century A.D. Josephus wrote:

> "I have proposed...for the sake of such as live under the government of the Romans, to translate those books into the Greek tongue, **which I formerly composed in the language of our own country, and sent to the Upper Barbarians**...[identified as the Parthians, Babylonians, Arabians and "the Jews **beyond Euphrates**..."][126] *(Emphasis added)*

Josephus, before writing his works in Greek for a Roman audience, had already written *Wars of the Jews* in his own Semitic language so the Parthians and people in their empire could read them. Note that Josephus again uses the phrase "beyond Euphrates" to designate Parthian territory. When he wrote to the Romans, he was mindful of his Roman audience in calling the Parthians "Upper Barbarians." Rawlinson states the following about Josephus' comments:

> "**Josephus...regarded the Parthians as familiar with Hebrew**, or Syro-Chaldaic, and wrote his history of the Jewish War **in his own native tongue...for the benefit especially of the Parthians**, among whom he declares he had many readers."[127] *(Emphasis added)*

Here is a "smoking gun" piece of evidence about Parthian origins. The Parthians were known to be so familiar with the Hebrew language that they could read whatever Josephus wrote "in his native tongue." The obvious conclusion is that the Jews and Parthians shared a common origin and language. The common elements in the Parthian and Hebrew languages further supports the conclusion that the Parthians were the descendants of the ten tribes of Israel. Combining the Parthian-Hebrew linguistic ties with Josephus' own testimony that the "ten tribes" had an immense population and lived in Parthia "beyond the Euphrates," results in a clear "positive identification." The Parthians were descendants of the ten tribes of Israel.

Why would the Parthians have a particular interest in the writings of Josephus, and why would Josephus have a special interest in communicating information to them? The clear answer is that both the Parthians and Josephus realized that the Parthians were the descendants of the ten tribes of Israel! Nothing else makes sense. Josephus was a product of the same Jewish culture that shaped the converts of the early New Testament church. That culture regarded non-Israelites

Parthian rock carving at Gotarzes

as "unclean" people with whom Jews could not interact. *(Acts 10:28)* Josephus, himself a Pharisee, would have shared these anti-gentile views, and would not have regarded the Parthians as "worthy" of extensive communication efforts on his part unless he realized that the Parthians were fellow Israelites of the ten tribes of Israel. Josephus even records that during the Jewish revolt against Rome which culminated in the destruction of the Temple in 70 A.D., the Jews had hoped that the people "beyond the Euphrates"—the Parthians—would have joined their war with Rome. That the Jews looked to Parthia for allies against Rome adds even more weight to the conclusion that many Jews knew the Parthians were their related kinsmen of the ten tribes of Israel.

The Parthians utilized coordinated lunar and solar calendars. Dr. G.R. Assar of Edinburgh, Scotland wrote the following observation about Parthian calendars:

> "...the Parthians operated two different but synchronized calendars...the first month of the [lunar] calendar was Nisanu(=March/April)... [they had] seven intercalary months in each 19-year period."[128]

The Parthian lunar calendar began in the Spring and its first month was named "Nisanu," a Babylonian term. The ancient Hebrews also began their lunar calendar in the Spring. It was originally called "Abib." *(compare Exodus 13:4-7 and Leviticus 23:4-6)* After the fall of Jerusalem, the Jews also adopted the name, "Nisan," for the first month of the year. *(Nehemiah 2:1, Esther 3:7)* Parthia's observation of a lunar calendar beginning in the Spring would have been consistent with the culture of Israel from the time of the Exodus. The similarity of names for the first month ("Nisan" and "Nisanu") and the use of seven intercalary months in a 19 year time cycle further confirm that the Parthians were the descendants of the ten tribes of Israel as the were still using Hebrew calendar calculations even though they had relocated into Asia.

Parthia maintained extensive trade relations with the Scythians and other people on their northern and eastern borders as indicated by the presence of Parthian coins being:

> "...found on the Volga, in the Caucasus, in Chinese Turkestan and elsewhere...At the same time Parthian-Chinese contacts overland are attested in Chinese sources."[129]

Ancient Chinese sources offer insightful observations about the Parthians. They provide a valuable perspective which supplements Roman accounts about the Parthians. One account from approximately 91 B.C. states:

> "When the first embassy was sent from China to An-hsi (=Ar-sak, Parthia) the king of Parthia ordered 20,000 cavalry to meet them on the eastern frontier...the wagons and ships of their merchants go to the neighboring countries..."[130]

China was impressed that Parthia sent 20,000 cavalry simply to meet and escort the Chinese delegation, and recorded that fact for posterity. It is noteworthy that China mentions that Parthia did conduct commerce via "ships" as well as via land routes. One Chinese account implies that both Parthia and China were aware of North America! It states:

> "From T'iao-chih [Chaldea] **by water you may go west over 100 days to come near the place where the sun sets**, they say...In the 9th year of Yung-yuan of Ho-ti (97 A.D.) the General Pan Ch'ao sent Kan-ying as an ambassador to Ta-ts'in [Syria], who arrived in Tiao-chih, **on the coast of the great sea**. When about to take his passage across the sea, **the sailors of the western frontier of Parthia** told Kan-ying: '**The sea is vast and great; with favorable winds it is possible to cross within three months**; but if you meet slow winds, it may also take you two years..."[131]

This account indicates the Chinese learned from the Parthians about a "place where the sun sets" which was far to the west across a "great sea." It indicates a voyage of at least 100 days was necessary to cross the great sea to a landfall on its western side. The "great sea" must be the Atlantic Ocean, as it would not take three months to two years to cross the Mediterranean Sea. However, if a voyage left from the eastern coast of the Mediterranean Sea on the shores of Syria, a problem exists. That was Roman territory except for a few years circa 40-37 B.C. when Syria and Palestine were subject to Parthia. It seems highly unlikely that Parthian vessels ever departed westward from the coast of Syria. However, the Chinese Ambassador Kan-ying considered embarking on a Parthian vessel while he was in Tiao-chih (Chaldea). Chaldea was in Mesopotamia and the Persian Gulf was a Parthian seacoast. The voyage to the land far to the west across the great sea more likely began in the Persian Gulf. This would also account for the voyage taking so long, as it would have to almost circumnavigate Africa before heading across the Atlantic Ocean to the Americas.

The fact that Parthian sailors told the Chinese that an area of "slow winds" could be encountered which would greatly prolong the voyage adds to the credibility of this account. There is an area known as "the Doldrums" in the Atlantic in which the winds rarely blow. Mariners who venture into this area with ships dependent on windpower could get marooned for a very long time as they waited for Ocean currents to drift them into a region where the winds would again be encountered. How would Parthian mariners know about sea-conditions in the Atlantic Ocean unless they had been there? There is an obvious answer.

Parthia had extensive trade relations with the Romans during their periods of "détente." During these times the Parthian merchant class imported metals and various manufactured items from Rome in exchange for textiles and spices supplied by the Parthians.[132] As evidence of the far-ranging trade between the Roman and Parthian empires, one Parthian coin was unearthed in the British Isles.[133] The above indicates that the Parthians were capitalists who took advantage of their strategic position as geographic middlemen between the Roman world and the Orient. During peaceful periods between Rome and Parthia, the trading vessels of each empire would have been welcome in each other's home ports. At the very least, Parthians accompanying Parthian cargo shipments likely sailed on Roman ships to Roman ports-of-call in Spain and the British Isles. Parthians would have learned about the dangers of "The Doldrums" during such voyages.

The Parthians were hardly "barbarians" when it came to scientific pursuits. It is known that their Scythian kinsmen were miners and expert artisans in gold artwork. The Parthians had an advanced military technology at the time of the first Parthian-Roman war: better bows, more protective body armor, and such. There is one more piece of evidence that will surprise modern readers. The Parthians had developed electricity! A 1996 issue of *Nexus* magazine revealed:

> "Wilhelm Konig, the then Director of the Baghdad Museum, reported the discovery of **an electric battery 2,000 years old**. You have not heard about this sensational discovery? We can tell you why. It did not fit in with the established viewpoint. Most archaeologists did not want to know about it and hoped it would go away. But Konig's electric battery did not go away. In fact, **a lot more of them were found in Parthian settlements** near Baghdad."[134] *(Emphasis added)*

Because "a lot" of these ancient Parthian batteries were found, there was a widespread use for them in ancient Parthia. This article explained the ancient batteries were pottery jars holding an acidic solution with metallic elements. Since each battery could only generate 1.5 volts of current, it was deduced that:

> "...these ancient people must have discovered how to link up several batteries in series to produce a higher voltage."[135]

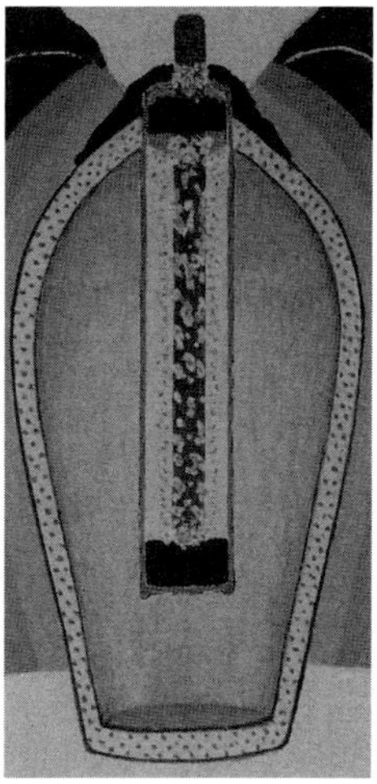

One suggested use of electricity in Parthia was for electroplating. The economic advantages of electroplating common objects with a gold exterior are obvious. One could command a much higher price for an object, or create a much more impressive collection to show off to others, if you could deceive buyers or viewers into thinking they were looking at a solid gold object instead of a gold-plated one. These ancient Parthian batteries are occasionally shown on cable television documentaries. These ancient batteries have also been mentioned or pictured in other books. Erich von Daniken's *Chariots of the Gods* states:

> "Electric dry batteries, which work on the galvanic principle, are on display in the Baghdad Museum."[136]

A photograph of an ancient Parthian battery appears in von Daniken's book, *In Search of Ancient Gods*.[137] It has also been proposed that the Parthians used the batteries for medicinal purposes. *Nexus* magazine stated:

> "Paul T. Keyser of the University of Alberta in Canada has...an alternative suggestion. Writing in the prestigious archaeological *Journal of Near Eastern Studies*, he claims that these batteries were analgesics ...They may have been [used] to apply electric shocks to the patient's stricken parts."[138]

Analgesic treatments for relieving pain would always be in demand in any society. Given the fact that Parthia's many wars with Rome produced many wounded and pain-ridden soldiers, small portable batteries may have been used to provide a measure of pain-relief for battlefield injuries. Seleucia was a city in the Parthian Empire, which was more than once caught in the crossfire of Roman-Parthian wars. Supporting the proposed use of the batteries for medicinal purposes is the fact that "bronze and iron needles were found alongside the battery devices found in Seleucia...these needles may have been used for acupuncture."[139] The Parthians traded with the Chinese so they could have easily become acquainted with the art of acupuncture.

Paul Keyser's article in the *Journal of Near Eastern Studies* states the following:

> "The Parthian galvanic batteries (electric batteries) have been known for some fifty years but have never been scientifically published, have heretofore seemed embarrassingly out of context, and have received little scientific treatment...The usual hypothesis...is that the purpose of the cells was electroplating, but I argue that this is impossible. Rather, I suggest a purpose...as a local analgesic...Such an application is supported by the modern clinical practice of transcutaneous electrical nerve stimulation."[140]

In modern medical usage, a "Transcutaneous Electrical Nerve Stimulation" device is called a TENS unit. Whatever the purpose served by the ancient Parthian electric batteries, they are an amazing find! Why has the truth about them been ignored? *Nexus* Magazine offers this apt explanation.

> "[It] was too much for the establishment. It did not fit with in with the usual concept of the development of Homo sapiens, the brilliant generation of modern man, which had slowly evolved from primitive ape-man to our sophisticated scientific society. **The Parthian batteries were before their time and were best forgotten.**"[141]

The blind adherence of "the establishment" to the theory of evolution has led to the suppression of truth about the ancient world whenever the "facts" don't support the theory of evolution. Not only has the existence of the ancient Israelite empires been censored from history texts, but also their advanced knowledge and technology has been suppressed as well. Why did "the establishment" suppress the knowledge that the ancient Parthians had electric batteries circa two millennia ago? Their existence is powerful evidence against the theory of evolution. Rather than abandon their flawed theory of evolution, it was easier to "go into denial" about the truths of the ancient world. However, you the reader are now learning those truths.

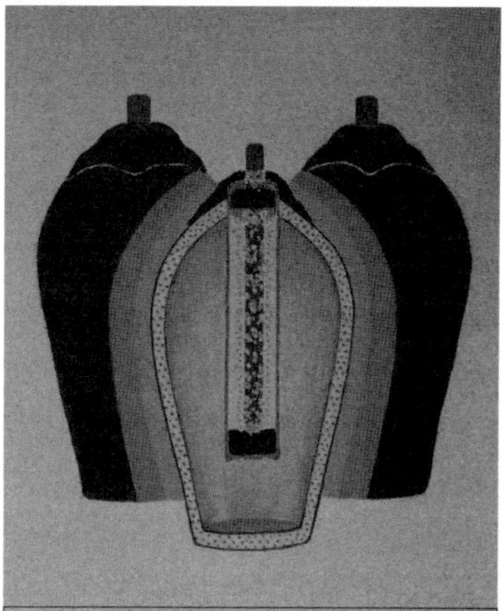
Parthian Batteries

Who in Parthian society invented and controlled access to the electric batteries? This author suggests it was the Magi, Parthia's priestly class (some of whom visited the Christ-child). The terms "magic" and "magician" are based on the Persian/ Parthian word "Magi."[142] Difficult-to-be understood technologies are often referred to as "magic." Electro-plating common objects to look like golden ones or relieving pain with mysterious methods would have been seen as "magic." Indeed, the private possession of such knowledge would have helped to preserve the influence and special status of the Magi. Because the term "**magic**" comes directly from the Parthian **Magi** and because these ancient batteries date to the Parthian period, the Magi were the likely inventors/custodians of the Parthian batteries.

Concerning Parthia's religion, we know that their empire contained sun-worshippers and other pagan religions. As discussed earlier, Judaism was common in Parthia, and Christianity had many adherents in the first and second centuries A.D. Indeed, Rawlinson wrote:

> "Christianity...penetrated the Parthian provinces to a considerable extent, and in one Parthian country... seems to have become the state religion. The kings of Osrhoene are thought to have been Christians from the time of the Antonines, if not from that of our Lord [the time of Christ]...and a flourishing church was certainly established at Edessa before the end of the second century."[143]

Parthia allowed considerable "freedom of religion" for its subjects,[144] a tolerant attitude not typical of the ancient world's empires. Rawlinson adds:

> "The Parthians had many liberal usages which imply a fairly advanced civilisation...in political matters they seem to have been free from the narrowness which generally characterizes barbarous nations. They behaved well to prisoners, admitted foreigners freely

> to offices of high trust, gave an asylum to refugees... were scrupulous observers of their pledged word, and eminently faithful to their treaty obligations."[145]

Parthia's empire was based on a feudal system that foreshadowed the feudal system of medieval Europe. The Parthians elected their monarchs via a bicameral body composed of the royalty, the priestly tribe and the nobility. They were capitalists who traded widely with other nations, and even with their enemies when possible. The Parthians were good hosts to large numbers of Jews within their borders, and even allowed home-rule privileges to some nations and cities in their empire. There were many adherents of Judaism and Christianity in the Parthian Empire, and their empire was known for many of the commendable traits of the "Judeo-Christian ethic."

In contrast, the Romans had a religion of superstitious polytheism, launched many wars of aggression to exalt the egomania of its emperors and commanders, enslaved other nations with tight controls, oppressed Jews, persecuted Christians, regularly violated treaties, etc. One of the clearest indicators of Rome's moral depravity was its love for gladiatorial "games." The reader is urged to look up "gladiator" in encyclopedias for a fuller accounting of Rome's degenerate pastime. Readers who saw the movie "Gladiator," released in the Spring of 2000, saw a graphic portrayal of this grisly activity.

The *Encyclopedia Britannica* notes that many Roman emperors sponsored these public murders. It states:

> "Julius Caesar engaged such extravagant numbers...that the Senate impos[ed] a certain limit...Claudius was devoted to this pastime...Under Nero, senators and even well-born women appeared as combatants. Even the emperor Titus ordered a show which lasted 100 days...Domitian at the Saturnalia of 90 A.D. arranged a battle between dwarfs and women."[146]

The *Encyclopedia Americana* makes this observation about the character of Rome's appetite for public murder as a sport:

> "Thousands of gladiators died annually in amphitheaters of the Roman Empire. Gladiatorial combat was probably the cruelest sport ever widely accepted in an advanced civilization."[147]

Restoration of the Hatra Palace-Temple (after Ainsworth).

The Romans possessed great engineering skills in designing and building roads, buildings, aqueducts, etc. Surviving Roman ruins attest to the remarkable Roman skills in such construction projects. Rome also was highly skilled in the art of warfare. However, Rome's character was deeply flāwed. The longstanding popularity of the gladiatorial contests testifies to Rome's barbaric cruelty and bloodlust. Given the fact that watching mass public murders was a favorite "sport" of Rome's leaders and citizens for centuries, Rome's society and culture exhibited a strong sociopathic aspect for much of its existence. If the leaders and citizens of any modern nation enjoyed public, mass murder spectacles as one of their major national "sports," would we call that nation "civilized?" Obviously, we would not! Modern societies would label such a practice as unspeakably degenerate and depraved!

Yet history texts paradoxically and routinely describe the degenerate Romans as "civilized," and call the Parthians and other rivals of Rome "barbarians." By any standard of comparison, which empire was "civilized," and which was "barbaric?" It was far more preferable to live under Parthian rule than under Roman rule, as the nations caught between the two empires regularly affirmed. The answer is obvious: the Parthian Empire was far more tolerant, humane and civilized than the Roman Empire.

There is also a myth that Rome was the custodian and preserver of civilized knowledge, holding back the Dark Ages until the "barbarians" sacked Rome. The reverse is true. Rome was largely responsible for the Dark Ages because it was the great destroyer of civilized knowledge! Consider the following quote by Rene Noorbergen:

> "The Romans' ruthlessness was an integral part of a wave of wanton destruction that struck the Library of Carthage in 146 B.C., reducing its irreplaceable 500,000 volumes to ashes...The most devastating blow, however, was struck by Julius Caesar when he burned the athenaeum of Alexandria, destroying 700,000 of the most valued scientific works of the classical world."[148]

Rome destroyed the great libraries that contained the world's historical and scientific knowledge. The Carthaginian library surely had the entire history of the Phoenician Empire, which had founded Carthage. This would have included many volumes on Israelite history. It also contained the nautical technologies and global maps that had been painstakingly developed over the centuries by Phoenician and Carthaginian mariners. If Carthage's library had survived, modern man would have realized that the ancient Phoenicians and Carthaginians knew the earth was round at least a millennium prior to the Greco-Romans. Who knows what technical knowledge was contained in Alexandria's library that had to be relearned when mankind emerged from the Dark Ages? Rome was too brutish to appreciate the priceless knowledge of other civilizations, so they destroyed it.

The modern western world thinks its societies are based on the Greco-Roman institutions, and students are force-fed the history of Rome while the extensive history of the Parthian empire is almost totally suppressed. An honest comparison indicates that the governmental and societal structure of medieval Europe and the modern western world have much more in common with the institutions and practices of the Parthian Empire than those of the Roman Empire. As will be seen in the next book, the modern world has been taught a major historical error. Even though European culture and the modern western world developed in the geographic region of the old Roman Empire, its social and political institutions are firmly rooted in the heritage of Parthia. The next book in this series will explain how this happened.

Before we examine the history of the Parthian migrations out of Asia in the next book, an important chapter will conclude this book. The next chapter will discuss the life of Jesus Christ and the history of the early Christian church within the historical context of the Roman-Parthian politics, which dominated the world into which Jesus was born. The full story of Christ's life cannot be understood apart from this Parthian-Roman context. The coming of the Magi, members of Parthia's ruling class, into Roman territory to worship the young Jesus as "a king" hints at many mysteries involving the life of Jesus Christ. The following chapter contains more major surprises!

ENDNOTES: CHAPTER TWO

1. Rawlinson, George, The Sixth Great Oriental Monarchy, preface, pp. v-vii

2.McClintock, John and Strong, James, Cyclopedia of Biblical, Theological and Ecclesiastical Literature, Vol. VII, see "Parthian," p. 711

3.Rawlinson, George, Parthia, p. 47

4.Josephus, Antiquities of the Jews, XI, VIII, 5

5.Rawlinson, George, The Sixth Great Oriental Monarchy, pp. 49-51

6.Ibid., pp. 54-57

7.Ibid., pp. 63-67

8.Ibid., pp. 94-95

9.Ibid., pp. 77 and 79

10.Ibid., p. 99

11.Ibid., pp. 104-105

12.Ibid., p. 105

13.Josephus, Antiquities, XIII, VIII, 4, and XIII, IX, 1 (also see footnote)

14.Strabo, The Geography of Strabo, translated by Horace Jones, 11, 9, 3

15.Rawlinson, George, The Sixth Great Oriental Monarchy, p. 85

16.Ibid., p. 85

17.Ibid., p. 86

18.Ibid., p. 393

19.Ibid., p. 87

20.Ibid., pp. 87-88

21.Encyclopedia Britannica, Vol. 17, Heading entitled "Persia," p. 578

22. Rawlinson, George, The Sixth Great Oriental Monarchy, pp. 88-89

23. Josephus, Antiquities of the Jews, Book XVIII, IX, 3 (see also footnote)

24. Rawlinson, Parthia, p.82-83

25. Josephus, Antiquities of the Jews, XI, V, 2

26. Rawlinson, George, The Sixth Great Oriental Monarchy, pp. 116-118

27. Frye, The Heritage of Persia, pp. 207-208; and the Encyclopedia Britannica, Heading entitled "Parthia," Vol. 17, p. 344

28. Rawlinson, George, The Sixth Great Oriental Monarchy, pp. 117-118

29. Ibid., see map after p. 78

30. Ibid., p. 115

31. Ibid., p. 118

32. Encyclopedia Britannica, Heading entitled "Ephthalites or White Huns," Vol. 8, p. 646

33. Ibid., Vol. 8, p. 646

34. Ibid., Vol. 8, p. 646

35. Encyclopedia Britannica, Heading entitled "Indo-Scythians," Vol. 12, p. 270

36. Ibid., Vol. 2, Heading entitled "Babylonia and Assyria," p. 857

37. Rawlinson, George, Parthia, p. 140

38. Rawlinson, George, The Sixth Great Oriental Monarchy, p. 146

39. Josephus, Antiquities of the Jews, Book XVIII, IX, 3-4

40. Rawlinson, George, The Sixth Great Oriental Monarchy, pp. 147-148

41. Plutarch, Fall of the Roman Republic (Crassus), 14

42. Ibid., 16

43. Ibid., Crassus, 25

44. Encyclopedia Britannica, Vol. 6, see "Crassus," p. 646

45. Encyclopedia Britannica, Vol. 17, Heading entitled "Persia", p. 579

46. Josephus, Antiquities, XIV, VII, 1

47. Ibid., XIV, VII, 1

48. Rawlinson, George, The Sixth Great Oriental Monarchy, p. 154

49. Ibid., pp. 155-156

50. Plutarch, Crassus, 18

51. Rawlinson, George, The Sixth Great Oriental Monarchy, p. 160

52.Ibid., p. 161

53.Encyclopedia Britannica, Vol. 17, Heading entitled "Persia," p. 581

54.Plutarch, Crassus, 21

55.Ibid., Crassus, 21

56.Ibid., Crassus, 23

57.Ibid., Crassus, 24

58.Ibid., Crassus, 24

59.Ibid., Crassus, 25

60.Ibid., Crassus, 31

61.Ibid., Crassus, 31

62.Rawlinson, George, The Sixth Great Oriental Monarchy, p. 172 (see also footnote no. 5)

63.Ibid., p.174

64.Frye, The Heritage of Persia, p. 214

65.Rawlinson, George, The Sixth Great Oriental Monarchy, pp. 174-175

66.Encyclopedia Britannica, Vol. 17, see "Persia," p. 577

67.Rawlinson, George, The Sixth Great Oriental Monarchy, p. 188

68.Ibid., p. 189

69.McClintock, John and Strong, James, Cyclopedia of Biblical, Theological and Ecclesiastical Literature, Vol. VII, see "Parthian," p. 711

70.Rawlinson, George, The Sixth Great Oriental Monarchy, pp. 190-191

71.Josephus, Antiquities, XI, V, 2

72.Rawlinson, George, The Sixth Great Oriental Monarchy, pp. 200-201

73.Ibid., p. 216

74.Ibid., pp. 218-219

75.Ibid., pp. 246-247, 266

76.Ibid., pp. 231-234

77.Ibid., p. 255

78.Ibid., pp. 270, 279-280

79.Ibid., p. 282

80.Ibid., p. 294

81.Encyclopedia Britannica, Heading entitled "Dacia," Vol. 6, p. 969

82. Rawlinson, George, The Sixth Great Oriental Monarchy, pp. 296-297

83. Encyclopedia Britannica, Vol. 1., Heading entitled "Alphabet," pp. 683-684

84. Rawlinson, George, The Sixth Great Oriental Monarchy, pp. 296-297

85. Frye, George, The Heritage of Persia, p. 232

86. Rawlinson, George, The Sixth Great Oriental Monarchy, pp. 304-305

87. Ibid., p. 308

88. Ibid., p. 309

89. Ibid., p. 312-313

90. Ibid., p. 315

91. Ibid., p. 317

92. Ibid., p. 318

93. Young's Analytical Concordance to the Bible, Old Testament Hebrew Lexicon, word "Melek," p. 26

94. Rawlinson, George, The Sixth Great Oriental Monarchy, p. 297 (footnote #1)

95. Eusebius, The History of the Church (The Ecclesiastical History), Book 3, 1, 1

96. Encyclopedia Britannica, Heading entitled "Persia," Vol. 17, p. 580

97. Harper's Bible Dictionary, Heading entitled "Aramaic," p. 43

98. Rawlinson, George, The Sixth Great Oriental Monarchy, p. 319

99. Ibid., pp. 322-325

100. Ibid., p. 328

101. Ibid., p. 328

102. Ibid., p. 329

103. Ibid., p. 329

104. Ibid., pp. 340-341

105. Ibid., p. 352

106. Herodian, iv. 20 (cited by Rawlinson, p. 354 in footnote 1)

107. Ibid., p. 356

108 Rawlinson, H.G., Intercourse Between India and the Western World, Second Edition, 1992 Reprint, p. 128

109 Ibid, p. 128

110. Herodotus, History, 4, 127

111. Rawlinson, George, The Sixth Great Oriental Monarchy, p. 357

112.Ibid., p. 358

113.Ibid., pp. 358-359

114.Ibid., p. 360

115.Ibid., p. 360

116.Benjamin, Persia, p. 170

117.Ibid., p. 173

118.Frye, The Heritage of Persia, p. 198

119.Encyclopedia Britannica, Vol. 17, see "Pahlavi," p. 30; and "Persia," p. 577

120.Frye, The Heritage of Persia, p. 213

121 Shahab Setudeh-Nejad, "Cultural and Cosmological Impact of Sasanian Civilization in Vietnam and Peninsular Areas of Southeast Asia," Asian Culture Quarterly, Vol. XXIV, No. 4, Winter 1996

122 Rawlinson, H.G., Intercourse Between India and the Western World, Second Edition, 1992 Reprint, Uppal Publishing House, New Delhi, pp. 114-115

123 Ibid, pp. 129-130

124 Shahab Setudeh-Nejad, , same article and issue

125 Ibid, same article and issue, pp. 76-80

126.Josephus, Wars of the Jews, Preface, 1-2

127.Rawlinson, George, The Sixth Great Oriental Monarchy, p. 424

128.Assar, Dr. G.R., Recent Calendar Research, website: www.parthia.com, links: "Calendars" and "Recent Calendar Research,"

129.Frye, p. 224

130.Hirth, China and the Roman Orient, from website: www.parthia.com, links: "Parthian Stations," "Parallel Passages from the Chinese Annals," citing: Shih-chi, ch. 123 and Ch'ien-han-shu, ch. 96a

131.Ibid., citing: Ch'ien-han-shu, ch. 96a and Hou-han-shu, ch. 88

132.Rawlinson, The Sixth Monarchy, pp. 425-426

133.Wilson, Daniel, The Archaeology and Prehistoric Annals of Scotland, p. 200

134.Nexus Magazine, June-July, 1996 issue, see Science News,

Why the Electric Battery was Forgotten," p. 43

135.Ibid., p. 43

136.von Daniken, Erich, Chariots of the Gods, p. 44

137.von Daniken, Erich, In Search of Ancient Gods, p. 174

138.Nexus Magazine, June-July, 1996 issue, see Science News, "Why the Electric Battery was Forgotten," p. 43

139.Ibid., p. 43

140.Keyser, Paul T. Journal of Near Eastern Studies, "The Purpose of the Parthian Galvanic Cells: A First-Century A.D. Electric Battery Used for Analgesia," April, 1993, p. 81

141.Nexus Magazine, "Science News: Why the Electric Battery was Forgotten," p. 44

142.Webster's New World Dictionary, see words "Magi" and "Magic," p. 449

143.Rawlinson, George, The Sixth Great Oriental Monarchy, p. 401 (see also footnotes 5-7)

144.Ibid., pp. 400-401, 426

145.Ibid., p. 426

146.Encyclopedia Britannica, Vol. 10, see "'Gladiators," p. 383

147.Encyclopedia Americana, Vol. 12, see "Gladiator," pp. 774-775

148.Noorbergen, Rene, Secrets of the Lost Races, New English Library, London, 1978

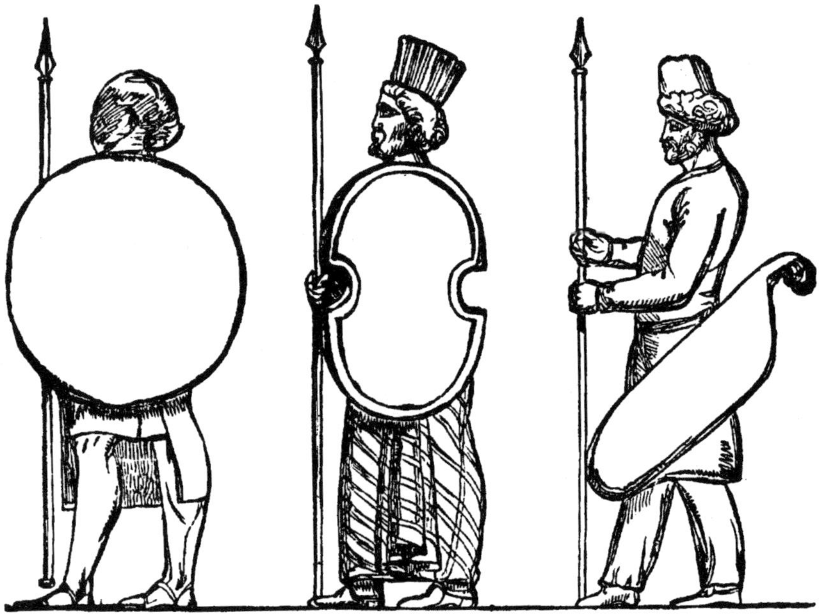

Parthian Soldiers

Chapter 3
The "Untold Story" Of Jesus Christ's Life

HIS CHILDHOOD YEARS (BIRTH TO AGE 12)

Much has been written about the life of Jesus Christ, the historical person whose name is attached to the many different denominations of Christianity that exist today. In fact, so much has been written that one might wonder whether anything truly new could be written about this one life. As the reader will see, new facts about the life of Jesus Christ can be ascertained by combining the accounts of the Bible with secular historical accounts and traditions about the time in which He lived. This chapter is not intended to be a complete history of the life of Jesus Christ. It will cover those aspects of His life and times which have not been generally known.

The prior chapter dealing with the Parthian Empire discussed historical events shaping the world into which Jesus Christ was born. When some surprising information about His life is added to the history contained in the previous chapter, it can be seen that Jesus Christ actually played a role in the great power politics which occurred between the empires of Parthia and Rome. The Bible hints that He could have played a much larger role in the political affairs of that era if He had chosen to do so.

Did Jesus Really Live?

There is no doubt that the person, Jesus Christ, actually lived in Palestine at the beginning of the first century A. D. While some skeptics doubt this fact, this chapter will begin by offering firm evidence that Jesus Christ was a real, historical person.

Josephus, a Jewish historian of the first century A. D., regarded the life of Jesus Christ as an established fact. In *Antiquities of the Jews*, Josephus wrote:

> "there was about this time, Jesus, a wise man, if it be lawful to call him a man, for He was a doer of wonderful works, — a teacher of such men as receive the truth with pleasure. He drew over to him both many of the Jews, and many of the Gentiles. He was Christ; and when Pilate [Pontius Pilate, Roman Procurator of Judea], at the suggestion of the principle men among us, had condemned him to the cross...He appeared to them alive again the third day, as the divine prophets had foretold these and ten thousand other wonderful things concerning him; and the tribe of Christians, so named from him, are not extinct at this day."[1]

In this account, written shortly after Christ died, Josephus not only gave us a powerful witness that Jesus Christ truly lived, but also provided an independent corroboration of many of the biblically-discussed events of His life. Josephus refers to him as "a wise man," and wonders whether He was more than a mere man because of the "wonderful works" He did. That a non-Christian, Jewish historian of the apostolic era writes of the miracles of Jesus as actual facts offers contemporary support to the Bible's accounts about them. Josephus agrees with the testamental writings that Jesus was sentenced to be crucified by Pontius Pilate at the behest of the Jewish Sanhedrin, "the principle men among us." Josephus also acknowledged that Jesus Christ fulfilled many prophecies of the Hebrew prophets about the Messiah, and **even refers to His resurrection as an historical fact!**

Josephus' reference to Jesus as "the Christ" acknowledges that Jesus was the Messiah, "the anointed." Since a non-Christian source so close to the actual time of Christ has confirmed these facts of His life, the musings of modern skeptics questioning Christ's existence are without merit. Josephus could speak with eyewitnesses of Jesus' life; modern skeptics are almost two millennia removed from the events, and their writings are merely speculative. Jesus Christ did live, and the writings of Josephus substantiate the Bible's claims of His performance of supernatural deeds as well as His being raised from the dead.

Roman secular sources agree with Josephus. Celsus, an anti-Christian writer of the Roman Empire in the second century A.D., wrote: "It was by magic that He [Jesus] was able to do the miracles which He appeared to have done."[2] Here a Roman opponent of Christianity grudgingly acknowledges the reality of Christ's "miracles," which he labels as "magic." However, Quadratus, writing in approximately 117-134 A.D., "urged people to believe in Jesus because the effect of His miracles continued up to the present — people had been cured and raised from the dead, and 'some of them...have survived even to our own day.'"[3] Tacitus, the famous Roman historian, writing about the Christians just decades after the death of Christ, stated:

> "Nero fabricated scapegoats — and punished...the notoriously depraved Christians (as they were popularly called). Their originator, Christ, had been executed in Tiberius' reign by the governor of Judea, Pontius Pilate."[4]

Tacitus' comment about Christ appears as a mere aside in an overall account of events in the reign of Nero. It is particularly compelling evidence that Jesus Christ really did live! Tacitus was no fan of Christ or Christianity, and he had no "axe to grind." His account that "Christ" was a real person crucified by Pontius Pilate is highly credible as Tacitus refers to it as an official act of Pontius Pilate within His overall accounting of Rome's activities.

Clearly, Roman accounts confirm that Jesus Christ lived, and that He was executed in Judea during the administration of Pontius Pilate. Even His detractors acknowledged that He performed supernatural deeds. Whatever your views about Jesus Christ, we begin with the fact that He, indeed, lived and died when the Bible states that He lived and died, that He performed marvelous deeds, and that He made a major impression on the civilization of His day.

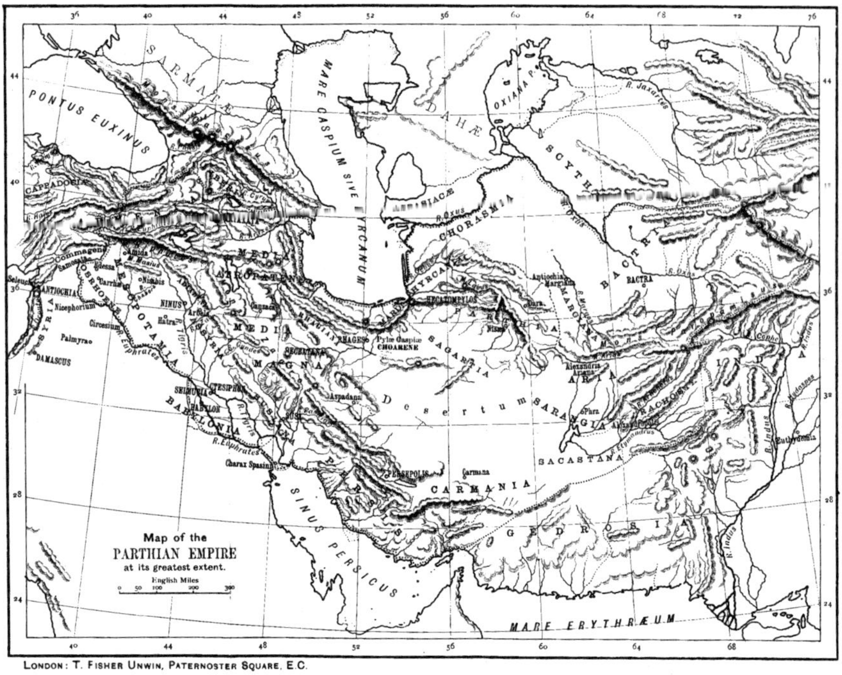

LONDON: T. FISHER UNWIN, PATERNOSTER SQUARE, E.C.

Let us now review the historical setting into which Jesus Christ was born. The Roman and Parthian Empires were both powerful, well-established "superpower" rivals at the time Jesus was born. Rome ruled the Mediterranean region, and Parthia ruled Asian lands from modern Syria to the Indus River. Palestine was located within the Roman Empire, but was close to the Euphrates River constituting the Parthian border.

Five decades before the birth of Jesus, Rome and Parthia fought several battles with one being fought near Antioch of Syria (very close to Palestine).[5] In about 40 B.C., the Parthians launched a major assault which drove the Romans out of Asia! For three years, 40-37 B.C., Palestine was within the Parthian Empire and was ruled by a Jewish vassal king of the Parthians named Antigonus. At that time King Herod, the Roman king of Judea, fled from the Parthians in fear of his life. While the Parthian-sponsored rule of Antigonus was brief, it was apparently popular with the Jews. When the Parthians withdrew across the Euphrates, Antigonus, with Jewish support, attempted to maintain himself as king of the Jews, but was defeated by Herod. Mark Antony, the Roman leader famous for his dalliance with Cleopatra, ordered Antigonus beheaded, and Josephus records that this was done to compel the Jews to accept the hated Herod as their king.[6] Mark Antony afterward led a massive invasion of Parthia in 37-36 B.C., but his army was utterly defeated by the Parthians.[7]

To help modern readers gain a frame of reference for these ancient events, these Roman-Parthian wars were more recent events for the people at the time Jesus was born than World War II and the Korean War are to modern readers. Parthian rule over Palestine was, therefore, vividly remembered by many in Jewish society as being preferable to Roman rule.

Parthia's victory over Mark Antony led to a long period of peace between Rome and Parthia, with the Euphrates River serving as the border between their two vast empires. This prolonged period of peaceful relations lasted from 36 B.C. until 58 A.D.,[8] including not only all of Jesus Christ's life, but also the early period of the Apostolic Church as well. Rawlinson records that it was an established Roman policy not to provoke a Parthian war during that period of time so long as both empires agreed to coexist on separate banks of the Euphrates River. Rawlinson comments on this peaceful interlude as follows:

> "It is a well-known fact that Augustus left it as a principle of policy to his successors that the Roman Empire had reached its proper limits, and could not with advantage be extended further. This principle, followed with the utmost strictness by Tiberius, was accepted as a rule by all the earlier Caesars..."[9]

As long as the Caesars wanted peace with Parthia, Roman officials along Parthia's border, such as King Herod and Pontius Pilate, knew they risked their positions and lives if they entangled Rome in an unwanted war with Parthia.

Without this period of Parthian-Roman detente, it would have been impossible for some of the events of Jesus Christ's life to have occurred, as we shall see. The first such event was the coming of the

Magi, or "Wise Men" to pay homage to Jesus. We read of this event in Matthew 2:1-12, which becomes more important when considered in the overall context of Roman-Parthian relations.

Parthia's Magi Visit Jesus (and Frighten Jerusalem)

As discussed in the previous chapter, the Magi were powerful members of the Parthian bicameral body that elected Parthian monarchs and wielded great influence within the empire. One assembly was composed of members of the royal family (the Arsacids), and the other consisted of the priests (the "Magi") and influential Parthians of non-royal blood (the "Wise Men"). The Magi and Wise Men were jointly known as the Megistanes.[10]

Matthew 2:1 states that "wise men from the east" came to worship Jesus. The term "Wise Men," which appears in Matthew 2:1, is not a generic description of these visitors, but was the proper title of Parthian Megistanes. The Greek word translated "wise men" is "magian," literally meaning "Persian astronomer or priest,"[11] from which we derive the word "Magi." Parthia governed Persia at the time of Christ, so the "Wise Men" cited in the Bible were Parthian nobles and/or priests. While traditional Christian accounts of this episode celebrate the coming of "the three wise men," the Bible does not limit the number of visiting Magi-Wise Men to three men. Indeed, biblical events and the realities of that time argue for a much larger contingent of Parthian Magi.

Since we saw in previous chapters that the Parthians were descended from the ten tribes of Israel and that their priests were likely descended from the tribe of Levi, it is likely that this delegation of Magi consisted of leading members of the ten tribes of Israel. Because there were numerous Jews of the tribe of Judah in Parthia's empire, they may have been represented as well. Consequently, the delegation of Magi could easily have consisted of at least ten or twelve men representing the various tribes of Israel.

Also, the Bible confirms that the Magi did not visit the young Jesus in the manger at Bethlehem as most nativity scenes depict, but rather visited Jesus in a house somewhat after His birth. Matthew 2:11 states that this visit of the Magi took place **in a house** (not at the manger) when Jesus was old enough to be called "**a young child**." Luke's version of Christ's birth *(Luke 2:8-40)* mentions the shepherds' arrival at the manger, but makes no mention of any Magi visiting Christ while He was "in the manger."

Matthew 2:8 adds that Herod sent the Magi "to Bethlehem" after conferring with the Jewish hierarchy about the prophesied location of the Messiah's birth. They cited Micah 5:2 that the Messiah would originate in Bethlehem, and they were likely familiar with Daniel 9:25-26 which predicted that the arrival of the Messiah was due at that time. Herod privately met with the Parthian delegation, and enquired when "the star" which they followed had first appeared. He apparently learned that this period of time was almost two years because he killed all male children in Bethlehem under two years of age in an attempt to kill the Messiah, whom he regarded as a competitor for his position as king of the Jews.

Although the Bible tells us that "the star" appeared to the Wise Men almost two years prior to His birth, this offers inexact information in determining how old Jesus was when the Wise Men came to him. The Wise Men were prominent people in Parthia when "the star" appeared, and they had to make a very time-consuming journey to reach Judea. It took time to prepare the costly gifts to present to the Messiah, set their affairs in order for a long absence, organize and equip a caravan, obtain an armed escort for protection and make the slow, lengthy journey to Judea in a caravan of pack animals. Since the "star's" appearance was not necessarily timed to coincide exactly with the time Jesus was born, He may have been a few months (or up to two years) old at the time of the Magi's arrival.

Consider also that Matthew 2:1-3 states:

> "Now when Jesus was born in Bethlehem of Judea in the days of Herod the king, behold, there came **wise men from the east to Jerusalem**. Saying, where is He that is born King of the Jews? for **we have seen His star** in the east, and are come to worship him. When Herod the king heard these things, **he was troubled, and all Jerusalem with him**." *(KJV)*

The arrival of the Magi's caravan in Jerusalem was a **very public affair** because "all Jerusalem" was "troubled" by their arrival. What was it about the Magi's caravan that scared the Roman leaders and the whole city of Jerusalem? The Magi, a delegation of high Parthian officials, came to Jerusalem in a caravan loaded with costly treasures and escorted by a strong force of armed Parthian soldiers! Since the Magi were high officials of the Parthian government, they would routinely travel with a substantial escort of Parthian soldiers to guarantee their protection. Since they were traveling with many costly treasures to present to the newborn Messiah, their escort may have been unusually large.

The Parthian Magi

The Magi's caravan would have included large numbers of servants, animal-handlers, cooks, etc. for such a long journey. These people alone would have constituted many hundreds of people! Given the fact that many high Parthian officials and very expensive treasures were in the caravan, there may have been many thousands of Parthian soldiers escorting the caravan! This is not an overstatement.

Josephus records that treasure caravans bringing expensive offerings to Jerusalem from Jews living in Parthian territory did so with "many ten thousand men" as escorts.[12] In ancient times, traveling with expensive items was dangerous. There was danger not only from brigands, but also from local satraps who might use their armies to conquer a treasure train passing through their territories. If Jewish commoners from Parthia were allowed to travel to Jerusalem with the equivalent of several infantry divisions as escorts, would an important delegation of Parthia's ruling class and a treasure train of gifts have been accompanied by any fewer armed escorts? If the Parthian column had included "many ten thousands" of soldiers, it would have justified the widespread fear in Jerusalem caused by their arrival. In the previous chapter, we learned that ancient Chinese historical accounts recorded that the Parthians sent 20,000 cavalry just to escort a Chinese ambassador into Parthian territory.

Plutarch records that Surenas — a Parthian military commander and, no doubt, a member of the Megistanes — traveled on routine business in a caravan of cavalry, servants, and attendants the size of "a baggage train of 1,000 camels...at least ten thousand men."[13] If one Parthian leader traveled with so large a caravan on routine business within Parthia, how large was the caravan of the Magi — a whole delegation of Parthian nobles carrying great treasures to worship a "new-born king?" It was large enough to frighten the whole city of Jerusalem!

The Wise Men coming to Jesus were not bringing just a few samples of gold and other precious things that they carried in their personal saddlebags. They were coming to worship a royal-born child, so they likely had a whole train of pack animals loaded with "gold, frankincense and myrrh!"

Bethlehem.

The Wise men presenting gifts to the child Jesus

Their caravan was so huge that it was a "cause celebre" in Jerusalem. The whole city was in an uproar over their arrival, and that argues for a **very visible and impressive** Parthian caravan arriving in Jerusalem. The sheer size of the caravan, its treasures and its escorts awed King Herod and the whole city to the point they were all "troubled." This indicates that the Parthian caravan had so many armed escorts that many feared it was an invasion force coming to besiege Jerusalem and start a new Roman-Parthian war. However, their announced reason — coming to visit a royal-born Messiah — could have electrified a city of Jews who intensely wanted the Messiah to come and free them from Roman rule! The Jewish hierarchy understood the Parthians were looking for the Messiah as they quickly looked for Messianic prophecies to locate the city of His birth.

After their consultations with Herod and high Jewish officials, the Parthian delegation traveled to Bethlehem to worship Jesus and present their gifts to him. By this time, Matthew 2:11 states Jesus and

The Flight Into Egypt

Mary were living in "a house," so they were no longer staying at the manger. The Magi's journey to Bethlehem would have been closely followed by Herod's spies.

Joseph was then warned by an angel to flee quickly into Egypt *(Matthew 2:13)* to avoid Herod's impending slaughter of Bethlehem's young male children. Since Herod's edict applied only to Bethlehem, there would have been no need for Joseph, Mary and Jesus to flee unless they were still in Bethlehem. Since Joseph and Mary actually lived in Galilee *(Luke 2:4)*, the fact that they were in a house in Bethlehem indicates that this must have been weeks after Jesus' birth while Mary was regaining the strength to make an overland trip back to Nazareth. Their flight to Egypt took them completely out of Herod's area of jurisdiction.

Herod made the mistake of assuming the Messiah would be born to a family native to the Bethlehem area. Since Luke 2:39 states that Joseph, Mary and Jesus returned to Galilee not long after Jesus was born, it seems apparent that the stay of Joseph, Mary and Jesus in Egypt was very brief. Historical sources disagree on the year of King Herod's death, but there is persuasive evidence that Herod died soon after giving his cruel order to murder the boy babies of Bethlehem. Matthew 2:14-19 states that Jesus and His parents returned from Egypt as soon as Herod was dead, and the account implies their stay in Egypt was brief.

This author acknowledges that there are differing scholarly and historical viewpoints concerning the year of Jesus Christ's birth. While many people assume that Jesus Christ was born in a theoretical "year zero," scholarly options for the year of Jesus' birth focus on the time frame of 5 B.C. to 2 B.C.

It is significant that Jesus' parents were faithful to God's law requiring circumcision on the eight day *(Leviticus 12:2-3)*, and to Jewish custom by making an offering to God at the Temple in Jerusalem to consecrate their firstborn male child. *(Luke 2:21-24)* This is an important observation as it shows Jesus was raised by a Jewish family that devoutly obeyed God's laws.

When the Parthian column arrived at Jerusalem, the Parthian Magi came directly to King Herod, quite open about their reasons for being in Roman-occupied Palestine. They informed Herod that they had come to worship "He that is born king of the Jews."

It is a tribute to the power of Caesar's policy that the Roman-Parthian peace be maintained that war did not result from this statement, for Herod could easily have taken it as an insult. He could have flown into a rage, and yelled "How dare you ask to see another 'king of the Jews' besides me; I am king of the Jews!" That Herod swallowed his gargantuan pride, and meekly answered the Parthians is quite noteworthy. This is a tribute not only to Caesar's policy to maintain the peace, but also to recognition that a sizeable Parthian army had come to Jerusalem as escorts of the Magi. Herod's meek response to the highly provocative question of the Parthian officials does imply that he was intimidated by the many Parthian soldiers who accompanied the Magi.

Because the whole city was "troubled" by the Parthians' arrival, the presence of so many Parthian soldiers surely sparked rumors in Jerusalem that a new Parthian-Roman war was imminent. Herod may even have suspected that the Parthians' question was designed to provoke an incident, which would lead to an outbreak of hostilities and his removal from the throne. Herod and all Jerusalem was surprised, but relieved to learn that the Parthian Magi and soldiers had arrived with peaceful intent. Herod may have been expecting to hear an ultimatum for the surrender of Jerusalem to Parthia when the Magi were ushered into his presence.

Some observations must be made about the "star" which led the Magi to Jesus. Some have proposed that this star was a comet or a celestial phenomenon although the biblical accounts indicate that this was not the case. The biblically-described "star" moved, leading the Magi over a long east-to-west route from Parthia to Judea, and Matthew 2:9 states that it finally "stood over where the young child was." **Simple logic confirms that no comet or celestial phenomenon in the sky could possibly pinpoint a single city, much less "stand over" an individual child on the earth's surface!** Nevertheless, that is what the biblical "star" did.

The Bible periodically uses the word "star" to represent angels *(Job 38:7, Revelation 1:20)*, and there is good reason to believe that the "star" which led the Parthian nobles to a specific child in a specific house in Judea was an angel of God. Nothing else makes sense. **Only an angel, a spirit being, could literally "stand over" the baby Jesus to designate one specific child to the Parthian nobles.**

Also, nothing in the biblical account indicates that this "star" was visible to anyone other than the Magi-Wise Men! Matthew 2:2 states that the Magi saw "the star," but the context argues no one else

The Guiding Star

The birth of Christ announced to the shepherds

ever saw it. Verse 7 relates that Herod asked the Magi when "the star" appeared **to them**, indicating no one in Judea was aware of any such "star." If a striking celestial object had appeared in the sky, Herod and his astrologers would already have known the exact date and hour on which it had appeared.

After leading the Parthians to Judea, the "star" disappeared, forcing the Parthians to ask Herod for directions. After the Magi left Herod, the "star" again appeared to them, led them directly to Bethlehem *(Luke 2:9)*, and finally "stood over" one specific child, Jesus. Verse 10 states the Magi rejoiced that the "star" had again appeared to show them where to go! Obviously, a "star" which appeared, disappeared and reappeared for the Magi (but which was apparently not seen by any other humans) had to be an angel. Supporting this fact is that Luke 2:8-15 records that the birth of Jesus was announced to shepherds **by**

angels speaking to them out of a heavenly light which accompanied their appearance. God also used **an angel** to warn Joseph to flee to Egypt. Since God used angels to direct the movements of persons in the events surrounding Christ's birth, it would have been completely consistent for God to also send an angel to guide the Magi's movements.

Having found Jesus, the Magi worshipped him, offering costly gifts of gold, myrrh and frankincense. They were then warned by God in a dream *(Matthew 2:12)* not to return to Herod, resulting in the prompt exit of the Magi and their many escorts from Judea. When Herod realized that he had been fooled, he wrathfully killed all the young male children of Bethlehem in a vain effort to kill the Messiah. However, there is no indication that Herod made any attempt to overtake or punish the Magi. As high Parthian nobles, they had "diplomatic immunity," and Herod dared not anger Caesar by provoking the Parthians. Also, Herod's garrison troops could have been vastly outnumbered by the size of the Magi's military escorts.

There is another important aspect of this remarkable episode. While it is not surprising that Jewish leaders during Herod's reign were sufficiently familiar with the prophetic writings to pinpoint for Herod exactly where the Messiah would be born, **it is surprising that God was working so closely with members of the Parthian ruling class! This makes no biblical sense unless: (A) the Parthians were descended from the ten tribes of Israel and (B) the Magi (Parthian priests) included some Levites**. During His ministry Jesus Christ asserted that He had not been sent to the gentiles, but only to the "lost sheep of the house of Israel." Matthew 15:24-28 shows the reluctance of Jesus to assist a gentile.

Throughout the Old Testament God worked almost exclusively with the House of Israel and the House of Judah. It was not until **after** the death of Christ that gentiles were given equal access to the God of Israel. The fact that God was working intimately with the Parthian nobility — sending them angelic messages, giving them divine messages in dreams — confirms that the Parthians had to be descended from the ten tribes of Israel which had migrated into Asia.

The fact that some of the Parthian ruling classes were apparently worshippers of the God of Abraham, Isaac, and Jacob is most revealing. God obviously considered these Parthians to be "righteous" men under the terms of His laws or He would not have been dealing with them so personally. That educated Parthians were ready to visit and worship the Messiah at the time of Christ's birth indicates they were also familiar with the prophecies of the Old Testament. Who but transplanted Israelites would have been looking for the Messiah at that time?

Although we are jumping ahead in the narrative, consider the events of Acts 2:9 which states Parthians were among those who made pilgrimages to Jerusalem for the Feast of Weeks, known to Christians as Pentecost Sunday. Verse 9 also mentions "Medes, Elamites, and dwellers in Mesopotamia" as being present at this feast, and all these regions were provinces of the Parthian Empire. We know that portions of the ten tribes had been relocated to "the cities of the Medes," so the presence of devout visitors from Media most likely designates people from the ten tribes of Israel who still lived in Media. Interestingly, verse 9 also mentions "dwellers...in Asia" were present. The word "Asia" has clouded origins, but the *Encyclopaedia Britannica* states, "It is probable that it ["Asia"] has an Assyrian or Hebrew root, and was used first...with a specific or restricted local application, a more extended signification having eventually been given it..."[14]

As briefly mentioned in chapter two, one of the Scythian tribes was called the "**Asii**" (or "**Asiani**").[15] Since the "Asiani" were one of the Scythian tribes bearing the name of Isaac, the Sacae or Saka, the Bible's reference to "**Asians**" attending the Feast of Weeks could indicate that Scythians were also present in Jerusalem at that time. This further indicates that the Parthians and Scythians were the displaced members of the "lost ten tribes of Israel." The non-Israelite populations of Asia had no cultural interest in the worship of the God of Israel; only the ten tribes of Israel would retain such a custom.

It was not unusual for large pilgrimages originating in Parthia to travel to Jerusalem to worship the God of Israel. Josephus' statement that caravans from Parthia arrived in Jerusalem under the protec-

Acts 2:5-11

"And there were dwelling at Jerusalem Jews, devout men, out of every nation under heaven. Now when this was noised abroad, the multitude came together, and were confounded, because that every man heard them speak in his own language. And they were all amazed and marvelled, saying one to another, Behold, are not all these which speak Galilaeans? And how hear we every man in our own tongue, wherein we were born? Parthians, and Medes, and Elamites, and the dwellers in Mesopotamia, and in Judaea, and Cappadocia, in Pontus, and Asia, Phrygia, and Pamphylia, in Egypt, and in the parts of Libya about Cyrene, and strangers of Rome, Jews and proselytes, Cretes and Arabians, we do hear them speak in our tongues the wonderful works of God."

tion of "many ten thousand men"[16] was noted earlier. These must have been magnificent treasure trains to have warranted the protection of a sizeable army. Such huge "offerings" going to Jerusalem from Parthia indicates that significant numbers of people within the Parthian Empire worshipped the God of Israel. This meant that, at the time of Jesus and Herod, there was a great deal of travel and trade between the Parthian Empire and the Roman province of Judea. It also shows that there was a strong sense of community between Judea and many regions of the Parthian Empire. If a caravan of Parthian commoners could be escorted by "many ten thousand men," how many escorts would accompany a caravan of Parthia's nobility?

The Parthian nobility did not "travel light." Plutarch records that Surenas, a high Parthian noble, had an entourage of ten thousand men when he traveled "on his own affairs" on routine business. Just one Parthian noble was accompanied by such a huge and imposing caravan when he traveled on routine business! Think how much larger would have been the caravan of a group of perhaps ten or twelve Parthian nobles, the Magi, travelling, not on routine business within Parthia, but through dangerous terrain with rich treasures and into Roman territory! Parthians believed in large numbers of armed escorts for VIPs. When an ambassador came to Parthia from China, an escort of 20,000 armed Parthian cavalrymen greeted him![18]

Now you can understand why the whole city of Jerusalem was frightened when the Parthian Magi arrived to look for the young child of royal birth. They were accompanied by a gigantic caravan from Parthia moving toward Jerusalem. This column was escorted by many thousands of Parthia's military cavalry. Many in Jerusalem feared the Parthians had come to start a war and besiege the city.

The Royal Lineages of Jesus Christ

In an earlier chapter it was shown that the Magi were loyal to one dynasty, the Arsacids, whose members continuously ruled Parthia. It was shown that many rulers of Parthian and Saka kingdoms had names incorporating the word "Phares" (PH-R-S). This indicates that the Arsacids were descended from the seed of David, who was the first king of the Phares family. *(Matthew 1:2-6)* The kings of Judah of the Phares dynasty are listed in I Chronicles 3:9-17, but verses 18-24 reveals that the royal lineage continued to flourish after Judah's captivity. Indeed, David's dynasty was given high status in the Babylonian Empire. *(II Kings 25:27-30)* This post-exilic elevation of the Davidic dynasty in Asia likely led to their serving as vassal kings over captive Israelites under Babylonian and Persian masters. Their later elevation to the throne of Parthia fulfilled the prophecy of Jeremiah 33:17 that David's descendants would always rule over the descendants of the ten tribes of Israel. This may explain the unshakable loyalty of the Parthians to the Arsacids. With the Parthians being Israelites, and the Arsacids being descended from King David, the Arsacids were the only dynasty in Asia that was racially, historically and culturally related to the Parthian people.

Since Matthew 1:3-17 tells us that Jesus Christ was a descendant of Phares and King David, Jesus was a distant relative of the Parthian ruling dynasty, which also descended from Phares and David. The bloodline relationship of Jesus to the Parthian Arsacids serves as a further explanation for the homage paid to Jesus by the Parthian nobility. It was customary for the Parthian Magi and Wise Men to keep track of male Arsacids in foreign nations. In some cases they sent to foreign nations, Scythia and Rome, to summon male relatives of the Arsacids to come to Parthia to serve as king. As mentioned in the previous chapter, some Parthian rulers killed every male relative they could find in an effort to eliminate potential rivals to their throne. This compelled the Magi to look for distant individuals who had the same bloodline as the Arsacids, the lineage of Phares and King David. At the time of the birth of Jesus, the recent Parthian emperor, Phraates IV, who reigned 37-2 B.C., had killed many male relatives, including his own father and almost thirty brothers.[19] Male Arsacids at the time of Jesus' birth were in very short supply.

When the Magi were led by God to pay homage to the young Jesus, they doubtless learned that Joseph, Mary and Jesus were all related to the Parthian dynasty! Indeed, they may already have known that Jesus was an Arsacid, related to Parthia's kings. When the Magi came to Herod, they said:

> "Where is **He that is born king of the Jews**?" *(Matthew 2:2, KJV)*

This statement confirms that the Magi arriving in Jerusalem already knew that Jesus was "royal-born," and it implies that they knew He was related to Parthia's kings. If they did not know that fact prior to their arrival, they learned it during their visit with Joseph, Mary and the young Jesus. Indeed, because Phraates IV, the emperor of Parthia, had killed so many of his male relatives, the Magi were surely delighted to find surviving males of the Davidic bloodline.

Consider some important information. When the Babylonians conquered Judah, they brought King Jehoichin of Judah and many of his royal family to Babylon. *(II Kings 24:15)* After languishing in prison for years, King Jehoiachin was exalted into the position of a favored vassal king in the Babylonian empire. I Chronicles 3:17 reveals that Jeconiah had many sons and grandsons, who very likely also became vassal kings in Asia after Jehoichin died. One of Jeconiah's sons was

"Salathiel" *(I Chronicles 3:17)*, who lived in Asia, not Judea. Salathiel, later spelled "Shealtiel,"[20] was the father of Zerubbabel. *(Ezra 3:2)* Matthew 1:12 and Luke 3:27 confirm this as well.

Zerubbabel's name includes the root word "babel," indicating he was born in Babylon. Zerubbabel was one of the leaders of the group of Jews who left Asia and returned to Jerusalem during the time of Ezra and Nehemiah under the auspices of Persian kings. Zerubbabel had a prominent role in the rebuilding of a Jewish presence in Jerusalem and Judea, and he is mentioned frequently in the books of Ezra and Haggai and once in the book of Nehemiah. Joseph, the human "father" of Jesus Christ was a descendant of Zerubbabel. *(Matthew 1:12-16)* So Jesus Christ was born into a very prominent and famous family in Judea, one known to be descended from the Kings of Judah. Since His royal progenitors formerly lived in Asia and had included vassal kings of the Babylonians, the Parthian Magi may have been very well aware that they were coming to visit a family of Arsacids! Babylon was then ruled by Parthia, so its records were available to the Magi. Because Phraates IV had killed so many males of the royal Parthian dynasty at that time, the Magi were compelled to look outside Parthia's borders for male Arsacids who were eligible for the throne of Parthia.

Now consider this: Because Jesus was eligible for the throne of Parthia, so was His human father "Joseph." Christian mythology tends to personify Joseph as an obscure, poor "carpenter" struggling "to make ends meet." But the possibility exists that he was, in fact, well-to-do. The account in Mark 6:3, for instance, indicates that Jesus himself was a "carpenter," but in that day someone in the building trades business was often more of a "building contractor," involving all aspects of construction. This could possibly have been a very responsible position.

The concept of Joseph and Mary being "poor" partly comes from the "manger scene" of them staying in a lowly manger when Jesus was born. However, they did not stay there for lack of financial resources. When they arrived in Jerusalem, they tried to stay in a lodging house, but everything was "booked solid" in the city. *(Luke 2:7)* As soon as the crowds thinned out, they promptly relocated to a rented "house" in Jerusalem. *(Matthew 2:11)* Also, it takes financial resources to travel. When God warned Joseph to flee to Egypt quickly, he obviously had the financial resources on hand to afford a hastily arranged, indefinite stay in a foreign nation. *(Matthew 2:13-15)* Either Joseph was not a "poor carpenter," or these funds came from the gifts of the Magi at Jesus' birth.

Jesus was descended from the kings of Judah through both His father and mother! While Matthew 1 gives Joseph's descent from Judah's dynastic line, Luke 3:23-33 gives Mary's descent from king

**Carpenter's shop in Nazareth,
From an original photograph**

David. Both Joseph and Mary were direct descendants of King David, the kings of Judah, related to the Davidic kings in Asia and had Salathiel and Zerubbabel as common ancestors. However, Joseph and Mary's immediate ancestors were descended from two different sons of Zerubbabel (Matthew 1:13-16, Luke 3:23-27). Some confusion exists on this point, as it is easy to not grasp that Luke 3's account gives Mary's lineage. Henry Halley explains this point as follows:

> "The commonly accepted view is that Matthew gives Joseph's line, showing Jesus to be the Legal Heir to the Promises given Abraham and David; and that Luke gives Mary's line, showing Jesus' blood descent, 'Son of David according to the flesh' (Romans 1:3). Mary's genealogy, in accord with Jewish usage, was in her husband's name. Joseph was the 'son of Heli' (Luke 3:23), that is, 'son-in-law' of Heli. Jacob was Joseph's father (Matthew 1:16)."[21]

Jesus was a "blue-blooded" son of parents descended from royalty. **This remarkable relationship meant both Joseph and Jesus were distant relatives of Parthia's kings.** Because Parthia could offer the kingship to **any** relative of the Parthian king line, not just the oldest son or closest relative of the previous king, both Joseph and Jesus Christ were potential claimants to the throne of the Parthian Empire! While the Bible does record Jesus' royal lineage of the seed of David, it does not specifically mention His relationship to Parthia's dynasty. However, as we shall see later in this chapter, the Bible implies that this relationship existed.

Since the Magi who worshipped Jesus were members of the body which selected the kings of Parthia and kept track of male Arsacids, they must been ecstatic to find living descendants of King David. The Magi no doubt discussed the possibility that this child Jesus, born under such unusual circumstances, might one day take the throne of Parthia. While the Bible is silent on their future contacts, this delegation of Parthian Magi likely would have stayed in contact with Jesus in future years and monitored the events of His life. If the Parthians had a Messianic understanding, Jesus would have been seen as an acceptable ruler because He was a son of David.

A Caravan of Camels.

Did the Magi Almost Cause a Roman-Parthian War?

Let us consider that the visit of the Magi to Jesus may have been a factor in a political crisis that almost led to a new Roman-Parthian war. Recall that from 40-37 B.C., Parthia had ruled Palestine and Syria before the Romans drove them back across the Euphrates River. That war ushered in a long period of Parthian-Roman detente which included the entire lifetime of Jesus Christ. However, a great Parthian-Roman war was barely averted in 1 A.D. when a "summit conference" was held between the Parthian emperor, Phraataces, and Caius Caesar, the grandson of Augustus Caesar on an island in the Euphrates River (i.e. neutral territory). Roman sources recorded that:

> "The armies of the two chiefs were drawn up on the opposite banks of the river [the Euphrates], facing one another; and the chiefs themselves, accompanied by an equal number of attendants, proceeded to deliberate in the sight of both hosts."[22]

This "summit conference" averted war, but how could the Magi's visit have had a role in this crisis?

The Bible's account of the Magi visiting Jesus ceases when the Magi left Judea and returned to Parthia, leaving the impression that the issue was concluded. However, if we consider the geopolitical realities of that time, there is no way that the Magi's exit from Judea ended the matter.

Matthew 2:3 records that Herod and "all Jerusalem" were troubled by the arrival of the Magi. Jerusalem was a commercial city at the nexus of major trade routes, and it commonly received caravans of thousands of people. Three tired Magi arriving from the east would not have made a ripple in the city's calm. For that matter, caravans from Parthian territory could arrive in Jerusalem with many thousands of armed escorts, and such events did not trouble the city. However, the arrival of Parthian Magi — Parthia's nobles and priests — in Jerusalem escorted by a large army of Parthian soldiers was unprecedented and unrepeated in the history of the city of Jerusalem. This occurred at a time when Parthia and Rome had a peace treaty, and no major Roman or Parthian military forces had crossed the Euphrates River in over three decades. The arrival of a large Parthian military force in Jerusalem escorting high Parthian officials was militarily provocative and could justifiably be seen by King Herod and the Romans as a treaty violation.

When Parthia had occupied Palestine, it had crowned its own vassal king, Antigonus, as ruler of Judea. When the Magi, Parthia's official king-makers, came to Jerusalem looking for "a new king of the Jews," it must have sounded to Herod and the Romans that the Parthians were trying to reassert their claim to Judea and dethrone Herod. Their speaking directly to Herod, who was Rome's "king of the Jews," about wanting to find a "**new** king of the Jews" could be seen by the Romans as very close to a declaration of war, given the region's history. The fact that King Herod "bit his tongue" and made no rash statement to

From a Photograph.

The Hill Machærus—the Site of Herod's Palace.

the Magi and treated them with deference argues that the Parthians must have had an intimidating number of troops at Jerusalem to compel Herod to be so uncharacteristically meek. Since a major Roman-Parthian treaty had been in effect for over three decades, Rome felt unthreatened in the region, and would, consequently, have had only a small garrison in Jerusalem.

Caesar's decree that no Parthian war be provoked also put Herod in an awkward position. While the Magi and Parthians were in Judea with no harmful intent, there is no way the Romans could be sure this "visit" was benign in nature. After the Parthians left, Herod "blew his stack" *(Matthew 2:16)* and vented his pent-up rage by murdering all male children in Bethlehem under age two. Official reports surely had to be filed with Augustus Caesar in Rome about this highly unusual event.

Herod was justifiably fearful of Parthian intentions in the area. Hadn't they come to anoint a replacement for him as "king of the Jews?" Hadn't they also deceived him by leaving the area without his knowledge? Herod's murderous act in Bethlehem would also have inflamed Jewish residents, and rumors of revolt against the hated Romans would have intensified. Faced with a possible Parthian invasion and/or a Jewish revolt, Herod needed more Roman soldiers in the region. In his reports to Caesar, Herod surely cast himself in a favorable light, warning Caesar that the Parthians had crossed the Euphrates, made a military reconnaissance to Jerusalem to spy out the city's weakness and were openly talking about crowning a "new king of the Jews." Because the Parthians' arrival in Jerusalem had scared the whole city, news of this extraordinary event would have spread quickly along the trade routes. Roman honor had been slighted, and Rome usually responded to such an insult.

However, the Romans could not respond immediately. Rome had been sapped by the costly civil wars between Brutus and Octavian and also Octavian against Mark Antony and Cleopatra. These wars were fought in the eastern half of the Roman Empire, so Rome's military forces in the east had been depleted and disorganized. Augustus Caesar could not be entirely sure whom to trust with an army, lest another civil war break out in the east. Herod the Great was a firm ally of Augustus, but Herod was soon to die, leaving Augustus with no close ally in the East to whom he could entrust an army. Also, Rome and Parthia were facing a possible conflict in Armenia over succession to the throne of Armenia. In both Armenia and Judea, the issue was whether Rome or Parthia would choose the kings of those nations. Also, Rome had to finance, train and equip an army to fight the Parthians. Rome's armies under Crassus and Mark Antony had been "clobbered" by the Parthians, so Rome would need extra time to assemble an army to challenge Parthia. Rome's leadership crisis is described by George Rawlinson as follows:

> "Augustus [formerly "Octavian"], from the time that he heard of the Armenian troubles, and of the support given them by Parthia, seems never to have wavered in his determination to vindicate the claims of Rome...[but] hesitated as to the person whose services he should employ...He would have been glad to employ Tiberius; but that morose prince had deserted him and...was living in self-chosen retirement. Caius, the eldest of his grandsons, was, in B.C. 2, only 18 years of age...the extreme youth of the prince caused him to hesitate...and the consequence was that Caius did not start for the East until late in B.C. 1."[23]

In other words, Rome's political situation compelled a delay in responding to Parthia's real provocation in Judea and apparent provocation in Armenia. The situation was further muddled by the death of Phraates IV, Parthia's emperor when the Magi visited Jerusalem.[24] Since Phraates IV and Herod the Great had died by the time Rome's army was ready, all the major principals had a fresh viewpoint by the time Rome and Parthia had their "summit conference" at the Euphrates River in 1 A.D.

Although historical accounts mention only the Armenian dispute, it is significant that the Parthian and Roman armies did not confront each other in Armenia. Their confrontation was along the Euphrates River, which had been crossed by the Parthian armed column led by the Magi. Everyone in the region breathed a huge sigh of relief when war was averted. As we shall soon see, if a war had been fought ending the Parthian-Roman detente, much of Jesus Christ's ministry in Judea could not have occurred.

Hall of the Sanhedrim.

If the armed Parthian column led by the Magi provoked the Roman-Parthian confrontation in 1 A.D. during which war was averted, a date of 2 B.C. for Christ's birth is more logical. If He had been born in 4 B.C., there would be too great a gap between that year and the Roman response in 1 A.D. However, a gap from 2 B.C. to 1 A.D. would be understandable given the political realities of that time.

The Bible says little else concerning the early years of Jesus Christ. Luke 2:40 states that Jesus "waxed strong," and was filled with wisdom and favored by God. Luke 2:41-50 tells us that Jesus, at age twelve, amazed the teachers in the Temple with His wisdom. This passage confirms that Jesus was being raised by His parents according to the Laws of God, as His family annually attended the Passover in Jerusalem, the location of the Temple. Jesus would have been seen by others as a devout, brilliant son of a prominent Jewish family.

Jesus in the Temple at age twelve

Luke's account states Jesus was absent from His family for a full day before they realized He was missing. They initiated a search, which located him in the Temple. How could Jesus, a twelve-year-old youth, be apart from His parents, and His parents not know about it for a full day on a journey? **How did a mere twelve-year-old lad even come into the presence of the teachers of the Temple**, the religious hierarchy of the Jewish religion? There is more here than meets the eye.

It would have been inappropriate for Joseph and Mary to have allowed Jesus to be wandering around Jerusalem unescorted by an adult. That Joseph and Mary were unconcerned about Jesus' absence for a full day before searching for him indicates that He must have been with an adult escort. It is recorded in the Jewish Talmud and in other sources that Joseph of Arimathea was the great-uncle of Jesus Christ.[25] It is likely that Joseph of Arimathea was the adult relative who was serving as Jesus' mentor and escort.

Joseph of Arimathea was a powerful figure in Jewish society, and was apparently a member of the Sanhedrin itself. Years later, when the Sanhedrin plotted the death of Jesus, Luke 23:50-51 asserts that Joseph of Arimathea **had not consented** to their action. That Joseph had not consented to the Sanhedrin's murderous plot implies that Joseph was a member of the body with the inherent right to consent to, or dissent from, the actions of the Sanhedrin.

There is a now a clear explanation for how the young Jesus came to be involved in a discourse with the Temple hierarchy. Since Jesus' great-uncle, Joseph of Arimathea, had easy access to the highest echelons of Jewish society, it is likely that Jesus accompanied Joseph of Arimathea to the Temple, and participated in a discussion between His great-uncle and the Temple teachers. Apparently, Jesus was with His great-uncle often enough that Jesus' prolonged absence from Joseph and Mary at that time was not a unique experience, but part of a pattern that was occurring frequently.

The remainder of Jesus' life until age thirty is a mystery. While the Bible is silent on the subject, it does give us a clue. By the age of twelve, Jesus was probably spending more time in the care of Joseph of Arimathea and less time in the care of Joseph and Mary. It appears that a major transition was occurring in Jesus' life. When Joseph and Mary found Jesus in the Temple after a three-day search, Mary reproved him with the words: "Why have you treated us so? Behold, your father and I have been looking for you anxiously."*(RSV)* Jesus replied: "How is it that you sought me? Did you not know that I must be in my Father's house?" Jesus, at the age of twelve, essentially told them: "Why were you even bothering to look for me?" The phrase "I <u>must</u> be in my Father's house" indicates that the Spirit of God was now leading him away from the household of His human family and into the work of His heavenly Father. The Bible adds that Jesus went back to Nazareth with Joseph and Mary, so Jesus did not yet make a "clean break" from His childhood home. However, the event at the Temple and Jesus' own words may have indicated His departure was imminent.

JESUS' "MISSING EIGHTEEN YEARS" (AGES 12-30)

Is it not incongruous that while Jesus Christ is the central character of the entire New Testament, it says almost nothing about the majority of His life? The Bible tells us a little about His first twelve years, a lot about His last three and one-half years, but contains an eighteen-year gap between ages twelve and thirty.

Biblical and Secular Evidence of Jesus' Absence from Judea:

Luke 3:23 observes that Jesus was "about 30" when He became a public figure in Judea due to the advent of His ministry, but where had He been and what had He done in the intervening eighteen years? Since the Bible makes no direct comment about this period of time, we must rely on non-Biblical sources for information about these "missing years."

The New Testament's silence about these eighteen years of Jesus' life is significant. Since Luke 1:2 and II Peter 1:16 state those New Testament narratives of Jesus' life were eyewitness accounts, it implies that the gospel writers had not witnessed any of the events of Jesus' life before age thirty. This would indicate that Jesus was not even present in Judea during the "missing" eighteen years. If He had been living in Judea or Galilee, it would have been impossible to hide such a precocious youth who had been worshipped by foreign nobility as a child, had awed the Temple's leadership with His brilliance at age twelve and came from one of the most prominent Jewish families in the region. Since Luke 2:52 says that Jesus continued to grow in favor with God and with men, it seems probable that He would have drawn a lot of attention from the common people with whom He'd have come in almost constant contact if He remained in Jerusalem. Leaving the country would have avoided that and also any possible conflicts with the rulers of Judea.

Did the spiritual power that was manifesting itself in Jesus at age twelve go dormant for eighteen years? Did Jesus "quench the spirit" at age twelve so He could pound nails as an obscure carpenter for eighteen years? That is highly unlikely. Indeed, the event at the Temple indicates that Jesus was in the process of separating from His parents to pursue the divine mission that He had been born to fulfill. It is the contention of this book that soon after the Temple incident, Jesus left Judea for eighteen years. There is biblical evidence supporting such a conclusion.

Matthew 13:54-56 indicates that **after this eighteen-year period, Jesus was scarcely known in His own hometown.** Whereas, at age twelve, Jesus is amazing the teachers in the Jerusalem Temple with His wisdom, the common folk in His home town synagogue are asking themselves eighteen years later, after hearing Jesus speak: "Where did this man (Jesus) get this wisdom?" If the exceptional wisdom of Jesus had been present in Nazareth for those eighteen years, such a question would have been ludicrous. Note also verses 55-56 where the listeners ask:

> "Isn't this the carpenter's son? is not His mother called Mary? and **His brethren** James, and Joses, and Simon, and Judas? and **His sisters, are they not all with us?**"

Jesus As A Child In Nazareth

This indicates that the members of His hometown synagogue were struggling to identify or remember who Jesus was. The fact that they easily named all His immediate family members, and said "are **they** not **all** **with** us?" seems to indicate that Jesus had not been "with them" as were His other family members. Their quizzical response to Jesus may in fact indicate that while Jesus had been gone from Nazareth for a **long** time, His immediate family members had remained there. If Jesus had been a carpenter in Nazareth all His life, the local citizenry would have easily recognized him. Yet they spoke as if they were unaware of either His wisdom or power!

Jesus' wisdom had awed the most learned Jewish leaders in the nation at age twelve! To believe that Jesus lived the next eighteen years in Nazareth as a "humble carpenter" and "stuffed inside" all His wisdom until age thirty, one must believe that for eighteen years Jesus "quenched" the Holy Spirit that was burning brightly in him at age twelve! Traditional dogma, that Jesus lived an obscure life in Nazareth until age thirty, requires such a view since the synagogue-attending folk in His own hometown were "astonished" that Jesus at age thirty exhibited wisdom and power.

The logical conclusion is that Jesus could hardly have worked as a "humble carpenter" in Nazareth during the missing eighteen years. In fact, the Bible offers no statement that Jesus was ever employed as a carpenter during His adult life. Matthew 13:55 refers to Jesus as a "carpenter's **son**," not as a "carpenter." Luke's account about Jesus' meeting with the Temple elders at age 12 records Jesus' open declaration that His future was not linked to the profession of His physical father, but with the calling of His spiritual Father in heaven. When His parents chided Jesus for being in the Temple rather than with them, Jesus replied "know you not that I must be about my Father's business?" This does not portray Jesus as a "rebel" since Luke 2:51 shows that He was an obedient youth, but it shows that as early as age twelve, God's Spirit was strongly drawing Jesus away from the "business" of Joseph, and toward the spiritual "business" of God.

(Drawn by W. HOLMAN HUNT.)

NAZARETH.

As a child growing up in a household in the construction industry, Jesus was certainly familiar with carpentry, but the Bible does not say that He was a carpenter in Nazareth during the "missing years." Mark's account of Jesus' visit to His old home synagogue (Mark 6:1-6) does quote townsfolk as calling Jesus a "carpenter." However, these were the same townsfolk who struggled to identify Jesus, as the context confirms. Note that the Bible itself does **not** declare "Jesus was a carpenter," but rather quotes the statements of people who hardly knew him.

Matthew 13:56 declares that Jesus had four brothers and at least two sisters — the word "sisters" is plural. Jesus was an oldest son in a family of at least seven siblings. Whatever the number of siblings, it is clear that Mary gave birth to a large family after Jesus was born. Mary was a "virgin" when she gave birth to Jesus *(Matthew 1:18-23)*, but she did not remain a virgin. Matthew 1:25 shows God had given Joseph permission to have normal marital relations with Mary as soon as Jesus was born.

The Bible never mentions Joseph, the human "father" of Jesus, after the episode of Jesus being in the Temple at age twelve. Since Mary, the mother of Jesus, and the siblings of Jesus **are** cited as being alive when Jesus is 30 years old and Joseph is not mentioned, it is apparent that Joseph died during those "missing years." Since Joseph of Arimathea was already spending much time with Jesus, he likely became Jesus' guardian after Joseph died. Joseph of Arimathea was a fine role model for Jesus as Luke 23:50 refers to him as "good" and "just." Since Joseph of Arimathea was a man of great prominence in the Jewish community, and the Temple elders knew Jesus' precocious wisdom even in His pre-teen years, why did people in Jesus' hometown struggle to identify him after the missing eighteen years of Jesus' life? The only logical answer is that He did not live in Judea during that time!

Ordinarily, with the death of a father, the oldest son (even a youth like Jesus) would have been compelled to begin work for a living to support the family. However, since Joseph of Arimathea was a wealthy relative who could guarantee economic security for Mary and her other children, Jesus was free to pursue His new calling in life. Also, Parthia's Magi had lavished gifts of gold, frankincense, and myrrh upon Jesus when they had visited him shortly after His birth. Since this large sum of wealth would have been held "in trust" for him by either His parents or Joseph of Arimathea, Jesus could have tapped that wealth to provide for His family's needs without local employment.

In *The Traditions of Glastonbury*, E. Raymond Capt cites evidence that Joseph of Arimathea was an international merchant who was involved with the tin trade in the British Isles. The previous two books in this series documented that the British Isles had been an Israelite region since at least the reign of King Solomon. Book Two presented evidence that large bodies of the tribes of Simeon and Dan entered Britain and Ireland around 721 B.C. when ancient Israel fell to Assyria, infusing more Israelites into the Celtic population of the British Isles. It is hardly surprising that Joseph of Arimathea, a prominent member of the tribe of Judah, would be in a commercial relationship with people descended from the other tribes of Israel.

Capt cites the account of Gildas Badonicus, an early British historian of the sixth century A.D., which refers to Joseph of Arimathea as a "nobilis decurio."[26] The fact that an early historian of Britain discusses Joseph of Arimathea at all gives weight to accounts that Joseph was involved with the events of early Britain. Capt asserts that Joseph's role was as follows:

> "The same title 'Decurio' [applied to Joseph of Arimathea] is used by St. Jerome in his translation of the Vulgate of St. Mark's 'honourable counselor' (Mark 15:43) and St. Luke's 'counselor.' (Luke 23:50) In the Roman world, a 'decurio' denoted an important Roman office, usually connected with the general management of a mining district. The implication is that Joseph was a provincial (Britain?) Roman Senator and in charge of Rome's mining interests in Britain. Such a position would require Joseph to spend a considerable amount of time away from his homeland."[27]

Roman Hall of Justice.

Joseph of Arimathea had to be a very prominent man in the Roman world to receive immediate access to Pilate, Rome's administrator of Judea, during the intense political turmoil surrounding the crucifixion. *(Mark 15:43-45)* Unless Joseph of Arimathea was both known to and trusted by Pilate and the Roman rulers of Judea, he would not have received swift access to Pontius Pilate himself at so sensitive and critical a time.

Capt also states that both Roman and Jewish law called for the disposal of the bodies of criminals in common pits with all memory of them removed, unless the body was promptly claimed by a relative.[28]

The fact that Joseph of Arimathea came forward to claim Jesus' body offers convincing evidence that he was a relative of Jesus. That he obtained such approval not by going to a lower official, but to Pilate himself, indicates that he was accustomed to doing business with the highest Roman officials.

An Anglican churchman, Rev. C.C. Dobson, also has asserted that Jesus Christ was absent from Palestine for many years. In his 1936 book, *Did Our Lord Visit Britain as they say in Cornwall and Somerset?*, Dobson writes:

> "We cannot help feeling, too, that our Lord's ministry would begin more effectively if he came as a stranger after an absence of some years.
>
> But while the association between St. John and Our Lord **suggests Our Lord's absence from Palestine, another incident certainly strongly implies it.**
>
> In Matthew 17:24, when our Lord arrives at Capernaum, St. Peter is asked by the tax gatherer whether his master paid the tax. From our Lord's subsequent remarks it is clear that it was the stranger's tax which was in question [Dobson here includes a long footnote documenting this point]. Now Capernaum was our Lord's domicile, to which we know that the Virgin Mary had moved earlier in our Lord's life.
>
> The question asked of St. Peter implies an uncertainty as to whether it was due. It is not demanded of Our Lord. The question would seem to imply that the tax gatherers knew that Our Lord was a native of the city, but absence for some time could be regarded as making him liable.
>
> Our Lord's words to St. Peter may be paraphrased: 'It is only strangers who must needs pay this tax. Residents of the town are exempt. However, as I have been absent for some years, there are grounds for regarding me as a stranger, therefore to avoid giving offense I will pay.'
>
> **We may thus infer from this incident...that prior to his ministry Our Lord was absent from Palestine.**"[29]

The reader is encouraged to examine this account in his or her own Bible. Matthew 17:24-27 contains this surprising account wherein Jesus agrees to pay a foreigner's tax to avoid giving offense to the local tax officials in Capernaum. The dialogue between Jesus and Peter shows Jesus making the point to Peter that this tax (referred to as a toll, duty or tribute in various Bible translations) should be paid by "strangers," not local residents. However, Jesus still sends Peter to get a coin miraculously supplied by a hooked fish to pay the tax due of foreigners to "not give offense." In doing so, Jesus quieted the concerns of the tax officials who no longer regarded him to be a "local" person. This biblical account makes no sense

Jesus And The Foreigner's Tax Coin

whatsoever if Jesus Christ had been living in the Capernaum region of Galilee for all his life. However, it makes a great deal of sense if Jesus had been absent for so many years that none of the tax officials had ever seen him and, therefore, identified him as a "foreigner." This biblical passage supports the conclusion that Jesus had been absent from Palestine for much of his adult life.

However, what of the activities of Joseph of Arimathea and Jesus during the "missing eighteen years?" If Jesus were under Joseph of Arimathea's tutelage during those years, He would have spent much time traveling, given that Joseph's business involved international trade between the nations of that day. While the information which follows is based on legends and traditions, they are buttressed by the Bible's implication that Jesus was absent from Judea for a prolonged period of time. Obviously, Jesus went **somewhere** during that time, and legends and traditions offer the only evidence that exists.

Many traditions assert that Joseph of Arimathea and Jesus were not only present in Britain, but had homes in the area of Glastonbury, England. Supporting these traditions, Capt cites evidence that Glastonbury bore two titles from ancient times — "Secretum Domini" and "Domus Dei" (Latin for "The Secret of the Lord," and "The House of God").[30] William Steuart McBirnie, in his book, *The Search for the Twelve Apostles*, wrote concerning these traditions:

> "There certainly is no other tradition known concerning the history of St. Joseph of Arimathea and since the British tradition is vigorous we see no reason to challenge it...If in any country there is a strong tradition concerning some Apostolic figures, and no counter-tradition elsewhere, then we at least stand on the ground of possibility and even probability. So it is with...St. Joseph."[31]

Capt cites a 15th century source, *Hardynge's Chronicle*, that asserts Joseph of Arimathea converted King Arviragus of 1st century A.D. Britain to the Christian religion, and that this early king gave Joseph and his party twelve portions of tax-free land in the area of Glastonbury.[32] This tax-free land in Glastonbury is confirmed in the 1086 A.D. Domesday Book of early English history under the title "Domus Dei."[33] The fact that there were **twelve** portions of land is significant...was there one portion representing each of the twelve tribes of Israel?

A Druid as depicted by Aylett Sammes in 1649

Another fact cited by Capt is that the Druids worshipped gods "known as 'Beli,' the Creator as regards the past; 'Taran,' the controlling providence of the present, and 'Yesu,' the coming saviour of the future."[34] The name "Beli" preserves a Semitic word for "Lord",[35] and in its expectation of a coming "Yesu" savior, Capt opines that "Druidism thus anticipated Christianity and pointed to the coming saviour under the very name by which Christ was called."[36] The name "Jesus" is from the Greek, but the Hebrew name of Jesus was likely "Yeshuah," meaning "salvation."[37] The similarity between "Yesu" and "Yeshuah" is obvious. It is not surprising that Semitic words are found in the Druidic religion of Celtic Britain. The previous two books in this series offered abundant evidence that the Celts of Britain were descended from Israelite-Phoenician settlers. Given their Hebrew-Semitic origins, it is not surprising that an expected Messiah-like figure would have a Hebrew-Semitic name.

Cited above was the account of Anglican churchman C. C. Dobson, who asserted Jesus Christ had been absent from Palestine for years during his adult life. He also agrees that Jesus Christ and Joseph of Arimathea had journeyed to and lived in ancient Celtic Britain. Dobson writes:

> "Most authorities agree that the Virgin Mary became widowed while Our Lord was still a youth, and that the Holy family moved from Nazareth to Capernaum. By Roman Law, and we believe also by Jewish Law, guardianship of a fatherless son devolved upon an uncle. If Joseph of Arimathea was an uncle of the Virgin Mary, then he would be the one upon whom the guardianship would be most likely to rest. This fact would provide a simple explanation for his taking Our Lord with him to Britain on one of his voyages."[38]

Dobson also buttresses this assertion with an account of the British historian, Gildas, who cites an event during the reign of Tiberius Caesar. Dobson cites:

> "...an even earlier statement by Gildas, the first British historian, A.D. 516-570: 'Christ...afforded His Light, the knowledge of His precepts, to this island during the height of, or the last year of the reign of Tiberius Caesar."
>
> Tiberius Caesar died in A.D. 37. Our Lord's crucifixion we may take as having occurred in A.D. 30. And His suggested visit to Britain would be concluded before A.D. 27, when He began His Ministry. It was in this year that Tiberius retired from Rome to Caprae.
>
> Gildas' statement is commonly regarded as referring to the coming and preaching of Joseph of Arimathea and his companions, subsequent to the resurrection.
>
> But Gildas' statement explicitly refers to an event *during* the reign of Tiberius...and could, therefore, hardly refer to Joseph of Arimathea ."[39]

C.C. Dobson correctly notes that Gildas recorded that Jesus Christ himself was present in early Britain prior to the retirement of Tiberius Caesar in 27 A.D. Some sources spiritualize this away to mean only Joseph of Arimathea was present in early Celtic Britain, but the text indicates that Jesus was with Joseph of Arimathea in Britain prior to his Judean ministry, and that this could not have referenced only Joseph of Arimathea. The time-frame of Jesus' presence in Britain coincides with the reign of Tiberias Caesar and allows for Jesus' later arrival in Judea to begin his ministry there.

Dobson also agrees with the above assertion by E. Raymond Capt that Jesus lived in Glastonbury, and that his teachings attracted the interest of the Celtic Druids. He writes further:

> "...Glastonbury was a leading Druid center, and he [Jesus] would meet those Druids, and tell them of the principles of His own Jewish religion. He would compare the two, and point out...that both looked forward to the coming Saviour under the same name, Hesus the Druid form, and Jesus, the Jewish. He would point out the remarkable similarity between the dress of the Archdruid and the Jewish Highpriest...Druidism never opposed Christianity and was quietly merged with it subsequently."[40]

Dobson further supports his conclusion that Jesus Christ was present in early Celtic Glastonbury via a statement by William of Malmesbury, who cites a charter given by King Ina to Glastonbury in approximately 700 A.D. He cites the following language in King Ina's Charter and adds his own commentary:

> "'To the ancient Church, situate in the place called Glastonbury (which Church the Great High Priest and Chiefest Minister formerly through His own ministry...sanctified by many an unheard of miracle...) do grant ...etc.'
>
> The Great High Priest and Chiefest Minister are clearly a reference to Our Lord Himself, and it thus asserts that he personally ministered there...Thus King Ina in his famous charter records the belief then commonly held that Our Lord Himself had resided there and ministered. This is certainly a confirmation of our interpretation of Gildas' statement that Christ 'afforded His Light and a knowledge of His precepts' [there]."[41]

Dobson thus bases his assertion that Jesus Christ was present in early Britain on the account of Gildas, a 6th century A.D. historian, the charter of King Ina from around 700 A.D., and the account of William of Malmesbury, who lived in the 11th century A.D. That so many ancient British historical accounts regard Jesus Christ's presence in early Britain as factual gives considerable weight to such a belief. All these sources wrote far closer to the actual events than modern writers, and they had no motivation, obviously, to affect viewpoints in the 21st century!

However, Dobson is not finished supporting his thesis. There is more evidence yet that Jesus Christ was physically present in early Celtic Britain. He cites:

> "...a very remarkable statement in a letter written by St. Augustine to Pope Gregory: 'In the Western confines of Britain there is a certain royal island of large extent [identified by Dobson as Glastonbury]...In it the first Neophites of Catholic Law, God beforehand acquainting them, found a Church constructed by no human art, BUT DIVINELY CONSTRUCTED (OR BY THE HANDS OF CHRIST HIMSELF), for the salvation of his people. The Almighty had made it manifest by many miracles...
>
> We must remember that St. Augustine arrived in A.D. 597 believing the whole island to be pagan. He found, however...that in the Western parts into which the [Celtic] Britons had been driven there existed a powerful British Church with its own bishops."[42] *(Emphasis by Dobson.)*

St. Augustine arrived in the British Isles as a Catholic emissary, but found already there a "powerful British Church with its own bishops." Where else could this well-established church have begun except via the early presence of Jesus Christ, Joseph of Arimathea and their companions? Is there evidence to support such a viewpoint? Of course! The following material is lengthy but it not only supports the concept that Jesus Christ was in ancient Britain during his "missing 18 years," but also gives fascinating insights to a forgotten era of the early church.

An earlier quote by Anglican churchman C.C. Dobson mentioned that if Jesus Christ had met the Druids at Glastonbury, he would have taught them "His own Jewish Religion." This is a remarkable and historically accurate assertion! Most people, including Christians, gloss over the fact that Jesus Christ lived his entire life as an observant Jew! Consider also that Joseph of Arimathea was a prominent member of Jewish society and that the Bible indicates he was a voting member of the Sanhedrin itself as he had a right to "consent" or "not consent" to its actions Luke 23:50. It is easy to forget that the early Christian Church began as a "sect of the Jews" and that the early leadership of the Apostolic Church was composed entirely of observant Jews. The New Testament confirms that Jesus

Jesus preaching on Lake Galilee

Christ, the Twelve Apostles, the Apostle Paul, and other early Church leaders all practiced the lifestyle of observant Jews (they kept a 7th-Day Sabbath, the "Jewish" Holy Days, etc.). Given this fact, one would expect that if the early Celtic Church had been founded by Jesus Christ, Joseph of Arimathea, and other 1st century Jewish Christians that such a church would have practiced and perpetuated the "Jewish" doctrines of the Apostolic Christian Church. That is exactly what happened!

In fact, the early Celtic Christian Church and the Roman Church, represented by the arrival of St. Augustine in 597 A.D., practically lived in separate religious universes. Leslie Hardinge's book, *The Celtic Church in Britain*, extensively documents the history and practices of the now-forgotten Celtic Christian Church. He makes the following observation:

> "The Celtic Church began at a date unknown…That [it] held special doctrines and usages, differing in several respects from those of Italian Christianity, is vouched for by the sources.
>
> The weight of this evidence tends to underline the fact there existed fundamental and far-reaching differences between the Celtic and Roman churches. Rome was ignorant of these discrepancies until the opening decade of the 7th century. It seems reasonable to conclude that the Celts were, for their part, also unaware of the beliefs and usages of the Roman Christians."[43]

The Celtic Christian Church had many adherents in Scotland, Wales and Ireland. Anglo-Saxon England was mostly pagan at that time, and they readily accepted the Roman version of Christianity. The Celtic Churches had well-established Hebraic (i.e. "Jewish

Christian") practices and doctrines that they were not readily willing to abandon. From the arrival of St. Augustine in 597 A.D. until the Celtic Churches of Wales surrendered to the Roman forms of Christianity in 768-777 A.D., there was often strong resistance on the part of the Celtic Christians to give up what would now be called "Jewish" doctrines.

The Celtic Christian Church found by St. Augustine observed the 7th Day Sabbath, commemorated Passover on the 14th day of the month of Nisan, and observed many customs based on the Old Testament (the Law of Moses). Hardinge writes concerning the Celtic day of rest: "The 'eve of the Sabbath' was Friday at sunset."[44] This Celtic custom was based on the biblical practice that days were numbered from sunset to sunset, a custom found in the Hebrew calendar.

St. Adamnan was an Irish Abbot and historian who lived in the 7th and 8th centuries, and St. Columba was an Irish ecclesiastic who lived in the 6th century A.D. The 7th Day Sabbath was still important in the Celtic Churches in their lifetimes. Hardinge writes concerning these two prominent Celtic Church figures:

> "Adamnan made several references to the Sabbath in the life of Columba... Adamnan invariably employed the original biblical name, Sabbath, for the seventh day of the week, and spoke of it in a manner betokening a respect which is not detected in writers two centuries later...."[45]

St. Columba himself is recorded as declaring:

> "This day is called in the sacred books 'Sabbath,' which is interpreted 'rest.' And truly this day is for me a sabbath...In it after my toilsome labour I keep Sabbath..."[46]

The Celtic Christians also observed the biblical Holy Days such as Passover instead of the Spring celebration of the Roman Church (Easter). Leslie Hardinge's book documents the struggle as parts of the Celtic Church fought for almost two centuries to retain the 7th day Sabbath and the Passover in its doctrines. For a time, Celtic Christians reverenced both the Sabbath and Sunday as a transitional period occurred before Sunday observance replaced Sabbath-keeping altogther. The Venerable Bede, an English historian and churchman, recorded that Popes Honorius and John wrote the Scots urging them to adopt the Easter celebration and abandon their practice of observing the Hebrew Passover. The following cites Pope John's letter to the Celtic Scots:

> "[We] learned that certain persons in your province...refuse to observe our Easter...arguing that it should be observed with the Hebrew Passover on the fourteenth of the moon."[47]

The Hebrew calendar was a lunar calendar, and Passover was commanded by God to be observed on the 14th day of Nisan, the first month of the Hebrew calendar (Exodus 12:1-6). Therefore, the Celtic Scots to whom Pope John addressed were still observing the Passover centuries after the crucifixion of Christ.

The early Celtic Churches had the scriptures as well. Even the patron saint of Ireland, St. Patrick, who lived in the 4th or 5th century A.D., is reported to have left copies of "the books of the Law and the Books of the Gospels" in all the churches he founded.[48] While we do not have copies of the earliest Celtic Bibles, surviving copies of the *Liber ex Lege Moisi,* dating no earlier than 800 A.D., preserved the Decalogue, and sections of the Books of Exodus, Leviticus, Numbers and Deuteronomy.[49] The prominence of those biblical books indicated the early Celtic Church venerated the Torah, known as the books of Moses. Leslie Hardinge states this concerning the scriptural foundations of the early Celtic Christian Church:

> "The Celtic Church developed a deep love of the Bible, and from the epistles of Paul developed their theology. The Psalms were used in worship...The legislation of Moses pervaded social, economic, and legal relationships to an extent seldom seen in the history of other branches of the Church...Celtic teachers stressed the Bible."[50]

The fact that early Celtic Christian life was regulated by a devotion to "the legislation of Moses" affirms that their Church's founders had to be observant Jews who lived at the very earliest days of the Christian Era. The additional fact that "the gospels of Paul" gave them their theology confirms that they had access to Paul's

Roman Galley.

writings, which had to be brought to the British Isles from the Mediterranean Region by 1st century Christians. Interestingly, the Celtic Christian Churches saw no conflict between the "legislation of Moses" and the "gospels of Paul," but blended them together in their religion. It is remarkable that the Celtic Churches were still strongly based on the Christianity of the early (read: "Jewish") Apostolic Church even as late as the 7th century A.D. when the Roman Church began the process of removing such practices from the Celtic churches in Scotland, Ireland and Wales.

Christianity began as a "sect of the Jews." Acts 24:5 and 28:22 record that the first Christians were called the Nazarenes, and were seen as a sect of the Jews. It is precisely the doctrines of the Nazarenes that were perpetuated by the Celtic Christian Church, confirming its founders were members of the earliest Nazarene Christians who still embraced the Torah. Its unique doctrines strongly indicate the Celtic Church was founded at a time contemporaneous with the earliest years of the Christian Church.

There is even an ancient Norwegian record that the Celtic Christian Church had adherents in Iceland and the islands north of Scotland. Hardinge writes:

> "The ancient Norwegian chronicler noted that 'these islands were at first inhabited by the...*papae*...the *papae* have been named from their white robes, which they wore like priests...as is observed from their habit and the writings of their books abandoned there, they were Africans, adhering to Judaism.' Here is a very early record of Celtic Christian settlers who were 'accused of adhering to Judaism.' This expression is used to describe observers of the Jewish Sabbath. This evidence suggest that early Celtic Christians followed this custom."[51]

The ancient record that Celtic Christians had their religious roots from "African" regions is important. We know that early Christianity spread throughout the Mediterranean World of the Roman Empire. The Apostle Paul (whose epistles made their way to the Celtic Churches) was particularly responsible for spreading this faith throughout the Empire. The "African" regions of the Roman Empire included the remaining Punic cities that had survived as Roman Provinces after Carthage fell. The second book in this series identified the Punic Culture of Carthage ("Kirjath Hadeschath") as having been founded by colonists from the ten tribes of Israel. That book also documented the ethnic and commercial relationships between Carthaginians and the Celts. By the time Christianity reached Celtic Britain in the 1st century A.D., there had been well-established sailing routes between Punic North Africa and Celtic Europe for centuries.

The Bible confirms that there were devout followers of the Torah in Africa at the time the Christian Chuch began. Matthew 27:32 records a Simon of Cyrene was impressed into carrying the cross of Christ. Cyrene was located in the Punic region of North Africa, and Simon would have been a devout Jew or Israelite of the ten tribes who had come to Jerusalem on a pilgrimage to observe the Passover in Jerusalem at the time Christ was crucified. Acts 2:10 records that Torah-observant people from Egypt and Cyrene (near Libya) were at the Pentecost observance after which the early Christian Church added 3,000 converts (verse 41). Africans from Cyrene are mentioned as emissaries of the early Christian Church in Acts 11:20 and 13:1, so there is biblical evidence that early Christians journeyed to Celtic Britain from African ports with the faith of the original Jewish

Christians. All of these early Christians would have been Sabbath-keepers who observed the laws of Moses, which is precisely the custom followed by the Celtic Christian Church for centuries.

The depth of the Celtic Church's fidelity to the Christian Church's early Jewish roots is as astounding as it is unappreciated by the modern Christian world. Hardinge's book documents that the Celtic Christians avoided swine's flesh and unclean animals, practiced Mosaic marital and sexual purity regulations for men and women, and observed both the seventh-year land-Sabbath and the 50-year Jubilee year cycles.[52] Celtic Christians in Scotland even practiced the Old Testament custom of Levirate marriages, in which a man would engender a child with a deceased brother's wife to ensure that a male heir would be born to his brother's name.[53]

However, there is no indication that the Celtic Church practiced either circumcision or animal sacrifices as religious requirements. That would identify the Celtic Church as not actually "Jewish," but rather that it had been founded by the original Jewish Christians who no longer required circumcision or animal sacrifices (I Corinthians 7:18-19, Hebrews 9:7-14). That would be consistent with the doctrines of Jesus Christ, Joseph of Arimathea and the earliest Apostles. The Celtic Christian Church, for centuries, consisted of "Torah-observant" people, and its founders had to be the Jewish Christians who dominated the Christian Church in the earliest decades of its existence. The fact that the Celtic Christian Church was firmly established on the Christianity taught by Jesus Christ, Joseph of Arimathea and the early Apostles argues that its founders were those very people! Its ability to flourish for six centuries in the British Isles after the death of Jesus Christ was a result of its being founded beyond the reach of the Roman Empire, which came to be dominated by the Roman Church. Jesus Christ's parting words to his Apostles before he rose to heaven included the charge that they be "witnesses unto me...unto the uttermost parts of the earth (Acts 1:8)." The existence of a strong Celtic Church in the British Isles, based on the doctrines of the initial Jewish Christians, indicates that his followers did exactly what they had been told to do by Jesus. They planted the faith far from Judea and the confines of the Roman Empire. History records it took firm hold in the British Isles.

C.C. Dobson's material (cited above) noted that the early English writers preserved accounts that Jesus Christ and Joseph of Arimathea had been present in the British Isles. Where would the early English writers have obtained such information? The early English historians were not Celtic Christians. Surely the information was not derived from Roman Christians, who opposed the Celtic Church's doctrines and would have opposed any effort to so credential Celtic Christian origins! English historians could only have received this information about Jesus Christ and Joseph of Arimathea from sources within the Celtic Christian Church, with whom they lived in the British Isles. Early British historians such as Gildas and the Venerable Bede lived at a time when the Celtic Christian Church still had adherents who preserved the origins and history of their own church! Leslie Hardinge's book confirms the early Celtic and Roman Christians had considerable communications with each other as they debated religious doctrines, so there was ample opportunity for the English writers to learn about the "Jewish" origins of the Celtic Christian Church. In conclusion, the early English historians preserved the records that the Celtic Christian Church had been founded by Jesus Christ, Joseph of Arimathea and other early Jewish Christians. The "Jewish" doctrines of the Celtic Church powerfully support such an origin.

However, the above British accounts do not assert that Jesus visited Britain after his resurrection, but rather prior to his Judean ministry. They also do not assert that Jesus spent the entire "missing 18 years" of his life in the British Isles. The account of Gildas indicates that Jesus was in Celtic Britain during the latter years of the reign of Tiberius, which would have been immediately prior to his departure for Judea to begin his recorded biblical ministry.

Where else did Jesus go during his youth and early adulthood? Other ancient legends assert that Jesus traveled as far East as India.[54] There is a biblical basis for legends that Jesus could have traveled both in the British Isles, and as far into Asia as India. In Matthew 15:24, Jesus said: "**I am not sent but unto the lost sheep of the House**

of Israel." The House of Israel refers to the ten tribes of Israel who, in Jesus Christ's lifetime, included the Celts of Europe, the Sacae/Saka Scythians and the Parthians in Asia. Since the area of Parthian and Saka dominance extended as far as India,[55] portions of the ten tribes of Israel could be found that far into Asia. **Since Jesus was "sent" to those ten tribes, it is logical that He traveled to where the ten tribes of Israel lived in the first century A.D.** Since the tribes of Israel then inhabited the British Isles and even portions of India at the eastern edge of Parthia's empire, Jesus' presence among these people would be a fulfillment of that scripture.

As seen earlier, Jesus lived during a period of peace between Parthia and Rome. During this period, trade flourished between the merchants of both empires. Rawlinson records that this trade was "considerable," and that merchants brought "various metals and numerous manufactured articles" from Rome into Parthia.[56] Given the indications that Joseph of Arimathea was involved in the Roman mining (metals) trade, and that Joseph's homeland in Judea was ideally located to facilitate exports into Parthia and Asia via overland trade routes, it is likely that Joseph's business included the export of metal products into Parthia and Asia. As Jesus grew, He likely became a trusted member of Joseph's international trading business. Who could possibly be better suited than Jesus to supervise Joseph's business trade with Parthian territories? Jesus had already been worshipped by members of the Magi, the Parthian ruling elite! Jesus was assured of a very warm reception in Parthia due to the Magi's favor, and would have been given access to any portion of Parthia's sphere of influence that He wished to visit. Joseph's international trading business could have given him an ideal opportunity to visit those regions to which the ten tribes of Israel had migrated — Britain, Parthia, Scythia and other Asian locations.

Did Jesus Visit the New World?

Another possibility exists. The previous two books in this series documented that both the Israelite-Phoenician Empire and the

Carthaginian Empire of the first millennium B.C. planted Semitic colonies in North America. It was also shown that some Carthaginians possibly fled North Africa during the Punic Wars to seek refuge in their North American colony. In the previous book in this series we saw evidence that the Punic civilization existed in the Americas even after Christ's crucifixion, so there was a significant Hebrew-Phoenician civilization in North America during the life of Christ. Since Christ was visiting the regions of the earth inhabited by the descendants of the ten tribes, did He visit ancient North America as well? The surprising answer may be "Yes!"

Consider the Quetzalcoatl legends of the ancient New World. While "Quetzalcoatl" is usually depicted as a serpent god, the legends record that some Quetzalcoatl legends are quite different. In *Voyages to the New World*, Nigel Davies includes a compilation of various Quetzalcoatl legends. These legends include the assertions that Quetzalcoatl:

> "**had a white skin** and...**was traditionally expected to return**..." [and that] "amid the lamentations of his people, Quetzelcoatl thereafter set out on his long journey **to the place in the East where he was destined to meet his end**"...[that] "**he rose to heaven and entered therein**"..."he remained four days in the land of the dead and, on the eighth day, reappeared as **the Morning Star**."[57] *(Emphasis added)*

Davies also comments that Quetzelcoatl is depicted as being a "**god in human form**," and that he was the "**creator God**" as opposed to a member of a pantheon.[58] It is also significant that the humanized Quetzelcoatl legends appear **only** in the **Christian era**. The Bible asserts that Jesus was a Semite, was destined to "meet His end" in a sacrifice for mankind, was buried and rose again to life, entered heaven and is even called "the Morning Star." *(Revelation 22:16)* The similarity between biblical accounts of Jesus Christ and the early legends about Quetzelcoatl are striking.

There is even more striking evidence. James Boland's book, *They All Discovered America*, adds that "the first Quetzelcoatl is said to have sprung from a **virgin birth**."[59] Accounts of the above attributes of Quetzelcoatl combined with his being born of "a virgin birth" point dramatically to a single historical personality: Jesus Christ! The many Christian themes attached to the early Quetzelcoatl strongly indicate that the humanized Quetzelcoatl represented Jesus Christ who visited the New World during the eighteen hidden years of His life. These ancient legends even record that He returned to the Old World aware of the destiny of self-sacrifice, which was just ahead of him. Those legends imply that He departed the New World to perform His ministry in Judea and there fulfill His self-sacrificial role.

Fanciful legends depict Quetzelcoatl as a serpent god. Since Satan is depicted as a "serpent" in the Bible *(Genesis 3:1-13, Revelation 12:9-15)*, one possible connection is that the worship of Quetzelcoatl was subverted from initial biblical themes into the worship of pagan gods, even including the rites of human sacrifice which Carthaginians had brought to the New World. Another intriguing possibility is found in Numbers 21, where we read that Moses lifted up a serpent in the wilderness and put it on a pole, "and it shall come to pass, that every one that is bitten, when he looketh upon it, shall live." *(Num 21:8)* In the New Testament, this symbolism is applied to Christ:

> "And as Moses lifted up the serpent in the wilderness, even so must the Son of man be lifted up: That whosoever believeth in him should not perish, but have eternal life." *(John 3:14-15)*

There are Peruvian accounts about a legendary figure named Viracocha, who "departed across the sea," but was "destined to return."[60] Viracocha is also portrayed in Spanish sources "like Quetzelcoatl — as a benevolent figure, who traveled from place to place, preaching repentance and performing miracles.[61] The legends about the person called Viracocha may be based on Jesus Christ's life, or even one of the Apostles who were sent by Christ to "all nations." *(Matthew 28:19)* Acts 1:8 records Jesus sent His apostles not just to "Judea and Samaria" (meaning "Judah and Israel"), but also to "the uttermost part of the earth." Jesus knew there were lands and civilizations on the planet that were a long, long way from Judea.

The two previous books presented much evidence that Israelite civilizations were established in the New World by the Hebrew-Phoenicians, Carthaginians, and Iberians. Indeed, these Semites brought Old World knowledge and customs to the New World. For example, the Carthaginians who colonized the New World included degenerate Israelites who practiced human sacrifice as part of their Baal worship. The fact that ancient New World cultures practiced human sacrifice indicates this grisly practice was planted in the New World by the Carthaginians. Since Carthaginians were also North Africans who were very familiar with Egypt's culture and its pyramids, the presence of pyramids in the Mesoamerican civilizations of the New World attests to linkages between the two regions because of Carthaginian voyages. More extensive evidence documenting this linkage was presented in the previous book in this series.

At this juncture, we will digress to more fully examine the possibility that Jesus visited the New World, and that Christianity was planted in the New World soon after Christ's earthly ministry was concluded. This will confirm that the Christian religion was present in the New World many centuries before Columbus, demonstrating that the sea route to the New World was also known during Christ's lifetime.

Matthew 15 contains a germane argument on this point. In Matthew 15:21-28, a gentile woman asked Jesus to heal her daughter — something that Jesus readily did for Jews. Jesus initially rebuffed the woman, stating He was sent only to "the lost sheep of the house of Israel." Only via a humble persistence did this gentile woman move Jesus to help her. Jesus' reluctance to help gentiles "in His own backyard" argues that He would not have journeyed across the Atlantic to visit, evangelize or help inhabitants of the New World **unless they were Israelites!** When Jesus stated that He had been "sent to the lost sheep of the house of Israel," He was acknowledging that He had been directed to go to the members of the "lost ten tribes of Israel" which were the "house of Israel." The eighteen-year gap in the biblical accounts of His life allows for a prolonged journey by Jesus Christ among the scattered tribes of Israel. Jesus' comment also indicates that He knew they lived in places to which He could actually go — that the ten tribes of Israel were not "lost" at all!

The first two books in this series contain abundant evidence about a substantial Israelite presence in the New World both before and during Christ's lifetime. There is also evidence that Israelites were present in the New World after His lifetime as well.

The Toltec civilization flourished in Meso-America from 900 A.D. until 1200 A.D. The *Encyclopedia Americana* states:

> "Their capital was Tollan, now Tula...the name 'Toltec' is derived from the name of their capital...the most important figure in Toltec history was...Topiltzin."[62]

One of the branches of the Israelite tribe of Issachar was named after an Israelite named "Tola" (Numbers 26:23). Notice the similarity between the Israelite name **Tola** and the root words **Tolla**n, **Tula**, and **Tol**tec, indicating the tribe of Issachar was involved in founding the Toltec civilization. An intermediate location where they may have also left their tribal name is found in **Thule**, Greenland. An analysis of Topiltzin's name points to a Viking/Scandinavian origin. His name concludes with the syllable "-zin." The letters "z" and "s" are phonetically similar. Substituting an "s" for the "z" in his name, we get Topiltsin, or Topilt-**son**. As many readers know, the suffix "-son" or "-sen" is extremely common at the ends of Scandinavian names. The consonants "S-N" or "Z-N" at the end of Topiltzin's name argues for a Scandinavian origin for this man.

An article by Lawrence Athy, Jr. printed in the *Epigraphic Society Occasional Publications*, and entitled "Foreign Influences on the Priesthood and Nobility of Pre-Columbian America" maintains that the Olmec and Toltec civilizations were ruled and directed by foreign elites who were characterized as tall, fine- or aquiline-nosed, thin-lipped, and bearded people. This foreign elite was in sharp contrast to the squat, flat-nosed and rarely-bearded Indian peasants over whom the foreign elites ruled. Clearly, the foreign elites exhibited characteristics of Semitic people from the Old World. Athy notes that the various foundings and revivals of cultures in pre-Columbian America were linked to the arrivals of new waves of these foreigners, and that by the time of the founding of the Toltec civilization, these "tall bearded elites" had been present in the New World for "over two thousand years."[63]

The Toltec ruler named Topiltzin was "a venerable and devout person...an old man with a long red beard turning white...who had come from a foreign country."[64] Athy further relates:

> "Topiltzin and his Toltecs were gentle people, were opposed by a wicked leader of many of the native people, and were persecuted to the point that the 'Toltecs abandoned this country and returned to their place of origin.' Topiltzin called together the people of Tula explaining that he was leaving due to persecution, and 'prophesied the arrival of strangers who would come...from the east'...thus the people were to be punished for their mistreatment of the Toltecs. 'No one was to escape from the hands of his sons who were to come to destroy them...Topiltzin also told them that the arrival of the strangers would not be witnessed by them...but would be seen by the fourth or fifth generation.'"[65]

The Spaniards under Cortez arrived approximately three hundred years later and fulfilled Topiltzin's prophecy about the destruction of the Aztec culture, which had followed the Toltecs. Athy adds that the Aztecs regarded the Spaniards as the prophesied "sons of Topiltzin," and that:

> "Cortez had arrived in the year 1 Reed in the Aztec calendar...the year in which Topiltzin had been born — the year in which the return of his sons had been forecast."[66]

Interestingly, Topiltzin and the Toltecs are called "gentle" foreigners. Since the ability to fulfill prophecy is a trait which God claims for himself *(Isaiah 41:21-26)*, the fulfillment of Topiltzin's prophecy may indicate that Topiltzin was an actual prophet in whom the Spirit of God was present. The Conquistadors could even have been God's hand of judgment for their persecution of Christians within the Toltec society.

Christianity in the New World before Columbus

In Volume 2 of this book series, it was noted that Christian inscriptions dating from the first to the third centuries A.D. were found in the Mayan ruins of Comalcalco. Since Christianity clearly existed in the New World very soon after the life of Jesus Christ, it takes no stretch of the imagination that it could still be present in the New World during the Toltec period, approximately 900-1200 A.D. There is further evidence that Christianity was at one time well established and widespread in the New World, but that it had degenerated over time as Christian symbols and practices were blended into the sun-worship religion of the native populations found by the Spaniards. Consider the following:

> "Many of the Catholic rituals taught to the Maya were already familiar to them, to the great surprise of the early missionaries. The Maya practiced baptism in water, confirmation, fasting...The cross was a familiar icon...When the friars explained that the cross was the sign of God, who had died on the Tree of Good and Evil and now lives in the heavens, the Maya accepted it as another version of a story they already knew."[67]

The cross, in particular, was a well-known symbol in the New World, especially among the ruling elites. Walter Stender wrote the following in the *Epigraphic Society Occasional Publications*:

> "When the Spaniards conquered Peru, they were astonished and puzzled to find crosses in the temples and palaces of the royal Inca family...For the Incas **the use of the cross was a continuance from preceding cultures...it becomes evident that the cross had a religious significance."**[68] *(Emphasis added)*

Stender also wrote:

> "The Mayas used it [the cross]...in one of their glyphs...Legends exist from various sites in South America that **white men came to the natives to teach them a better way of social life**. A similarity is obvious with the well-known Mesoamerican traditions, where white men arrived and tried to develop the cultural level of the natives...all these white men... were bearded, and another feature is particularly remarkable: **the garments of these white visitors have been decorated with white and black crosses**...At the time

> of the Spanish conquest there was a broad awareness in South America of an early presence of white residents..."[69] *(Emphasis added)*

Stender's article documents that the symbol of the cross had been present in the New World at least as early as the middle of the first millennium A.D. Combined with the evidence that Christian inscriptions were placed at Comalcalco in the 1st to the 3rd centuries A.D., it is clearly shown that Christianity had been present in the New World from virtually the beginning of the Christian era! It is also important to note that the symbol of the cross is associated with elites of white men who ruled over the natives. After white men disappeared, crosses were adopted by the subsequent ruling classes as a symbol of their authority.

That so many legends about previous white elites in the New World existed at the time the Spaniards arrived confirms that white men were widely present in the New World during various times in the history of the New World. That the cross and other Christian rituals were still present testifies to the previous existence of a Christian community that had degenerated into a sun-worship religion with vestigial Christian symbols and practices.

"Cassi" Sun Cross on prehistoric monument at Sinniness, Wigtonshire.

It would seem, however, that the Christianity found in the New World by the Spaniards was not necessarily a direct descendant of the Christianity that existed in the New World in the initial centuries after the life of Jesus Christ. It was also noted that the native populations "incensed and dressed their idols just as the friars would later ask them to do for the statues of the saints."[70] The incensing and dressing of statues was not the practice of the Early Apostolic Christian Church. Indeed, the early Christians would have regarded such a practice as rank idolatry. However, "statues of the saints" can be associated with Roman Catholicism, and it was being practiced in the New World **prior** to the arrival of the friars who accompanied Cortez. How did this happen? There are ready answers.

James Boland's book, *They All Discovered America*, includes a chapter on the efforts of Irish monks to flee westward in the tenth century A.D. across the Atlantic to escape the pillaging Vikings. He follows their travels to Iceland, Greenland and the New World.[71] However, during the thirteenth through the fifteenth centuries A.D., there were Christian Norsemen who worked closely with the Catholic papacy of Rome. The *Epigraphic Society Occasional Publications* reproduces a series of letters from three different popes, dated 1282, 1448 and 1492 A.D., written to Norse bishops and a church in Greenland. The letter of Pope Martin IV to a Norwegian Archbishop in 1282 A.D. addresses tithing practices for the Greenland churches, and the letter of Pope Nicolaus V in 1448 A.D. contains even more interesting information. Pope Nicolaus V wrote:

> "as regards our beloved sons, the natives and all **the inhabitants of the Island of Greenland**, which is said to lie...in the extremity of the Ocean, in the northern region of the Kingdom of Norway...whose inhabitants and natives, **for almost six hundred years**, have kept the faith of Christ..."[72] *(Emphasis added)*

This extraordinary papal letter acknowledges that Christianity had been present in Greenland "almost six hundred years" prior to his writing that letter. This would place Christian Norsemen in Greenland in the ninth century A.D., even before the Irish monks mentioned by Boland voyaged there to seek refuge from pillaging, pagan Vikings. Pope Nicolaus V's letter lamented the fact that Greenland's Christians were being attacked by fleets of pagans in the following words:

> "the barbarians, gathering together in a fleet on the neighboring shores of the pagans, attacked this entire people in a cruel invasion, devastating their fatherland and sacred temples...leaving in the island only nine parochial churches."[73]

Viking voyages to the New World had been taking place for centuries prior to Pope Nicolaus V's letter, and Icelandic history records that a Catholic bishop named Eric Gnuppson was sent from Iceland to Vinland in the New World in the year 1121 A.D., three centuries prior to Pope Nicolaus V's letter.[74] **This indicates that a Roman Catholic bishop was assigned to the New World at least four centuries before the arrival of Cortez and his Spaniards!**

Consider again the Toltecs of Mesoamerica, who flourished approximately 900-1200 A.D. Their ruling White elite, who arrived from a foreign land, were called a "gentle" people, indicating that they exhibited characteristics of Christianity (peacefulness, non-oppressiveness, etc.). Their capital city **Tula** (or **Toll**an), and their name (**Tol**tec), bore a connection to the name of a clan of the Israelite tribe of Issachar (the sons of **Tola**). The city of **Thule**, Greenland exhibits that same Israelite root word, and provides a link between the Christians of Greenland (confirmed by Pope Nicolaus V's letter to have been in Greenland at the time the Toltec civilization was founded) and the founding of the Toltec civilization in the New World.

This concludes the above digression on the evidence of Christianity in the New World. It was deemed necessary to confirm to the reader that Christianity has been present in more than one form in the New World since soon after the life of Jesus Christ. It also confirms that **Christians** were voyaging to the New World not only in the first century A.D., but at many other times prior to the arrival of Columbus or Cortez. While not directly relating to the life of Jesus Christ, it **does** provide firm documentation that Old World voyages to the New World were occurring from the time of Jesus Christ through many centuries afterward. Therefore, it is not so revolutionary a proposal to assert that Jesus Christ visited the New World during the eighteen-year period about which the Bible is silent. We will now return to our narrative for specific evidence that it was very possible for Jesus Christ to have made a journey to the New World in His lifetime.

There is no doubt that it was physically possible for Jesus Christ to have traveled to the New World. The first two books in this

Phoenician Trireme sailing vessel

series abundantly document that Phoenician and Carthaginian vessels crossed the Atlantic throughout the first millennium B.C., and that Roman vessels also sailed these routes in later centuries. In addition, there is evidence that the European Celts, contemporaries of Julius Caesar, had many large vessels that sailed to the New World.

Records exist that the Romans had ocean-going vessels capable of carrying a cargo load of 1200-1300 tons, and that such vessels could be 180 feet in length, have a beam of 45 feet and a cargo hold 44 feet deep.[75] Josephus records that he rode in a Roman passenger ship carrying 600 people,[76] and Acts 27:9-36 records that Paul rode in a Roman vessel carrying 276 people in a dangerous sailing season when a reduced passenger total was likely. Roman artifacts have also been found in the New World. Boland comments in his book on Roman artifacts found on the American East Coast.[77] In *Saga America*, Dr. Fell documents that Roman coins, artifacts and inscriptions have been found in the American states of Alabama, Tennessee, New Hampshire, Massachusetts, Connecticut, Georgia, and others.[78] Dr. Fell's comments on Jewish coins from the first and second centuries A.D. being found in Kentucky and the Missouri-Arkansas border region confirm that **sailing routes from Judea to ancient North America**

were known in the early Christian era.[79] Dr. Fell also wrote concerning a Hebrew inscription found in Tennessee:

> "...the Bat Creek stone from Tennessee, supposed by the Smithsonian finders to be Cherokee, but recognized by all Hebrew scholars who have studied it as **a Hebrew text of the first century A.D.** Dr. Robert Stieglitz of New York reads it as 'A comet for the Hebrews," with reference to Halley's comet, which 'hung over Jerusalem like a flaming sword' in the year 69 A.D. during the first revolt...The evidence suggests that Kentucky and Tennessee became havens of refuge for persecuted Hebrews..."[80] *(Emphasis added)*

Dr. Cyrus Gordon has also written about the validity of the Bat Creek stone found in Tennessee, and he also documents that Jewish/Judean coins dating to 132-135 A.D. were found in ancient America.[81] He dismisses those who assert "no one was here before Columbus" in the following strong words:

> "Trying to explain away the Bat Creek stone as anything other than **American contact with Palestine around the second century A.D.** can only amount to obscurantism that no sensible scholar or layman should elect. The Atlantic was crossed long before the Vikings, by different peoples during different centuries. The significance of the excavations at Bat Creek is that **they attest inscriptionally and archaeologically a migration in early Christian times from Judea to our [American] Southeast**."[82] *(Emphasis added)*

The above evidence places Judean Jews travelling to ancient North America for refuge during the 1st and 2nd centuries A.D., very soon after Jesus Christ's lifetime. Given the above evidence, it seems obvious that transatlantic sailing routes between Judea and ancient America existed during the lifetime of Jesus Christ. Since Joseph of Arimathea was involved in an international trading firm that necessitated long oceanic voyages, Jesus would have ready access to Roman vessels and oceanic sailing routes. If Joseph were also a Roman official (a "decurio"), he would have had privileged access to Rome's knowledge of routes to North America. Joseph could have taken Jesus himself, or he could have provided Jesus with a Roman vessel equipped to cross the Atlantic Ocean to the Americas.

An episode in the Bible indicates that Jesus was physically adapted to the effects of long ocean voyages. Mark 4:35-41 describes an event in which Jesus and His disciples were crossing the Sea of Galilee and were caught in a storm. Verse 37 states: "there arose a great storm of wind, and the waves beat into the ship, so that it was now full." Afraid for their lives, the disciples found Jesus "in the hinder part of the ship, asleep on a pillow." After being forcibly awakened by the disciples, Jesus commanded the wind to "be still," and an immediate calm prevailed.

Hebrews 4:15 tells us that Jesus was a human being as well as the Son of God, and that He "was in all points tempted like as we are." If Jesus experienced all the pulls and sensations which humans experience, His human body was subject to seasickness and nausea. That Jesus was able to sleep on a ship that was rolling and pitching in a

Jesus calms the storm

severe storm indicates that He had become adapted to the buffeting of waves and the movements of sea swells. His involvement with Joseph of Arimathea's international trading business would have given him ample time to get His "sea legs." While the context of this account shows that this storm was the most severe experienced by these fishermen on an inland lake, it was likely less severe than the storms and sea swells experienced by Jesus on the open ocean, enabling him to sleep through a lesser storm on an inland lake.

Another biblical account also supports the concept that Jesus was outside of Palestine during the "hidden years." In John 10:16, Jesus had a discourse with the Jews in which He said:

> "And **other sheep I have, which are not of this fold**, them also must I bring, and they shall hear my voice; and there shall be one fold, and one shepherd." *(KJV)*

In Matthew 10:6 and 15:24, Jesus referred to the "lost sheep" of the House of Israel, the ten tribes of Israel. In Mark 6:34, Jesus regarded the multitudes who followed him as "sheep," and most of those multitudes would have been Jews of Judea. Since sheep dwell in "folds," what was meant by Jesus' imagery of John 10:16 that He had "sheep" in more than one "fold?" Jesus refers to Judea where His Jewish followers were as "this fold," but informs them that they did not constitute His only "fold." Clearly, the other "fold" was where the descendants of the ten tribes of Israel lived. Since Jesus told them "**Other sheep I have** [in other folds]," His use of the present tense indicates that it was already an accomplished fact: He already had "sheep" (followers) in "folds" other than Judea. Since there is no evidence of Jesus being in Judea from ages 12 to 30, He had abundant time to gain followers in the distant lands inhabited by the descendants of the ten tribes of Israel during those eighteen years.

The gospel books of the Bible (Matthew-John) are eyewitness accounts of Jesus' ministry **to the House of Judah**, which lasted 3 and 1/2 years. None of His ministry **to the House of Israel** is recorded for us in the Bible even though the Bible implies it had occurred prior to Jesus' ministry in Judea. The life of Jesus, as presented in the Bible, is like a book in which only the first and the last few chapters are included, with all the middle chapters, covering the majority of His life, left out!

The Apostle John wrote that the Gospel accounts did not provide a comprehensive account of the life of Christ. John 21:25 states:

> "And there are also many other things which Jesus did, the which, if they should be written every one, I suppose that even the world itself could not contain the books that should be written." *(KJV)*

John's assertion that the life of Jesus was extraordinarily active and eventful is significant in light of the fact that the Bible says nothing about His life from age 12 to age 30. It is logical that many of Jesus' undescribed activities spoken of in John 21:25 were not done in Judea, or they would have been discussed in the "eyewitness" accounts in the gospel books. Many of Jesus' unwritten exploits must have been performed **outside** of Judea, and this is consistent with legends that Jesus traveled to many parts of the ancient world.

There are reasons to believe that the response of the ten tribes of Israel to Jesus was favorable. Since some of the Magi in Parthia's

ANCIENT DRUIDIC WORSHIP AT STONEHENGE, ENGLAND.

ruling class had worshipped Jesus when He was a child and knew He was related to Parthia's royalty in the Davidic-Arsacid dynasty, they likely welcomed him eagerly in Parthia's Asian empire when He was a young man. The positive legends about the first Quetzelcoatl, paralleling many biblical facts about Jesus' life, indicate that He made a lasting, favorable impression in the New World. The Druids of the British Isles and Northwest Europe had long expected a savior named "Yesu," very similar to "Yeshuah," and the legends of early Britain record a warm response to Joseph of Arimathea and other early Christians. It seems apparent that Jesus was right in telling the Jews He had "sheep" in other "folds" which predated His final ministry in Judea.

The New Testament also records that Jesus was well-received by the common people of the House of Judah. Who could respond negatively to one who miraculously healed so many people? It was the Jewish hierarchy that reacted negatively to Jesus. The reason is simple. The nations of the ten tribes of Israel were mostly independent, sovereign nations at the time Jesus visited them. Therefore, they were not bothered that Jesus' mission did not include physical "salvation" from oppressors. They generally didn't need any! In contrast, the House of Judah — the portion that lived in Judea — was hungry for physical "salvation" from Roman oppression. Their leaders had little interest in a message of **spiritual** salvation; they wanted a Messiah bringing **physical** salvation from Rome!

As Jesus approached age thirty, He said good-bye both to His great-uncle's international mining and trading business, to His "sheep" living in the "folds" of the ten tribes of Israel, and journeyed toward His native land of Judea. The satisfying years of international responsibility and warm welcomes among many diverse and distant Israelites were over. The difficult years of His earthly mission were now ahead of him, and He knew it.

The New Testament teaches that if Jesus Christ had failed in His mission to atone for mankind's sins, God the Father — the "Most High God" of the Old Testament — could not have permitted a single human being to ever taste eternal life since mankind would have had no atoning sacrifice. If Jesus failed, all mankind died with him. This young Jewish man, with the royal blood of King David in His veins, and filled with the Holy Spirit of His Father (the "Most High God"), must have had a tremendous load on His mind as He made what was to be His last trip home. He must have felt like He was "carrying the world on His shoulders" as He returned to Judea, for so He was.

THE JUDEAN MINISTRY AND DEATH OF JESUS CHRIST

The Bible records that Jesus Christ began His ministry at the age of thirty. *(Luke 3:23)* This is significant because the Old Testament required a man to be thirty years old in order to serve in the priesthood. *(Numbers 4:3)* Jesus Christ, as God in the flesh, was not subject to the normal human maturation schedule. His discourse with the Temple elders indicated that He was spiritually maturing at the age of twelve. However, the Bible records that Jesus chose not to enter Jewish society in a leading religious role until He attained the age of thirty.

After Jesus returned to Judea, one of His first public acts was to be baptized by John the Baptist in the Jordan River. *(Matthew 3:13-16)* In doing so, Jesus affirmed the ministry of John the Baptist, and became a role model to His future followers concerning the need for baptism.

Satan Offers World Rulership to Jesus Christ

After His baptism, Matthew 4:1-11 and Luke 4:1-15 tell us of a direct confrontation between Jesus and Satan the devil. Satan repeatedly tempted Jesus in an effort to entice him into doing something sinful or idolatrous. If Jesus had failed the test, He could not have served as the sinless "Passover lamb" which mankind needed for its salvation. Luke 4:2 asserts that Jesus fasted for 40 days to prepare for His spiritual battle with Satan. Fasting is frequently discussed in the Bible as a means of humbling one's self for purposes of drawing nearer to God.

Luke 4:5-7 relates one of Satan's temptations involved His showing Jesus "all the kingdoms of the world" and making Jesus this offer:

> "**All** this power will **I give thee**, and the glory of them: for **that is delivered unto me**; and to whomsoever I will I give it. If thou therefore wilt worship me, **all shall be thine**." *(KJV)*

Satan here claimed to be the unseen ruler of the earth, who had the authority to select national leaders and put them in positions of power as he wished. He offered temporal power over **all** the earth to Jesus if He would accept Satan as His lord. Most significantly, Jesus did not dispute Satan's claim to being the unseen lord of the world's nations and rulers. However, the Bible is clear that God intervenes to select national rulers whenever He wishes to do so to fulfill His will.

The Bible states that Satan is the "prince of **this world**" *(John 12:31 and 14:30)*, and acknowledges he was still "the prince" of **this world** even after the death of Christ. *(Ephesians 2:2)* He will remain the "prince" of **this world** until Jesus dethrones him at His second coming, at which point Revelation 20:1-3 states that Satan will be imprisoned and restrained from invisibly manipulating the nations. At that point, Jesus Christ is prophesied to rule as king over the earth's nations for 1000 years with His resurrected saints. *(Revelation 20:1-4)*

Consider Satan's sweeping offer and Jesus' response. Jesus did not challenge Satan's right to give the world rulership which he offered; however, He declined a temporal world rulership under Satan's auspices in favor of a future, eternal world rulership under God. *(Revelation 19:11-16, 20:1-6)*

Could Satan have made good on his offer if Jesus had accepted it? Consider these facts: (A) Jesus had already been worshipped by some of the kingmaking Magi of Parthia (an ancient "superpower"), and His status as a relative of the Arsacids made him eligible for Parthia's throne, (B) Jesus had been well-received in Britain, and His Hebrew name identified him as the promised Messiah (the "Yesu") expected by the Celtic Druids, (C) Jesus had already gained a following in the New World, and was likely the subject of the first Quetzelcoatl legends, and (D) the Jews were expecting the Messiah at that time due to the timetable of Old Testament prophecies. In other words, Satan's offer was quite practical in human terms. The physical conditions were already in place for Jesus to be made a powerful world ruler! Satan was offering his services to use the above circumstances to make Jesus a world emperor if He was willing to choose short-term gain instead of long-term good. Thankfully, Jesus resisted his offer.

It should now be apparent that Jesus Christ was hardly an obscure carpenter in Galilee. At the time He began His ministry in Judea, He had concluded visits to the far-flung ten tribes of Israel, utilizing His excellent relations with the Parthian Magi to travel east into Asia. He could also have traveled westward to Europe, the British Isles and the New World via the transoceanic routes available to him through Joseph of Arimathea's business. Jesus would have been known

Jesus in the Temple

to the influential classes of the Parthian Empire, Celtic Britain, portions of the New World, and even the Roman officials of the countries in which Joseph's mining and trading concern conducted business. Luke 2:52 records that after Jesus amazed the teachers in the Temple with His precocious wisdom at age twelve, He:

> "...**increased** in wisdom and **stature**, and in **favor** with God **and man**." *(Emphasis added)*

Luke's comment that Jesus' wisdom and favor with people continued to increase after age twelve contradicts the modern viewpoint that Jesus' went "dormant" to live as an obscure carpenter in Galilee until He "burst" onto the scene at age thirty. Since Jesus declared at age twelve that He had to "be about His [spiritual] Father's business," it is clear that His precocious brilliance was used to serve the "business" of His heavenly Father during His missing eighteen years, not that of His human father. Also, since Jesus was unknown in His Judean hometown at the time He began His ministry at age thirty, it is apparent that the "favor" He had in the eyes of other people occurred in regions far beyond the awareness of people in Judea and Galilee.

Jesus Widely Accepted Except In His Home Town

After the confrontation between Jesus and Satan, Jesus began His ministry with miraculous events and numerous appearances in synagogues. *(Matthew 4:23-25 and Luke 4:14-15)* He did mighty miracles, and people commonly "glorified" him. *(Luke 4:15)* On the other hand, Luke 4:16-30 describes His visit to the synagogue in Nazareth, His hometown, where the people tried to kill him. This event contained several harbingers of the future impact of Jesus' ministry in Judea.

Luke 4:16 begins by stating that Jesus "came to Nazareth, **where He had been brought up.**" *(both KJV and RSV)* Notice that Luke did **not** say Nazareth was "where Jesus lived," but rather that Nazareth is "where He **had been brought up,**" This language indicates that Jesus had lived in Nazareth **only** during His formative years. The *New Testament In Basic English* renders this passage as, "He came to Nazareth, **where He had been as a child.**" Luke's comment clearly indicates that Jesus had not lived in Nazareth as a young man or adult!

Luke then tells us that Jesus "**as His custom was**, went into the synagogue **on the Sabbath Day**, and stood up for to read." Jesus was still an observant Jew, and it was customary for Jesus to observe the Sabbath Day. In other words, Jesus was acting as would any devout Jew of the period. If Jesus had been present in His hometown

The Sermon On The Mount

synagogue from ages twelve to thirty, His wisdom and fame would have been well known to them as Jesus, even at age twelve, made no effort to conceal His spiritual maturity. Yet verse 22 shows that the congregation "wondered at the gracious words" of Jesus and said "Isn't this Joseph's son?" To reiterate an earlier argument, the local congregation had not experienced Jesus' power or wisdom during the intervening years, and was struggling to identify him. Clearly, Jesus had not been there in many years!

If Jesus had lived in Nazareth, one must also believe that God's Spirit, which moved Jesus so powerfully at age twelve, went completely dormant for eighteen years and suddenly reawoke in him one day after a very long hiatus. This author finds such a viewpoint untenable. All scriptural examples show that once God's Spirit is moving a person, it either waxes stronger or is "quenched." It is not a commodity that can stagnate or go dormant for almost two decades. Indeed, in the parable of the talents *(Matthew 25)*, Jesus likened a servant who "went dormant" with His gift to be worthy of punishment! It is impossible that Jesus "went dormant" for eighteen years!

Jesus then read and applied to himself a passage from Isaiah 61 which states: "the spirit of the Lord is upon me because He [God] hath anointed me to preach the gospel..." Jesus openly claimed to be the Messiah, the "anointed one" of God when He stated to His audience: "this day is this scripture fulfilled in your ears." In verse 23 Jesus tells them "Ye will surely say unto me this proverb, Physician, heal thyself." Jesus is here speaking in the future tense, indicating He already knew how He would be mocked during His eventual suffering on the cross.

Mark 6:4 parallels Luke's account, and quotes Jesus as saying: "**a prophet is not without honor, but [except] in his <u>own</u> country, and among his <u>own</u> kin, and in his <u>own</u> house**." This speaks volumes. Jesus affirmed that He was a prophet, but predicted that His own country (the Jews) and His own relatives would not accept him as the Messiah. There is another implication of this statement that could easily be missed. This statement also implies that while He would not be honored in His own country as a prophet, **He would receive honor outside His own country, community and family — He would not be "without honor."** It even implies that He already had been "honored" elsewhere **outside** His own nation.

Jesus' message infuriated His listeners. They attempted to kill him, and Jesus escaped this "lynch mob" by "passing through the midst of them." *(Luke 4:30)* The fact that those who sought to kill him did not recognize him as He passed through the angry crowd further illustrates two points. It supports the contention that He had been absent from His hometown a long time — if He had lived there for 30 years, they would all have recognized him. It also indicates that Jesus was an average-looking Jew who did not stand out in a crowd.

That Jesus was an average-looking Jew exposes another modern myth about him. The average Jew of Jesus' day did not have "hippie-length" hair, as Jesus is depicted as having on modern pictures. If His hair were very long, He would have **easily** been recognized in a crowd of Jews. Since Paul the Apostle, himself a Jew, wrote in I Corinthians 11:14 that it is a "shame" for a man to have long hair, it is evident that Jesus could not have had "long" hair. What constituted "long hair" in Jesus' time? There can be honest disagreements about this issue, but it seems safe to assume that men usually had hair shorter than the hair of females.

Some confusion on this issue can result from a misunderstanding of the terms "Nazarite" and "Nazarene." A "Nazarite" was one who, during the length of a vow, refrained from drinking alcohol or cutting His hair. *(Numbers 6:2-5)* Since growing long hair would separate them from the rest of the male population, Nazarites could easily be identified by their long hair. Unless you were a Nazarite, the indication is that Jewish men cut their hair to a shorter length. Jesus was a "Nazarene," indicating that He was from Nazareth, but He was not a Nazarite, since He drank alcohol. Matthew 11:19 records that Jesus' detractors called him a "winebibber" because they thought He drank too much wine!

This episode is atypical of Jesus! It shows Jesus going to the synagogue of His boyhood home and rebuking them so strongly that even the "religious" people of the synagogue tried to murder him! This would sound strange if it were not for several hints in the text. The account of this episode in Mark 6:1-6 shows that while the locals voiced no ill feelings toward His mother and siblings, verse 3 states that the townspeople "were offended" at Jesus! Why? There is a logical answer to this question.

Since Jesus had the Spirit of God from birth, there are many ways in which Jesus would never have "fit in" with the attitudes, actions and interests of other children in the area. Since Jesus lived a sinless life, He would have been unwilling to participate in the usual trouble-making and mischief that characterize young boys, making him a target of considerable "hazing" by other children. Also, since He could confound the Temple elders at age twelve, Jesus was "light years" ahead of His peers in maturity, and would have had almost nothing in common with other boys His age. Also, the strange visit of foreign dignitaries, the Magi, to lavish gifts on Jesus as a little child would have made some townspeople jealous or suspicious of him. If the Magi continued to send emissaries to him over the years (a distinct possibility), this action would have further complicated His life in a rural town in Galilee.

After the death of Joseph, His mother, Mary, may have thought it was best for Jesus to leave the area, and become an "apprentice" to His great uncle and international businessman, Joseph of Arimathea. When Jesus came back to His home area after an eighteen year absence, many of the people in that synagogue were likely the very ones who had hazed and ostracized Jesus when He was a boy. When He claimed to be the Messiah, their reaction was "Oh no, not him!" They were "offended" when they learned that the wise teacher speaking to them was the same Jesus they had hazed and taunted years ago. This analysis is supported by Luke 4:15, which indicates that Jesus was commonly "glorified" in other Jewish synagogues, but rejected only in His own hometown.

It is also evident that the teachings of Jesus were consistent with the beliefs of devout Jews at that time or He would have not have been "glorified" in their synagogues. Devout Jews in those synagogues found nothing heretical in His teachings.

Before proceeding further, it is worth recalling that Josephus, the Jewish historian who wrote soon after the death of Jesus, didn't express doubts that Jcsus was the Messiah. Josephus openly stated of Jesus — **"He was [the] Christ**."[83] He affirmed the divine miracles of His life with the words "**He was a doer of wonderful works**," and spoke of the resurrection of Jesus as a historical fact with the words "**for He [Jesus] appeared to them [His followers] alive again the third day, as the divine prophets had foretold...**"[84]

When Josephus, a prominent Jewish leader and historian of that time acknowledged that Jesus was the promised Messiah, and when the Bible records that He was widely "glorified" among the masses, it would seem that many Jews did perceive Jesus to be the promised Messiah. Even some Jewish religious leaders accepted Jesus as one sent by God.

Jesus chooses His first disciples

Another early act of Jesus was His selection of twelve men from the Jewish community to serve as the initial apostles of His church. *(John 1:35-51)* Jesus knew that these men would serve not only as contemporary spiritual leaders, but also as future kings over the twelve tribes of Israel after His second coming. *(Matthew 19:28)* Therefore, He was selecting men who would fit the distinct temperaments and needs of each of the twelve tribes of Israel! Where had Jesus gained first-hand knowledge of the unique personalities of the scattered tribes of Israel so He could select a suitable apostle/future king for each of them? It is evident that He obtained such knowledge during His visits to them between ages twelve and thirty. Since only two of the tribes of Israel were present in Judea at the time of Jesus, a fact confirmed by Josephus, the only way He could have gained personal knowledge of the scattered ten tribes of Israel was via international travel to visit them where they lived!

The Reaction of Jewish Leaders to Jesus

John 3:1-3 states:

> "there was a man **of the Pharisees**, named Nicodemus, **a ruler of the Jews** [who] came to Jesus by night, and said unto him, Rabbi, **We know that you are a teacher come from God**: for no man can do these miracles that you do, except God be with him."

Nicodemus came to Jesus "by night," implying that he was on a secretive mission. He was representing other Jewish leaders, because he spoke for a larger group in saying **"we know..."** The leaders of the Jews were not ignorant men; they could see from the Old Testament prophecies that the Messiah was due in their time period, that Jesus was doing miracles that only someone with the power of God could do, and that Jesus was fulfilling Messianic prophecies. The words of Nicodemus make that evident. Then why did they later kill Jesus when they **knew** He was sent from God? There are two plausible answers.

William Steuart McBirnie, in his book, The Search for the Twelve Apostles, has offered one possible answer. He states:

> "...the greatest reason for His condemnation was the fact that Jesus had lanced through the swollen hypocrisy of the Jewish political and ceremonial religion and the religious bureaucracy of professional priests, Pharisees and Sadducees. So all the main Jewish leaders, including the official party of the Herodians...consented to or sought His death."[85]

Josephus essentially agreed with the modern opinion of McBirnie in stating:

> "He [Jesus] was the Christ; and when Pilate, **at the suggestion of the principal men among us**, had condemned him to the cross..."[86] *(Emphasis added)*

This is a very candid statement by Josephus. After declaring the righteousness of Christ and affirming the status of Jesus as "the Christ" — the "anointed one" — Josephus acknowledges that the "principal men among us" (i.e. the Jewish leaders) arranged for the death of Christ. The Jewish religious leaders held much power over the people in Judea. Their conduct clearly showed that they were more interested in selfishly clinging to their power than in serving the people by a fair administration of the laws of God as given through Moses. Because Jesus was exposing their hypocrisy and venality, the religious leaders saw Jesus as the symbol of a "reform movement" which could sweep them from power. The Bible records that Jesus was "glorified" in many Jewish synagogues. *(Luke 4:15)* He was such a popular figure with the Jewish population that Luke 5:15 records that "great multitudes came together to hear, and to be healed by him." Josephus agreed with Luke that Jesus was very popular in Judea by stating that Jesus "drew over to him many of the Jews, and many of the Gentiles."[87] Jesus' rising popularity with the Jewish population was seen as a threat to the power structure of the Jewish leaders.

The Pharisees were surely familiar with prophecies that the Messiah would set up a kingdom of His own. Therefore, it was clear to the Pharisees that if Jesus was the Messiah and was destined to set up a kingdom, He would oust them from their authority. Obsessed by their desire to cling to their temporal power, they determined to slay Jesus to prevent the loss of their status...even if it meant killing the Messiah! In arranging the execution of Jesus, they actually fulfilled the prophecies pertaining to the Messiah's betrayal and death. Matthew 26:15 fulfilled Zechariah 11:12's prophecy about "thirty pieces of silver," and Jesus' death to redeem mankind fulfilled the messianic prophecy of Daniel 9:26 that the Messiah would be "cut off, but not for himself."

This first possible explanation suggests that the Jewish leaders did not really respect the scriptures or fear God: that they viewed religion simply as a means of perpetuating their power over the people. Matthew 27:1 states that "the chief priests and elders took counsel against Jesus to put him to death." It does not say the whole Jewish nation wanted to slay Jesus. Their middle-of-the-night trial and condemnation of Jesus was designed to thwart any opposition to their plan from the Jewish masses who held Jesus in high esteem.

There is also a second possible answer to the question of why the Pharisees arranged the sentencing of Jesus. Consider the life of the Jews under the Roman yoke. They hated the loss of their independence, and keenly resented being ruled by gentile Romans.

Some recalled the relative freedom they had enjoyed a few decades previously when the Parthians had briefly freed them from Roman rule. Having had a taste of freedom, they hungered for more of it! The Bible stresses the hatred the Jews felt for the "publicans," the collectors of the Roman taxes, and Luke 13:1 refers to a violent confrontation in which the Romans executed a number of Jews. Josephus confirms that this was a time of tremendous discontent on the part of the Jews with their Roman rulers, leading to verbal and violent confrontations.[88]

The Jewish leaders were expecting a Messiah who would free them from Roman tyranny. No doubt many were familiar with such Messianic prophecies as Zechariah 14 and Isaiah 61 which promised that the tribes of Israel would be exalted over the gentiles and that Jerusalem would become a world capital. The Jews must have thirsted for these prophecies to be fulfilled in their day and for the Messiah to lead them in a great war against Rome.

As Jesus fulfilled many Messianic prophecies and confirmed His Messiahship by manifesting divine powers, it is logical that many Jews would expect Jesus to start using His divine power against the hated Romans! This expectation must have grown like wildfire, and Jesus' own disciples shared this expectation!

After all, Jesus had promised His twelve closest disciples that they would each **rule** over one of the tribes of Israel when He (Jesus) would "sit in the throne of His glory." *(Matthew 19:28)* Jesus consistently spoke of the coming "**kingdom of heaven**" in many comments and parables. It was common knowledge that Jesus was a direct descendant of King David and the ancient Jewish kings. *(Luke 2:4)* There are many instances cited in the Gospel accounts of people addressing Jesus as the "**son of David**." Jesus was even given a royal procession just before His crucifixion when the masses hailed him with the words "**Hosanna: blessed is the King of Israel that cometh in the name of the Lord**!" Also, in Matthew 10:34 Jesus proclaimed that He had come "to bring a sword, not peace." The disciples even quarreled about who would be the greatest in the kingdom that Jesus would rule. *(Matthew 18:1, Mark 9:33-37)* Small wonder there was a widespread expectation

Jesus' triumphal entrance into Jerusalem

that Jesus was about to oppose the Romans and establish the "Messianic kingdom" in their day.

It is possible that some Jewish leaders of the day felt they had to "assist" or "push" Jesus into confronting Rome in order to fulfill all the Messianic prophecies at that time. After all, did not Ezekiel 37:15-28 prophecy that the House of Israel and House of Judah would be united under "David" their King? Since Jesus was a direct descendant of David, a relative of the Parthian kings, and had great favor with the Parthian nobility that picked Parthian kings, the Jews could easily assume that Jesus was positioned to fulfill this prophecy by uniting Parthia (the House of Israel) and the Jews (the House of Judah) in a war against Rome! Those expecting and wanting such a war must have been very frustrated and disgusted at what they perceived to be a "cozy" relationship between Jesus and the Romans.

Rome was a despotic empire that tightly controlled its subjects. Yet the entire life of Jesus exhibited a lack of Roman control over His activities. He could travel where He wanted, when He wanted and with whom He wanted without the supervision or permission of Roman authorities. This freedom was permitted by the Romans in spite of the fact that Jesus was drawing huge crowds and talking about a new "kingdom," a message that Rome could easily have seen as fomenting a Jewish revolt. Why did the Romans allow freedoms to Jesus that they regularly denied to others? There are four reasons for Rome's permissive attitude toward Jesus.

A Parthian Offer of Sanctuary to Jesus Christ

To begin with, it was discussed earlier in this chapter that Jesus was related to the rulers of the Parthian Empire at a time when Caesar wanted peace with Parthia. The Roman rulers of Judea risked Caesar's wrath if they provoked the Parthians into a war Caesar didn't want! They were surely aware that Jesus Christ was related to Parthia's emperor, an Arsacid, because of the widespread knowledge that Jesus was of the royal seed of David. The Romans were not ignorant of Jesus' special relationship with the Parthian Magi, who elected Parthian emperors from male Arsacids. Rome had great interest in matters that could affect the political relationships between Rome and Parthia, and Rome's actions regarding Jesus could affect Roman-Parthian relations.

Coupling Jesus' "special relationship" with the Parthians with Caesar's decree that good relations with Parthia should not be disturbed, Roman officials in Judea had to be very careful not to antagonize the Parthians by mistreating Jesus Christ! There is an historical account that supports the contention that Parthia's ruling class was closely watching the affairs of Jesus while He was in Judea.

This legend relates that a Parthian provincial ruler, King Abgar of Edessa — a city of Northern Mesopotamia — carried on a correspondence with Jesus during His ministry in Judea. William Steuart McBirnie relates the legend as follows:

> "[the] legend has come down to us from Eusebius...This legend tells of a correspondence between Jesus and Abgar, King of Edessa (in what is now southern Russia)...Eusebius claims to have seen this correspondence in the archives of Edessa and to have translated it himself from the Syriac language."[89]

McBirnie misidentifies "Edessa" as a city in "southern Russia," apparently confusing it with "Odessa," a Russian city on the Black Sea. King Abgar's "Edessa" was a city in the northern Mesopotamian region of Parthia's Empire, in southeastern Turkey on a modern map. It was located near the Euphrates River, near the border where the Parthian and Roman Empires met. Vassals of the Parthian Emperor ruled Edessa.

Eusebius was a famous Christian historian who lived from 260 A.D. until 340 A.D. The *Encyclopaedia Britannica* writes concerning him:

> "Eusebius was one of the most learned men of His age, and stood high in favour with the emperor Constantine ...Eusebius' greatness rests upon his vast erudition and his sound judgement. He is best known by his *History of the Christian Church* completed in 324 or early in 325 A.D."[90]

Eusebius was not a man given to wild claims. Consider Eusebius' own account about the exchange between King Abgar of Edessa and Jesus Christ. Eusebius begins:

> "...when King Abgar, the brilliantly successful monarch of the peoples of Mesopotamia, who was dying from a terrible physical disorder which no human power could heal, heard continual mention of the name of Jesus and unanimous tribute to His miracles, he sent a humble request to Him by a letter-carrier, begging relief from his disease."[91]

This record that news of Jesus' miracles was well known in Parthia's western provinces confirms that the trade routes must have been full of news about Jesus' exploits. At the beginning of this chapter, Roman historical accounts were offered confirming that Jesus' miracles really happened. Now we also have historical confirmation from within the Parthian Empire that Jesus' miracles did occur! The following excerpt from King Abgar's letter to Jesus is taken from Eusebius' account:

> "Abgar...to Jesus, who has appeared as a gracious saviour in the region of Jerusalem — greeting.
>
> "I have heard about you and about the cures you perform...If the report is true, you make the blind see again and the lame walk about; you cleanse lepers...and raise the dead...I concluded that...either you are God and came down from heaven to do these things, or you are God's Son doing them. Accordingly I am writing you to beg you to come to me, whatever the inconvenience, and cure the disorder from which I suffer. I may add that I understand the Jews are treating you with contempt and desire to injure you: my city is very small, but highly esteemed, adequate for both of us."[92]

This account is most intriguing! The reports heard by Abgar parallel biblical accounts about the miracles of Jesus. King Abgar professes his faith in Jesus, is desperate for Jesus to come, and even offers him refuge in Edessa from the risks faced by Jesus in Jerusalem. It is remarkable that Eusebius preserved a record that Jesus was given an official offer of sanctuary in Parthian territory from the dangers He faced in Jerusalem! According to Eusebius, the following reply was sent by Jesus Christ himself to King Abgar by a courier named Ananias. The reply is reproduced in its entirety:

> "Happy are you who believed in me without having seen me! For it is written of me that those who have seen me will not believe in me, and those who have not seen me will believe and live. As to your request that I should come to you, I must complete all that I was sent to do here, and on completing it must at once be taken up to the One who sent me. When I have been taken up I will send you one of my disciples to cure your disorder and bring life to you and those with you."[93]

This letter attributed to Jesus Christ would have been about three hundred years old when Eusebius read it in the Royal Records of Edessa, and it reflects thoughts entirely consistent with those expressed by Jesus in the Gospel accounts. Jesus' words give the impression that His crucifixion may have been imminent at the time He wrote this letter. Significantly, while Jesus was reluctant to perform a healing for a non-Israelite in Palestine *(Matthew 15:21-28)*, He quickly agreed to send someone to heal King Abgar. This argues that King Abgar and his Parthian subjects were Israelites from one of the ten tribes of Israel. If Jesus had traveled in Parthia's empire during His missing eighteen years, He would have known this to be true from personal experience and, therefore, He exhibited no reluctance to heal King Abgar. Indeed, because of the likelihood that Jesus traveled to many areas where the ten tribes of Israel lived, Jesus surely visited the Israelites living in nearby Parthian regions. It is even possible that King Abgar and Jesus were already acquainted with each other as a result of Jesus' travels in Parthia. This possibility is supported by King Abgar's boldness in approaching Jesus, and Jesus' very favorable response.

There is more to the story. According to Eusebius, the archives of Edessa recorded that after Jesus' death and resurrection, Thaddeus, mentioned in Mark 3:18, was sent by the Apostle Thomas to Edessa. Once there, he not only healed many of King Abgar's subjects, but also laid hands on King Abgar himself and healed the king. King Abgar ordered his subjects to assemble and hear the preaching of Thaddeus, and offered him silver and gold, which Thaddeus refused. King Abgar is quoted as stating to Thaddeus:

> "I believed in Him (Jesus) so strongly that I wanted to take an army and destroy the Jews who crucified Him, if I had not been prevented by the imperial power of Rome from doing so."[94]

Remarkable! Here is a record of a Parthian vassal king wishing to mount a military campaign to punish those responsible for crucifying Jesus Christ! This Parthian support for Jesus Christ is very consistent with the fact that Jesus enjoyed tremendous favor with the Magi, Parthia's priests and nobility. The willingness of a Parthian vassal king. who bordered Rome's territory, to go to war to rescue Jesus Christ from physical dangers in Judea gives an insight into how sensitive the political situation was for Rome in dealing with Jesus Christ. Rome was surely not ignorant that there was sentiment in Parthia to mount an armed invasion of Judea to rescue Jesus! The account of Pilate handling the crucifixion matter will confirm Rome's great reluctance to harm Jesus Christ.

However, King Abgar acknowledges that he alone did not have the power to challenge the Roman army in Judea — the Parthian Emperor would have to mass the armies of many of his feudal kings, like Abgar, to fight the Romans. But this account confirms that Jesus had strong supporters within the Parthian Empire, justifying Rome's reluctance to interfere with his life. While Rome maintained a hands-off policy toward Jesus, their spies undoubtedly kept a constant watch on all that Jesus did — enabling them to know that Jesus had very strong supporters in Parthia's ruling class.

Roman Reluctance to Execute Jesus

The second reason for amicable relations between Jesus and the Romans is that Jesus was likely well known to Roman officials who had met him through contacts with Joseph of Arimathea's company. If Joseph was a Roman "Decurio," a Roman mining official who traveled between Judea and Britain, people affiliated with Joseph's company came in contact with Roman officials on a constant basis. This would have occurred in Britain, the Mediterranean region, and wherever the goods of Joseph's company were shipped and transported within the Roman Empire. It is likely that Jesus assisted in Joseph's business as He traveled under Joseph's tutelage. At any rate, it would have been well known that Jesus was the protege of Joseph the Roman Decurio. During those years, Jesus must have developed a personal rapport with a number of Roman officials. Indeed, while most of the Jewish community recoiled from personal contacts with Romans as "unclean gentiles," Jesus was even willing to use miraculous power to heal the servant of a Roman centurion. *(Matthew 8)* While this won for Jesus goodwill with the Roman administrators of Judea, it must have infuriated the Jewish leaders who wanted their Messiah to fight the Romans, not heal them!

If Joseph of Arimathea were a Roman Decurio, he surely possessed Roman citizenship. Since Jesus was a blood relative and youthful protege of Joseph of Arimathea, **it is also very possible that Jesus Christ became a Roman citizen during His "lost" eighteen years!**

JESUS WAS EVEN WILLING TO USE MIRACULOUS POWER TO HEAL THE SERVANT OWNED BY A ROMAN CENTURION. *(MATTHEW 8)*

If Joseph of Arimathea and Jesus Christ possessed Roman citizenship, it further explains why (A) Joseph was given prompt access to Pilate, the Roman governor, after Jesus was crucified; and (B) why Jesus came and went as He pleased! If Jesus was a Roman citizen, He had the **right** to travel as He wished within the Roman Empire! It was not unusual for some Jews of that period to be Roman citizens. The apostle Paul, who was first named Saul, was also a Roman citizen. *(Acts 16:37-38, 22:22-29)*

A third reason that enabled Jesus to go wherever He wished and do whatever He pleased was the fact that Jesus was wealthy! Does this surprise the reader? It should not. Remember that the Parthian Magi had given Jesus costly gifts of "gold, myrrh, and frankincense." We are not told how much gold and costly spices were given to Jesus, but it was no doubt a substantial amount. The Parthians regarded Jesus as royalty, and it was the ancient custom to give a royal person a truly worthy gift when coming into his presence. Since the Parthian Magi were directed to Jesus by an angel of God, their sense of awe likely resulted in unusually large gifts being given to Jesus. This gold was likely held in trust for him until He was older, first by His physical "father" Joseph, and then by Joseph of Arimathea after Joseph's death. When Jesus reached adulthood, He would have controlled His own wealth. Also, if Jesus' relative and mentor, Joseph of Arimathea, was independently wealthy, one can be sure Jesus shared in that wealth. In all cultures and times, wealth can open many doors.

Jesus' financial resources were confirmed by the fact that He and His large band of disciples traveled for years without any visible means of support! In spite of their itinerant lifestyles Jesus' band had monetary resources, and John 13:29 shows that Judas Iscariot was their treasurer in charge of disbursements. John 12:3-6 reveals that people around Jesus could afford expensive purchases and that Judas, the treasurer, was an embezzler. Judas was, therefore, handling sums of money so large that he thought his embezzling would not be noticed. Judas' comment in John 12:5 also indicates that Jesus' group was in the habit of making donations to the poor. The fact that Jesus never asked for "tithes, offerings and donations" from people, but rather gave money to the poor confirms that Jesus traveled with plenty of financial resources to take care of His followers.

The fourth reason why Rome allowed Jesus to travel and speak as He did is that Rome had reason to believe that part of His message actually served Roman interests. The Roman rulers, knowing about Jesus' connection to Parthian royalty and seeing His divine powers, were likely quite relieved to hear Jesus preaching a message that did not include inflammatory remarks toward Rome.

For example, Matthew 22:15-22 records one attempt by Jewish leaders to push Jesus into a confrontation with Rome. The Pharisees wanted to entangle Jesus politically on the subject of the hated Roman taxes, and they made sure the "Herodians" — Roman sympathizers — were there to listen. They asked Jesus whether it was lawful for the Jews to pay Roman taxes. They apparently expected Jesus to answer "no," and wanted the Roman sympathizers to hear His answer, hoping to bring Jesus and Rome into conflict. However, Jesus tactfully refused to become a "tax protester," saying: "render unto Caesar the things that are Caesar's, and to God the things that are God's." Hearing Jesus' response, both the Romans and Herodians had to be pleased with His answer. The non-confrontational relationship of Jesus and the Romans continued to the chagrin of the Jewish leaders.

Indeed, when the Jewish leaders urged Pilate to crucify Jesus, some of them may have seen it as a final attempt to make Jesus use His divine powers against Rome to save himself. Since similar desires for war existed among the disciples of Jesus, an alliance between some in the Sanhedrin and one of Jesus' disciples, Judas, to bring about this confrontation is understandable. They could easily have assumed that if Jesus' own life were put at risk, He would use His miraculous powers to save himself and fight the Romans as the "conquering Messiah."

Support for this possibility is found in the actions of Judas after Jesus Christ allowed himself to be crucified. Judas was so shocked at Jesus' death that he committed suicide. *(Matthew 27:3-5)* Clearly, Judas had not expected that the outcome of his actions would be the death of Jesus! Perhaps Judas also assumed that Jesus would, when

Jesus and Pilate

pushed to the point of death, finally oppose the Romans with His divine powers. If so, this hope was a result of wishful political thinking and flawed prophetic understanding. Daniel 9:26 had prophesied that the Messiah would be killed, and Jesus had tried to prepare His followers for this event, telling them He would be buried for three days and three nights. *(Matthew 12:40)*

Daniel's prophecy that the Messiah would "be cut off [killed]," was fulfilled on Golgotha. That He was to be killed "not for Himself" prophesied that He would sacrifice Himself for others. Even Jesus' own disciples discounted Daniel's prophecy about the Messiah being killed, as they were also shocked when Jesus died. The disciples had an expectation that Jesus would lead them in a war fulfilling the "conquering Messiah" prophecies. *(Acts 1:26)* Peter was armed at the time that Jesus was taken into custody, and his first instinct was to kill the first person who dared to seize the Messiah. *(Matthew 26:47-56)* They were aghast when Jesus offered no resistance to His captors, and fled from the scene.

Jesus was not only aware of His prophesied death, but realized the manner in which it would occur. He told His listeners that His death would involve "a lifting up from the earth" *(John 12:32-33)*, which occurred when He was lifted up on a cross. He also predicted it in John 3:14, saying His "lifting up" would be like an ancient event in which Moses placed an image on a pole and lifted it up for the deliverance of all who looked upon it. *(Numbers 21:8-9)*

The Pharisees, either not realizing or not accepting that the Messiah had to die, became the very instruments of fulfilling Daniel's prophecy that the Messiah would be "cut off." It never occurred to the Pharisees that the "conquering Messiah" prophecies would have to wait for a Second Coming of the Messiah.

It must be pointed out that the Jewish race, as a whole, is not collectively responsible for the death of Christ. As noted earlier, Josephus confirmed that it was the Jewish hierarchy (not the whole nation) who caused His death at the hands of the Romans. Those Jews who cried out to Pilate "crucify him...let His blood be upon us, and on our children" *(Matthew 27:22-25)* were an infinitesimally small fraction of the Jewish race. The Jews who uttered those rash words could not have numbered more than a few hundred people. The Jews crying for the blood of Jesus to be spilled were suborned agents of the Sanhedrin in a plot to engineer the death of Christ. Even if God had placed a curse on the offspring of those who uttered those words, it excuses the 99.9+% of the Jewish race who did not participate in the murder of Jesus and did not even know about it until it was over. The vast majority of the Jews living in Judea were not aware of Jesus' crucifixion until well after the event. The numerous Jews living in Parthian provinces were also completely innocent of Jesus' blood. One cannot blame those Jews or their descendants for causing Jesus' death.

Consider now the extremely delicate position of the Roman rulers of Judea in the crisis involving Jesus' trial and crucifixion. The first priority for Pontius Pilate and the Romans was to carry out the will of Caesar. What pleased the native population was secondary. Remember that the life of Christ occurred during a period of stability

Jesus tried by Pilate

between the empires of Rome and Parthia, a stability that Augustus Caesar wanted to maintain. Therefore, it was a top priority for Pilate to avoid incidents that could bring about a confrontation with the Parthian Empire. Pilate also knew that when Rome had provoked Parthia several decades prior to that time, Parthia had driven the Romans out of Palestine and controlled it for three years.

Rome had good intelligence about matters involving the political activities of people in their provinces, and was aware that Jesus Christ was a special favorite of high Parthian officials. Pilate was likely aware that communications took place between Jesus Christ and Parthian officials, including at least one king over a Parthian province: King Abgar. Rome surely knew that Jesus Christ was a blood relative of the Parthian emperor, an "Arsacid" via the "Phares" bloodline of King David, and had to tread lightly where Jesus was concerned.

Since Jesus espoused the payment of Roman taxes, fomented no revolts, and His non-violent message was popular with the masses, the Romans viewed him as a counterweight to the revolutionary zealots among the Jews.

Jesus was also very likely a personal friend of some Roman officials as a result of His involvement with Joseph of Arimathea's international business. Additionally, other Romans had undoubtedly witnessed some of the miracles of Jesus and had reported these events to Roman leaders.

Since Jesus was close to the ruling elites of Parthia and was seen as a stabilizing influence for Roman interests in Judea, Rome was disinclined to harm Jesus. In view of His miraculous powers, the polytheistic Romans were likely also averse to harming someone who was so "close to the gods."

When the Jewish religious leaders demanded that Jesus be crucified, Pilate was in a terrible quandary. He had compelling political reasons for not harming Jesus, yet he also needed to handle the situation in a manner that did not precipitate a Jewish rebellion. Another factor, which must have concerned him, was whether he was being "set up" by the Jewish leaders to do something that **would** precipitate a war not only with the Jews but also with Parthia. After all, there were many Parthians who served the same God of the Jews, and they were present in large numbers in Jerusalem during the annual Holy Days. *(Acts 2:9)* Since Jesus was crucified during the Passover season, many people from Parthia's provinces were surely present in Jerusalem at that time. Pilate could have wondered whether the Jews were plotting with the Parthians to provoke an incident which could precipitate a Parthian-Jewish war versus Rome. This would anger Caesar, so Pilate had to avoid that possibility at all costs.

Matthew 27:18 and Mark 15:10 record that Pilate knew the Jewish leaders had "framed" Jesus. Pilate's behavior showed that he did not want to crucify Jesus Christ, and he freely offered Jesus an opportunity to defend himself. *(Matthew 27:11-14)* Pilate "marveled greatly" when Jesus took no action to avail himself of Pilate's offer.

Ordinarily, a person would do or say anything to avoid the hideous fate of crucifixion! The implication is that if Jesus had made **any** effort whatsoever to defend himself, Pilate would have released Jesus. Knowing this and knowing that His central mission was to sacrifice himself for mankind, Jesus' silence thwarted Pilate's effort to free him.

Pilate.

DETAIL, CHRIST BEFORE PILATE, BY M. MUNKACSY.

Pilate grew exasperated with Jesus' refusal to defend himself, and said privately to Jesus: "You will not speak to me? Do you not know that I have power to release you, and power to crucify you?" *(John 19:10)* In modern words, Pilate was saying to Jesus: "C'mon, get with it Jesus, play ball with me, say something and I'll set you free."

Even though Jesus refused to defend himself, Pilate was still determined to find a way to keep Jesus alive. He next offered to free Jesus as part of a Passover tradition, giving the public a choice between Jesus and a prisoner named Barabbas. *(Matthew 27:15-23)* Pilate was likely again taken aback when the crowd requested freedom for Barabbas instead of Jesus. Pilate had been outsmarted by the Sanhedrin, which had "stacked the deck" against Jesus by having only their followers in the crowd. *(verse 20)* Pilate's own wife then urged him not to harm Jesus, saying she was having nightmares about the situation, and adding her view that Jesus was a "just man." *(Matthew 27:19)*

Pilate tried a third ploy to keep Jesus alive by an outright declaration of His innocence. Luke 23:4 quotes Pilate as telling the Jewish leaders and their mob, "I find no fault in this man." When the mob called for the crucifixion of Jesus, Pilate again publicly defended Jesus, saying, "Why, what evil has he done?" *(Matthew 27:23)*

Even though the suborned crowd was screaming for Jesus' death, Pilate tried again to save Jesus. Pilate was relieved to hear that

Jesus was a Galilean because it gave him a fourth option for keeping Jesus alive: a delaying tactic by giving the whole mess to Herod, who had jurisdiction over Galilee. Herod was "exceedingly glad" to see Jesus, and wanted to talk with him. So Herod was also disinclined to crucify Jesus. While the "chief priests and scribes" demanded Jesus' death, Jesus remained silent and did nothing to defend himself. *(Luke 23:6-9)* Herod finally gave this "hot potato" right back to Pilate. *(Luke 23:11)*

Most people have failed to appreciate that Pilate, the Roman governor, tried more than anyone else to keep Jesus alive! Here we see Pilate pursuing many options to prevent or stall the crucifixion of Jesus in spite of great pressure to the contrary. Luke 23:20 openly declares that Pilate was "willing to release Jesus." If Jesus were a Roman citizen as mentioned earlier, Pilate likely expected Jesus to "appeal to Caesar" (as did the Apostle Paul in Acts 25:10-12). Such an appeal would have prevented Jesus' execution in Jerusalem and transferred his case to Rome. Pilate probably expected Jesus to make such an appeal, but Jesus refused in order to fulfill all prophecy.

JESUS BEFORE PILATE.

Finally, Pilate realized he was out of options. As Matthew 27:24

puts it: "Pilate saw that he could prevail nothing, but rather that a tumult was made..." The mob scene was ready to turn into a riot. The Passover celebration was one of the biggest of the year, and a violent riot at that time could develop into a revolution. So, even though

Pilate washing his hands

he knew Jesus was innocent, he finally agreed to crucify Jesus to forestall the most immediate threat to Roman interests. Even in condemning Jesus, Pilate engaged in political posturing to keep this event from turning into a confrontation with Parthia. Washing His hands before the multitude, he proclaimed himself "innocent of the blood of this just person." *(Matthew 27:24)* In doing this, Pilate was disassociating Rome from the killing of a celebrity who was popular with many Jews as well as the powerful Parthians. Pilate wanted it publicly known that responsibility for Jesus' crucifixion lay with the Jewish hierarchy, not with Rome.

When Jesus was twelve years old, He had amazed the Temple's elders with His spiritual wisdom and insight. By the time Jesus was crucified about 21 years later, many of those same Temple teachers who had interacted with Jesus at age twelve were, no doubt, still alive. Some of them had surely progressed in the Jewish leadership hierarchy, and were members of the Sanhedrin at the time Jesus Christ was executed. Therefore, it is likely that some of the Sanhedrin's members who conspired to kill Jesus had been at the Temple and witnessed Jesus' wisdom at age twelve.

Now consider the attitude of Jesus in this episode. He knew that Daniel 9 prophesied that He, the Messiah, had to be "cut off" or slain. The divine side of him knew that He had to face the moment of sacrifice, but His human side recoiled from it as the time drew near. His prayer in the garden of Gethsemane showed that He wanted out of having to be sacrificed! His words in John 12:27, "Father save me from this hour: but for this cause came I unto this hour," reveal an inner conflict between His human side wanting to be spared, and His divine side which understood that He had to be sacrificed to fulfill the Messiah's role. Matthew 26:38-42 shows the depth of Jesus' anguish when He said, "my soul is exceedingly sorrowful, even unto death." When He prayed "Father, if it be possible, let this cup pass from me..." Jesus' human side was beseeching God the Father to find some other way to save mankind. Luke 23:42-45 adds that Jesus prayed with such intense "agony" that "His sweat was as it were great drops of blood falling down to the ground." Jesus did not want to die! He went through with it only because He was perfectly submitted to the will of His Father in heaven, and because His death represented the only possible atonement for mankind. By the time His tormentors came, He was reconciled to His fate.

In John 18:33-37, Pilate asked Jesus if He were really a king, confirming He knew about Jesus' descent from King David. Jesus replied: "**My kingdom is not of this world**; if my kingdom were of this world, **my servants would fight**, that I might not be handed over to the Jews..." Jesus added: "You say that I am a King, **For this I was born, and for this I have come into the world**..." Jesus acknowledged that He was born "a king," that His kingdom was "not of this world [the first century A.D.]," but that He would become a king in the future. Jesus also stated in verse 11: "You would have no power over me unless it had been given you from above." Jesus asserted that unless His death was according to the will of God, no temporal government could have had any power over him.

This is affirmed by a comment of Jesus Christ in Matthew 26:52-54. When one of His disciples tried to resist the taking of Jesus by attempting to kill a would-be captor, Jesus told him not to resist with the words:

> "Do you think that I cannot appeal to my Father, and He will at once send me more than twelve legions of angels? But how then should the scriptures be fulfilled, that it must be so?" *(RSV)*

This comment of Jesus is both sobering and revealing. His comment reveals that He was voluntarily refusing to use divine power to save himself in order to fulfill Scripture, such as Daniel 9:26. However, it is sobering to realize that Jesus affirmed that if He were but to ask, the Father would "at once" give him twelve legions of angels to rescue him. This statement shows that while it was the Father's will to save mankind, the final decision to "go through with it" belonged to Jesus, that if He chose not to "go through with it," the Father would have honored that choice and sent thousands of angels to slay all who threatened him! If Jesus had made that choice, mankind would have had no sacrifice, and the doorway of salvation would have been closed. Jesus knew the stakes, and put mankind's long-term good ahead of His short-term safety. Indeed, if Jesus had refused to "go through with it," the whole plan of salvation, which required a sinless, sacrificed Messiah for mankind's sins, would have been cancelled. This brings up a sobering possibility.

If Jesus had "opted out" of being a sacrifice and terminated the plan of salvation, the legions of angels might have destroyed not just Jesus' tormentors but **all** mankind since the very existence of mankind would have become moot. If there were no savior to ransom mankind, there would have been no purpose in a continued existence for mankind itself. Jesus may well have seen legions of death angels poised in the spirit world to terminate all mankind if He chose not to implement the plan of salvation for mankind. If so, Jesus had a very stark choice set before him that no human being could see. If Jesus called on the Father to rescue him and stop the crucifixion, mankind would die, but if Jesus chose to sacrifice himself, mankind would live. It was up to Jesus.

Jesus knew that if He asked for angelic rescue, none of His human friends could ever be saved. So He gave up His life, and made salvation available for not only His beloved friends, but for all humanity. If the people at the crucifixion scene had realized the awesome choice before Jesus, they would have all fallen trembling at His feet. Jesus chose to save mankind even as it tortured, mocked and reviled him. *(Matthew 27:39-44)*

When Jesus died, many supernatural events occurred to confirm that Jesus was the Divine Son of a very real God, the "Most High," who had watched the entire episode from heaven. Matthew 27:51-54 records that:

> "the veil of the temple was torn in two, from top to the bottom; and the earth did quake, and the rocks were broken apart; And the graves were opened; and many bodies of the saints which slept [were dead] arose, And came out of the graves...and went into the holy city and appeared to many."

The tearing of the curtain in the temple, which had sealed off the Holy of Holies, signified that the death of Jesus Christ meant that there were no longer any limitations on human access to God, and the

The Angel at the Tomb declaring the Risen Christ

concurrent resurrections of many people both testified that Jesus' death meant "life for the dead" and foreshadowed that there would be a future resurrection.

The key question concerning the death of Jesus Christ is "Did He really rise from the dead?" He foretold that He would rise again after a period of three days *(Matthew 12:40)*, and many eyewitness accounts are included in the Bible that He fulfilled His promise. Whether the reader believes His resurrection to be a fact depends on: (A) the faith the reader places in the eye-witness accounts in the Bible, (B) the credibility of the Bible based on fulfilled prophecies, the unity of the Bible with the record of ancient history, etc., and (C) the reader's experience with answered prayer offered in the name of Jesus. However, we do have the contemporary affirmation of Josephus, a non-Christian, Jewish historian who lived shortly after the time of Christ, that "He [Jesus] appeared to them alive again the third day."[95]

This chapter has provided information that permits the life of Jesus Christ to be viewed in a much broader perspective than was previously possible. It is clear from the evidence presented in this chapter that Jesus Christ was not only a **real** historical figure, but also a **prominent** personality of His time whose fame extended far beyond the borders of Judea. Two more biblical themes will be examined and then this chapter will conclude. One substantiates that Parthia's ruling dynasty was descended from King David. The second further supports the contention that the Scythians and Parthians were descended from the ten tribes of Israel.

Revelation 19:16 prophesies that when Jesus Christ returns, He will bear the title "King of Kings." Modern society does not appreciate the great significance of the use of this specific title. George Rawlinson, in his epic history of Parthia entitled *The Sixth Great Oriental Monarchy*, observed that Parthia's empire was organized as a feudal system with many vassal kings owing their allegiance to the overall Parthian emperor. He added:

> "...Parthian monarchs took the title of 'King of Kings,' so frequent upon their coins..."[96]

The previous chapter documented that the Parthia title "king of kings" was based on the Hebrew-Semitic word "Melek," which means "king." Rawlinson also recorded an incident that confirms this title was used by Parthia's emperors during the time of Christ. Discussing events that led to the Parthian-Roman "Summit Conference" in 1 A.D., he records:

> "Phraataces [Parthia's emperor]...responded to Augustus, dispatching to him a letter wherein he took to himself the favourite Parthian title of 'king of kings,' and addressed the Roman Emperor simply as 'Caesar.'"[97]

The book of Revelation's claim that Jesus will eventually rule forever as the "King of Kings" now carries new meaning! Those who read the Apostle John's words in the first century A.D. could recognize that this statement meant that Jesus Christ would inherit the title and throne of Parthia's Kings at His Second Coming! Jesus was often called the "Son of David" in His lifetime, and it was prophesied before His birth that Jesus would eventually inherit "the throne of His father David, and He shall reign over the house of Jacob forever." *(Luke 1:32-33)* Yet the Apostle John referred to Jesus' future throne as having the title given to Parthia's kings! These scriptures mean that "the throne of His father David" and the throne of the Parthian "king of kings" are one and the same! The Bible, therefore, confirms that Parthian kings literally sat "in David's throne." This also offers Biblical evidence that Jesus Christ was an Arsacid, a relative of Parthia's ruling dynasty!

Where Did the Twelve Apostles Go?

The missions of the twelve apostles confirm that the Scythians and Parthians were descendants of the ten tribes of Israel. In Matthew 10:5-6, Jesus gave the twelve apostles this charge:

> "These twelve Jesus sent forth...saying, Go not into the way of the Gentiles...But **go rather to the lost sheep of the house of Israel**." *(KJV)*

The ten tribes of Israel — the "house of Israel" — were spiritually, not physically "lost" at that time. The apostles stayed with Jesus during His ministry, but they obeyed this commandment of Jesus to go to the ten tribes of Israel after Jesus died. Just before He rose into heaven, Jesus told His apostles:

> "...and ye shall be witnesses unto me both in Jerusalem, and in all Judea, and in Samaria, **and unto the uttermost parts of the earth**." *(Acts 1:8 KJV)*

Since Jesus had earlier sent them to the ten tribes of Israel, and later said they would go "to the uttermost parts of the earth," it is clear that some of the descendants of the ten tribes of Israel lived "in the uttermost parts of the earth;" that is, "a very great distance from Judea."

The book of Acts indicates very few of the apostles remained in Judea after Jesus' ascension. Many of the Apostles heeded Jesus' charge to evangelize the ten tribes of Israel. Many legends exist about the nations of the earth visited by the apostles. We have already seen the account that Thaddeus was sent to northern Mesopotamia to heal the Parthian vassal king, Abgar, and evangelize his people. Eusebius also recorded:

> "Meanwhile, the holy apostles...were scattered over the whole world. Thomas, tradition tells us, was chosen for Parthia, Andrew for Scythia, John for Asia..."[98]

The *Encyclopedia Britannica* writes concerning Thomas:

> "...his bones were reputed to have been brought to Edessa from India...According to the tradition, St. Thomas founded the Christian churches in Malabar [India], and then crossed to Mylapur, now a suburb of Madras, where the shrine of his martyrdom...still stands on Mt. St. Thomas, where a cross is shown with a Pahlavi [Parthian] inscription."[99]

Chapter two documented that portions of the ten tribes established "Saka" kingdoms in India to the east of Parthia, so Thomas' presence in India is consistent with Christ's charge that they go to the ten tribes of Israel.

Peter wrote the epistle of I Peter while in Babylon *(I Peter 5:13)*, which was then within the Parthian Empire. Some have asserted that Peter's use of "Babylon" symbolized "Rome" but there is nothing in the text to support that view. Peter understood the difference between the cities of Babylon and Rome, and he was a simple fisherman not given to literary or scholarly devices. When Peter said "Babylon," he meant the city of Babylon.

Various legends state that the apostles Thaddeus, Matthias, Andrew, Bartholomew, and Simon the Canaanite (or "Zealot") all evangelized or passed through Armenia.[100] Armenia was settled by portions of the ten tribes after the fall of Samaria, as noted in the previous book in this series, and was a province of the Parthian Empire though often disputed with Rome. Armenia was a gateway to Scythia via the Caucasus Mountains, so it is possible that some of these apostles passed through Armenia on their way to Scythia.

One account places Simon and Jude together in northern Mesopotamia and Persia, also within Parthia's Empire.[101] Simon the

Zealot is also recorded as taking a missionary journey through North Africa, including the old Punic cities near Carthage, continuing on to the British Isles before going to Persia where he reportedly perished.[102] McBirnie also writes:

> "The Coptic Church of Egypt affirms that Simon 'went to Egypt, Africa, Britain and died in Persia.'"[103]

It would be logical for an apostle to visit "Africa" as the Punic-Israelite culture of old Carthage was still thriving in North Africa. McBirnie cites the book, *The Christian Centuries*, by Jean Danielou as recording:

> "Christianity was probably planted in Carthage as early as the end of the first century, otherwise it is difficult to explain how the city had such a large Christian population by the time of Tertullian [born circa 150 A.D.]...The Council of Carthage, in 216 [A.D.] was attended by 71 African bishops."[104]

Earlier, an account was cited that Joseph of Arimathea was present in Britain. A British historian, Aylett Sammes, wrote in 1676 that:

> "But the most-received opinion...which seemeth to carry the greatest antiquity, is that Joseph of Arimathea...was sent into Britain by St. Philip, where he preached the gospel, and founded a church in a place called...Glastonbury, which place was granted him by this Arviragus, king of Britain..."[105]

McBirnie also cites the writings of Eusebius, in which Eusebius wrote:

> "Surely later, the Apostles preached in Britain."[106]

Early historians knew that Christianity had reached Celtic Britain early in the Apostolic period. It is only after the advent of evolutionary dogmas that such accounts were censored out of the historical record.

Earlier in this chapter, we examined the legend of Viracocha, who "performed miracles and preached repentance" in ancient America.

Was "Viracocha" one of the apostles of Jesus Christ who really did travel to the "uttermost parts of the earth?" Someone brought Christianity to the New World soon after Christ's death, as Christian inscriptions were found in Comalcalco in the early centuries of the Christian era.

Ancient Briton lady, wife of Barates, a Palestinian Semite

There are many more legends about the lands visited by the twelve apostles, but the above will suffice for this chapter. All the regions and nations discussed earlier in this book as being places inhabited by the ten tribes of Israel are also cited as regions and nations visited by one or more of the twelve apostles. Since Jesus had sent His apostles to the ten tribes of Israel, these legends further confirm that "the lost sheep" of the ten tribes of Israel were located in Parthia, Scythia, Armenia, the North African Punic regions, the British Isles, the Saka kingdoms of India and perhaps even the ancient Americas.

This chapter has illustrated how the life of Jesus Christ impacted relationships between the empires of Rome and Parthia. The next book in this series on Israelite history will examine the migrations of the ten tribes of Israel after the fall of the Parthian Empire in the third century A.D., resuming the narrative at the point where chapter two of this book concluded.

ENDNOTES: CHAPTER THREE

1. Josephus, Antiquities of the Jews, XVIII, III, 3

2. Wilken, The Christians as the Romans Saw Them, p. 98

3.Ibid, pp. 99-100 (citing Eusebius, The History of the Church, 4.3.2)

4.Tacitus, The Annals of Imperial Rome, Part II, "The Burning of Rome," circa XV.42-47

5.Rawlinson, The Sixth Great Oriental Monarchy, pp. 178-181

6.Josephus, Antiquities, XV, I, 2

7.Rawlinson, The Sixth Great Oriental Monarchy, pp. 199-205

8. Ibid, The Sixth Great Oriental Monarchy, p. 216

9. Ibid, p. 210

10.Ibid, p. 85

11.Young's Analytical Concordance to the Bible, see word "Wise," subhead 8, p. 1060

12.Josephus, Antiquities, XVIII, IX, 1

13.Plutarch, Crassus, 21

14.Encyclopaedia Britannica, Heading entitled "Asia," Vol. 2, p. 512

15.Rawlinson, The Sixth Great Oriental Monarchy, p. 118

16.Josephus, Antiquities of the Jews, XVIII, IX, 1

17.Plutarch, Crassus, 21

18.website: www.parthia.com, see links: "Geography," "Parthian Stations," and "Parallel Passages from the Chinese Annals" (citing Friedrich Hirth's China and the Roman Orient)

19.Rawlinson, George, The Sixth Great Oriental Monarchy, pp. 195-198, 215

20.Young's Analytical Concordance to the Bible, see "Salathiel, Shealtiel," p. 831

21.Halley, Henry, Halley's Bible Handbook, see "Matthew," p. 415

22.Rawlinson, The Sixth Great Oriental Monarchy, pp. 218-219

23.Rawlinson, The Sixth Great Oriental Monarchy, pp. 213-214

24.Ibid, pp. 213-215

25.Capt, The Traditions of Glastonbury, p. 19

26.Capt, Ibid, p. 22

27. Capt, Ibid, p. 22

28.Ibid, p.20

29 Dobson, Rev. C.C., Did Our Lord Visit Britain as they say in Cornwall and Somerset?, pp. 22-23

30.Ibid, p. 10

31.McBirnie, The Search for the Twelve Apostles, p. 230

32.Capt, pp. 39-41

33.Ibid, p. 41

34.Ibid, p. 9

35.Young's Analytical Concordance to the Bible, see word "Lord," subheading 5, pp. 616-617

36.Ibid, p. 9

37.Young's Analytical Concordance to the Bible, Hebrew Lexicon, word "Yeshuah," p. 55

38.Dobson, p. 23

39. Ibid, p. 26

40. Ibid, p. 27-28

41. Ibid, p. 28

42. Ibid, p. 24-25

43. Hardinge, Leslie, The Celtic Church in Britain, Preface, xii-xiii

44. Ibid, p. 81

45. Ibid, p. 84

46. Ibid, p. 84

47. Ibid, p. 25 (citing Bede, Ecclesiastical History, II, 19)

48. Ibid, p. 50

49. Ibid, p. 50

50. Ibid, p. 51

51. Ibid, pp. 11-12 and map on page 13

52. Ibid, pp. 99-100, 197-198 and Appendix, p. 216

53. Ibid, pp. 198-199

54.Capt, The Traditions of Glastonbury, p. 7

55.Frye, The Heritage of Persia, pp. 200-201 and Encyclopedia Britannica, Vol. 17, see "Persia," p. 577

56.Rawlinson, The Sixth Great Oriental Monarchy, p. 425

57.Davies, Voyagers to the New World, pp. 125-126

58.Ibid, p. 131

59.Boland, They All Discovered America, p. 303

60.Ibid, pp. 126-127

61.Ibid, p. 136

62.Encyclopedia Americana, Vol. 26, Heading entitled "Toltec," p. 829

63.Athy, "Foreign Influences on the Priesthood and Nobility of Pre-Columbian America," Epigraphic Society Occasional Publications, Vol. 17, 1988, pp. 112-115

64.Ibid, p. 114

65.Ibid, p. 115 (Athy herein cites Book of the Gods and Rites and the Ancient Calendar by Fray Diego Duran)

66.Ibid, p. 115

67.Morris, Walter, Living Maya (as cited in Epigraphic Society Occasional Publications, Vol. 17, 1988, p. 196

68.Stender, "The Cross of the Inca," Epigraphic Society Occasional Publications, Vol. 17, 1988, pp. 179-181

69.Ibid, pp. 181-183

70.Morris, Living Maya, cited in Epigraphic Society Occasional Publications, Vol. 17, 1988, p. 196

71.Boland, They All Discovered America, pp. 127-152

72.1448 A.D. letter of Pope Nicolaus V, reproduced in the Epigraphic Society Occasional Publications, Vol. 17, 1988, pp. 255, 261

73.Ibid, p. 261

74.Boland, pp. 277-280

75.Casson, The Ancient Mariners: Seafarers and Sea Fighters of the Mediterranean in Ancient Times, pp. 208-209

76.Ibid, p. 209

77.Boland, pp. 54-78

78.Fell, Saga America, pp. 31-35, 124-132, 153

79.Ibid, p. 168

80.Ibid, p. 168

81.Gordon, Cyrus, Before Columbus, pp. 175-187

82.Ibid, p. 187

83.Josephus, Antiquities of the Jews, XVIII, III, 3

84.Ibid, XVIII, III, 3

85.McBirnie, The Search for the Twelve Apostles, p. 36

86.Josephus, Antiquities, XVIII, III, 3

87.Ibid, XVIII, III, 3

88.Ibid, XVIII, III, 1-2

89.McBirnie, p. 203

90.Encyclopaedia Britannica, Vol. 8, Heading entitled "Eusebius of Caesarea," p. 892

91.Eusebius, The History of the Church, I, 13

92.Ibid, I, 13

93.Ibid, I, 13

94.Ibid, I, 13

95.Ibid, XVIII, III, 3

96.Rawlinson, The Sixth Great Oriental Monarchy, p. 88

97.Ibid, p. 218

98.Eusebius, The History of the Church, III, 1

99.Encyclopaedia Britannica, Vol. 22, Heading entitled "Thomas, St." p. 143

100.McBirnie, The Search for the Twelve Apostles, pp. 199-202, 243

101.Ibid, p. 231

102.Ibid, pp. 207-211

103.McBirnie, p. 208 (citing Alkhrida, Precious Jewels, Coptic Church, 1915)

104.Ibid, pp. 209-210

105.Sammes, Aylett, Britannia, p. 212

106.Ibid., p. 209, citing Eusebius' Demonstration Evang.

CHRONOLOGICAL TABLE OF THE REIGNS

OF THE

PARTHIAN KINGS.

KINGS.			B. C.	Aer. Seleuc.	Reigned Years.	Extreme Dates on their Coins.
Arsaces	I.	.. .. ..	255	57	2	
....	II.	Tiridates I. ..	253	59	37	
....	III.	Artabanus I. ..	216	96	20	
....	IV.	Phraapatius. ..	196	116	15	
....	V.	Phrahates I. ..	181	131	8	
....	VI.	Mithridates I. ..	173	139	37	
....	VII.	Phrahates II. ..	136	176	10	
....	VIII.	Artabanus II. ..	126	186	3	
....	IX.	Mithridates II. ..	123	189	36	
....	X.	Mnaskires. ..	87	225	10	233 ?
....	XI.	Sinatroces. ..	77	235	7	
....	XII.	Phrahates III. ..	70	242	10	
....	XIII.	Mithridates III. ..	60	252	6	
....	XIV.	Orodes I. ..	54	258	17	
....	XV.	Phrahates IV. ..	37	275	41	275—311.
		Tiridates II.				
....	XV.	Phrahates IV. restored.				
			A. D.			
....	XVI.	Phrahataces. ..	4	316	1	
....	XVII.	Orodes II. ..	5	317		
....	XVIII.	Vonones I. ..	5	317	8	
....	XIX.	Artabanus III. ..	13	325	28	334—353.
		Tiridates III.				
		Cinnamus.				
		Artabanus III. restored.				
Arsaces	XX.	Bardanes. ..	42	353	4	353—357.
....	XXI.	Goterzes. ..	45	357	6	357—362.
		Meherdates. ..	50	362		
....	XXII.	Vonones II. ..	51	363		363.
....	XXIII.	Vologeses I. ..	51	363	11	364—369.
....	XXIV.	Artabanus IV. ..	62	374	15	374—388.
....	XXV.	Pacorus. ..	77	389	31	389—404.
....	XXVI.	Chosroes. ..	108	420	13	421—431.
		Parthamaspates. ..	115	427	1	
....	XXVI.	Chosroes restored. ..	116	428		
....	XXVII.	Vologeses II. ..	121	433	27	433—460.
....	XXVIII.	Vologeses III. ..	148	460	44	460—502.
....	XXIX.	Vologeses IV. ..	192	504	17	504—520.
....	XXX.	Vologeses V. and Artabanus V.	209	521	18	521—539.

Epilogue

This book has presented the facts about the rise and fall of the Parthian Empire, an ancient "superpower" rival of Rome. Given the dominant role in world history played by the Parthian Empire for almost five centuries and the additional fact that Greek and Roman writers preserved a multitude of information about Parthia's history, is it not strange that this book is likely the first time you have seen a detailed discussion of Parthia's history?

Has the glaring omission of Parthia's proper place in history been a accidental oversight? It is hard to imagine that intelligent and gifted historians could all make the same mistake because readily-available source material, the classical Greco-Roman writings, clearly discuss Parthia's dominant role in world history. The same observation could be made about the incredible absence of information about Phoenician, Carthaginian and Scythian history. Greek writers wrote much about Phoenicia and Scythia and the Romans recorded a great deal about the Carthaginian Empire. Since much evidence exists about these ancient empires, why have modern historical accounts ignored these prominent ancient empires?

The real reason why Phoenicia, Carthage, Scythia and Parthia are so slighted in historical accounts is that the evolutionary dogmas and fantasies which pervade the modern educational system would experience a mortal blow if these forgotten empires were given their rightful place in history. As the reader has seen in the first three books of this series on Israelite history, the Hebrew/Israelite origins of Phoenicia, Carthage, Scythia and Parthia become very obvious when examined in any depth. Because the histories of these empires offer strong evidence that the Creator God of the Bible has kept his promises to the numerous descendants of the tribes of Israel throughout history, modern historical accounts choose to ignore or de-emphasize them. The truth would verify the Bible, so the truth has been "covered up."

You are now invited to read the fourth book in this series on Israelite history. It resumes with hordes of Parthian refugees beginning a mass migration toward the Black Sea where their kinsmen, the western Scythians, could offer them refuge against their Sassanian Persian conquerors. However, the Caucasus and the Black Sea region could not begin to support the masses of Parthian refugees pouring through the Caucasus Mountains toward Europe. The millions of Parthian refugees migrating through the Caucasus Mountains came to be known afterwards as the "Caucasians."

Many Parthian refugees were called "Goths" by the Romans who had given that name to Scythians living near the Black Sea. Without the mighty Parthian Empire to act as a buffer against invaders from East Asia, the Goths became exposed and in following centuries, their masses of people were also forced to flee into Europe in search of new homelands. Over several centuries, millions of Parthian and Scythian refugees, accompanied by many of their former subject peoples, flowed from Asia into and across Europe like the alluvial fan of a great human river.

Some Parthian and Scythian names were retained as their descendants conquered new homelands in Europe. The "Sacae or Saxa" of Scythia and Parthia became known as "Saxons," the "Kermans" from Parthia were renamed the "Germans," the Asian "Jats" (once allied to the Massagetae of Scythia) became "Jutes", etc. The feudal system of Parthia was reestablished in Europe by the migrating tribes of Caucasians. Parthian/Scythian culture was moved from Asia into Europe by migrating Caucasians. The next book will convincingly document that many of the modern nations of Europe (as well as nations in North America, Africa and Australia founded and settled by

Europeans) are directly descended from the Caucasian refugees of the mighty Israelite Empires of Asia: Parthia and Scythia.

Parthia's hordes of refugees invaded Roman Europe after their flight from Asia. Their torrent of migrating tribes fought the Romans, wresting province after province from the Romans until the Roman Empire was conquered and supplanted by Parthian refugees. The Parthian and Scythian refugees were so numerous that they even fought each other in their search for "lebensraum." They also fought and merged with the Celtic peoples of Europe, who like the invading Parthians and Scythians, were descendants of the original Kingdom of Israel.

The second book in this series showed that the Celts descended from Israelite/Phoenician colonists who had lived in Europe and the British Isles from at least the time of Kings David and Solomon of ancient Israel. The invading Caucasian refugees from Parthia and Scythia (now called Goths, Germans, Saxons, etc.) were Israelites who had descended from the ten tribes of Israel who had relocated into Asia and lived there approximately a millennium before Parthia and Scythia fell.

The invaded Celts and the invading Saxons, Goths and Germanic people were all part of the "lost sheep of the House of Israel" and they were being shepherded by the God of Abraham, Isaac and Jacob into the specific places where his prophecies required them to be in our modern age. The next book will examine biblical prophecies about each of the tribes of Israel and demonstrate how dramatically these prophecies have been fulfilled in the history and locations of modern nations, offering further evidence that the Creator God of the Bible is still ruling supreme in the affairs of men.

The exciting account of how the descendants of the tribes of Israel were pushed from Asia into Europe and the revealing analysis of where they are located in the modern world await the reader in the next book. More startling surprises will be encountered when we learn that God is still conferring the Abrahamic Covenant's blessings upon the Israelite nations in the modern world.

Parthian Prisoners from the arch of Marcus Aurelius

Bibliography

Alexander, Caroline, "Alexander the Conqueror," National Geographic, March, 2000, p. 72

Assar, Dr. G.R., Recent Calendar Research, website: www.parthia.com, links: "Calendars" and "Recent Calendar Research"

Athy, Lawrence F. (Jr.), "Foreign Influences on the Priesthood and Nobility of Pre-Columbian America," Epigraphic Society Occasional Publications, Vol. 17, 1988

Encyclopedia Americana, Grolier, Inc., Danbury, CT, 1988 Edition

Benjamin, S.G.W., Persia, T. Fisher Unwin, London, 1887 and G.P. Putnam's Sons, New York, 1888

Boland, Charles M., They All Discovered America, Doubleday, 1961

Encyclopaedia Britannica, Encyclopedia Britannica, Inc., Chicago, 1943 (175th Anniversary) Edition

Capt, E. Raymond, The Traditions of Glastonbury, Artisan Sales, Thousand Oaks, California, 1983

Casson, Lionel, The Ancient Mariners (Seafarers and Sea Fighters of the Mediterranean in Ancient Times, Second Edition, Princeton University Press, Princeton, 1991

Charles-Picard, Gilbert and Colette, Daily Life in Carthage, MacMillan, New York, 1961

Church, Alfred J., Carthage, T. Fisher Unwin, London, 1890

Culican, William, The Medes and the Persians, Praeger, New York, 1965

Davies, Nigel, Voyagers to the New World, Morrow, New York, 1979

Epigraphic Society Occasional Publications, Vol. 17, 1988, Citing the 1448 Letter of Pope Nicholas V, pp. 255-261

Eusebius, The History of the Church, Penguin Classics, 1989 Edition

Fell, Barry, America B.C., Wallaby, New York, 1976

Fell, Barry, Saga America, Times Books, New York, 1980

Frye, Richard N., The Heritage of Persia, Mentor, New York and Toronto, 1966

Gawler, Colonel J.C., Our Scythian Ancestors Identified With Israel, Guest, London, and MacLaren & MacNiven, Edinburgh, 1875

Gordon, Cyrus, Before Columbus, Crown Publishers, New York, 1971

Halley, Henry, Halley's Bible Handbook, Zondervan, Minneapolis, 1964

Harper's Bible Dictionary, Harper & Row, San Francisco, CA, 1985

Herodotus, The History, Translated by David Grene, University of Chicago Press, Chicago, 1987

Hirth, China and the Roman Orient, from website: www.parthia.com. Links: "Parthian Stations," "Parallel Passages from the Chinese Annals," citing: Shih-chi, ch. 123 and Ch'ien-han-shu, ch. 96a

Josephus, Antiquities of the Jews and Wars of the Jews, Contained in Complete Works of Josephus, Translated by William Whiston, Kregel Publications, Grand Rapids, Michigan, 1969

Keyser, Paul T., Journal of Near Eastern Studies, "The Purpose of the Parthian Galvanic Cells: A First-Century A.D. Electric Battery Used for Analgesia," April, 1993

McBirnie, William Steuart, The Search for the Twelve Apostles, Living Books, Wheaton, Ill., 1986

McClintock, John and Strong, James, Cyclopedia of Biblical, Theological and Ecclesiastical Literature, Baker Book House, Grand Rapids, 1981

Morris, Walter, Living Maya (as cited in Epigraphic Society Occasional Publications, Vol. 17, 1988

Nexus Magazine, "Science News: Why the Electric Battery was Forgotten," June-July, 1996

Noorbergen, Rene, Secrets of the Lost Races, New English Library, London, 1978

Plutarch, Fall of the Roman Empire, Penguin Books, London and New York, 1972

Ragozin, Zenaide, Media, 4th Edition, T. Fisher Unwin, Circa 1890

Rawlinson, George, Ancient History, Barnes & Noble, New York, 1993 Edition

Rawlinson, George, Intercourse Between India and the Western World, Second Edition, 1992 Reprint, Uppal Publishing House, New Delhi

Rawlinson, George, Parthia, G. P. Putnam's Sons, New York, 1893

Rawlinson, George, The Sixth Great Oriental Monarchy, Dodd, Mead & Co., New York, 1872

Rawlinson, Henry, Bactria, T. Fisher Unwin, London

Rice, Tamara Talbot, The Scythians, Thames and Hudson, London, 1958

Sammes, Aylett, Britannia (Antiquities of Ancient Britain), Tbo. Roycroft, London, 1676

Schoff, Wilfred H., Parthian Stations (citing Hirth, China and the Roman Orient), see website: www.parthia.com

Shahab Setudeh-Nejad, "Cultural and Cosmological Impact of Sasanian Civilization in Vietnam and Peninsular Areas of Southeast Asia," Asian Culture Quarterly, Vol. XXIV, No. 4, Winter 1996

Stender, Walter, "The Cross of the Inca," Epigraphic Society Occasional Publications, Vol. 17, 1988

Strabo, The Geography of Strabo, English Translation by Horace L. Jones, William Heinemann, London and Harvard University Press, Vol. 5, 1969 and Vol. 7, 1966

Tacitus, The Annals of Imperial Rome, Penguin Classics, London and New York, 1989

von Daniken, Erich, Chariots of the Gods, G. P. Putnam's Sons, New York, 1970

von Daniken, Erich, In Search of Ancient Gods, G. P. Putnam's Sons, New York, 1973

Waddell, L. A., The Phoenician Origin of Britons, Scots, and Anglo-Saxons, Williams & Norgate, London, 1924

Website: www.parthia.com (various links)

Webster's New World Dictionary, Second Concise Edition, World Publishing Co., 1975

Wilkin, Robert, The Christians as the Romans Saw Them, Yale University Press, New Haven, 1984

Wilson, Daniel, The Archaeology and Prehistoric Annals of Scotland, Sutherland and Knox, Edinburgh, 1851

Young, Robert, Young's Analytical Concordance to the Bible, Wm. B. Eerdmans Publishing Co., Grand Rapids, 1978

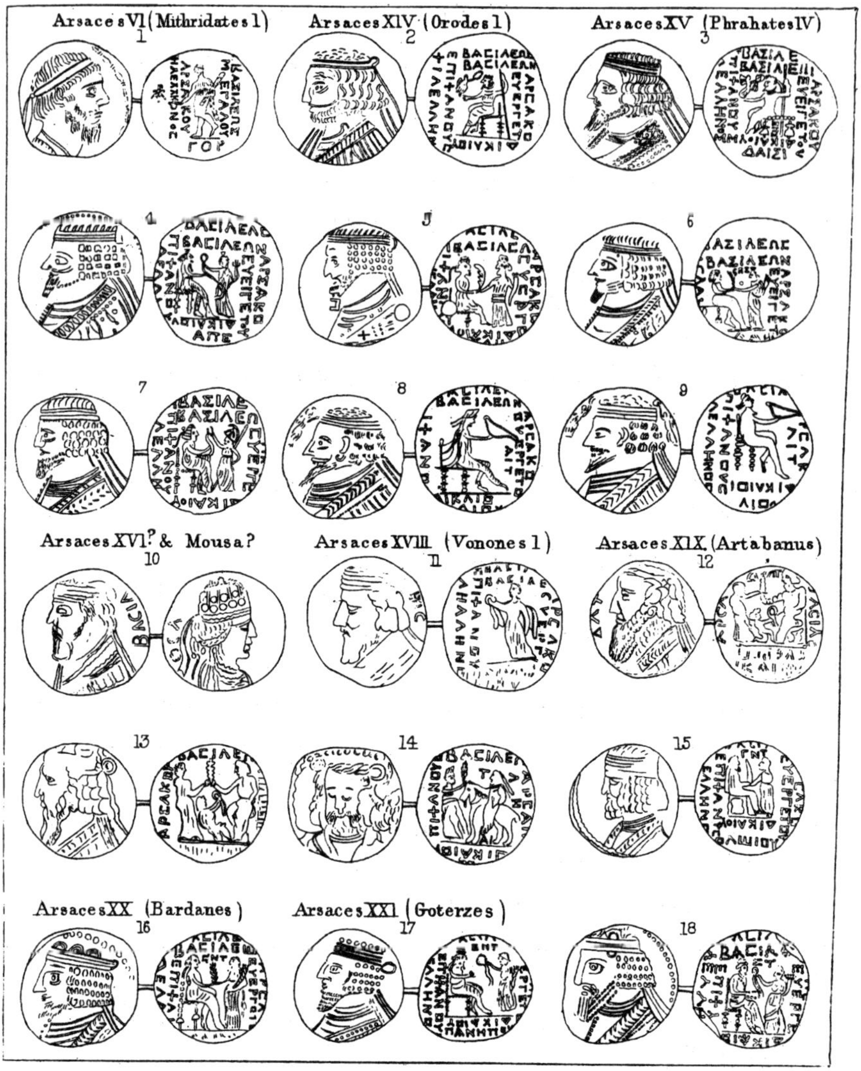

PARTHIAN COINS: The illustrations above are taken from John Lindsay's, *A View of the History and Coinage of the Parthians,* published in Cork, England in 1852. Concerning the coin of **Arsaces VI** (shown at top left above), Mr. Lindsay says, "The coins of this great prince, are as may be expected from the length of his reign and the extent of his conquests extremely numerous... he is also the first of the Parthian kings of whom tetradrachms appear; the execution also of his coins is superior to that of almost any others in this extensive series, the portraits from the strong likeness exhibited by coins struck at different times and in different places, being evidently good likenesses, the legends more legible, and the silver of a greater degree of finess than that of most of the Parthian coins." *(p.137)*

Index

Persons, Places, Subjects

D

E

F

G

J

N

O

Q

R

S

T

[End]

Index:
Scripture References

OLD TESTAMENT

NEW TESTAMENT

[End]

Recommended Reading
Available from Bible Blessings

Additional copies of this book:
PARTHIA: THE FORGOTTEN ANCIENT SUPERPOWER
Part Three of the Lost Tribes Of Israel Series

By The Same Author:
THE LOST TRIBES OF ISRAEL SERIES, by Steven M. Collins
I. Origins and Empire Of Ancient Israel
II. Israel's Lost Empires
III. Parthia: The Forgotten Ancient Superpower, And Its Role In Biblical History
IV. Israel's Lost Tribes Today
(See a review and pictures of these books at **www.israelite.info**)

Also Recommended:
THE STORY OF CELTO-SAXON ISRAEL

This is the story of a missing branch of God's People: ten tribes known in Scripture as the House of Israel. Historian and scholar, W.H. Bennett, a long-time Fellow of the Royal Geographical Society, spent fifty years following their trail. In separate chapters, he examines twelve early tribes who entered Europe from Asia, showing that each of them had very distinctive Hebrew-Semitic cultural features. Over 175 maps, charts, and illustrations, as well as 12 valuable appendices, help tell the story of these lost Israelites. A unique study! Almost 250 pages (236+ xii). Hard or soft cover. Please see our current order form or visit our website for prices: